Christianity
THE WESLEYAN WAY

Principles and Practices for Life and Ministry

BRIAN E. GERMANO

Nashville

First published in 2020 by the General Board of Higher Education and Ministry, Wesley's Foundery Books imprint, under ISBN 978-1-945935-69-5.

ISBN 9781791043247

Copyright 2020, 2025 by Abingdon Press. All rights reserved.

No part of this work may be reproduced or transmitted in any form or by any means, electronic or mechanical, including photocopying and recording, or by any information storage or retrieval system, except as may be expressly permitted by the 1976 Copyright Act, the 1998 Digital Millennium Copyright Act, or in writing from the publisher. Requests for permission can be addressed to Rights and Permissions, The United Methodist Publishing House, 810 12th Avenue South, Nashville TN 37203, or emailed to permissions@abingdonpress.com.

All web addresses were correct and operational at the time of publication.

Scripture quotations in Wesley's reproduced sermons are taken or adapted from the Authorized (King James) Version (AKJV). Rights in the Authorized Version in the United Kingdom are vested in the Crown. Reproduced by permission of the Crown's patentee, Cambridge University Press.

Scripture quotations marked ASV are taken from the American Standard Version (public domain).

Scripture quotations marked NRSV are taken from the New Revised Standard Version Bible, copyright © 1989 the Division of Christian Education of the National Council of the Churches of Christ in the United States of America. Used by permission. All rights reserved worldwide. http://nrsvbibles.org/

Printed in the United States of America.

To my sources of inspiration for this book.

My Lord and Savior, Jesus, who knows the worst I'll ever do and loves me anyway; my wife, Trish, who has been God's tangible expression of that same love and support throughout my years of ministry; Hal, who first introduced and taught me most of what I know about John Wesley and continues to teach me even today; my Course of Study students over the years, whose need for a more concise text encouraged me to write this.

CONTENTS

List of Illustrations ix
List of Wesley's Sermons Referenced x
Introduction. 1

Part One: Introduction to Early Methodism

Chapter 1. The Spiritual Context of Wesley's England 7
    A. Martin Luther and Lutheranism .7
    B. Philipp Jakob Spener and Pietism. 9
    C. John Calvin, Ulrich Zwingli, and "Reformed" Christianity 10
    D. Jacob Arminius and "Arminian" Christianity 11
    E. The Church of England's *"Via Media*/Middle Way" 12
    F. Puritanism (Nonconformist/Dissenter Tradition) 14
    G. Roman Catholic Mysticism. 16
    H. Early Church (Patristic) Authors 17
    I. Discussion Questions 19

**Chapter 2. The Life and Legacy of John Wesley
and the Early Methodists.** 21
    A. Early Life (1703–25) 21
    B. Oxford and the "Holy Club" (1725–35) 22
    C. The Search for More: Georgia and the Moravians
       (1735–38) 24
    D. Aldersgate: A Turning Point (1738) 26
    E. Unorthodox Evangelism: Field Preaching (1739). 27
    F. Wesley and the Poor: Social Holiness 29
    G. The Development of Methodism: Organizing the Revival. 32
    H. Growth and Legacy of the Movement. 40
    I. Discussion Questions 41

Part Two: The Christian Life and Wesley's "Way of Salvation" (*Via Salutis*)

Chapter 3. Turning to God: The Work of Prevenient Grace 45
    A. Humanity's "Original State" and the *"Imago Dei"* 45
    B. Humanity's Natural State and Original Sin 46
    C. The Goal/Purpose of Salvation: Restoration of the
       Image of God 59
    D. Prevenient Grace 75
    E. The Legal State: Conviction and Repentance 78
    F. Discussion Questions 82

Chapter 4. Becoming a Christian: The Work of Justifying Grace 85
    A. Justification 99
    B. New Birth/Regeneration 101
    C. Assurance/Witness of the Spirit 104
    D. Discussion Questions 107

**Chapter 5. Growing in Salvation: The Work of Sanctifying
Grace** 109
    A. Sanctification 109
    B. Fruit of the Spirit 114
    C. Evangelical Humility/Repentance of Believers 116
    D. Backsliding 118
    E. The Goal of the Christian Life: Perfect Love 122
    F. Discussion Questions 147

Part Three: The Means of Grace and the Sacraments

Chapter 6. The Means of Grace 151
    A. The Instituted Means of Grace 152
    B. The Prudential Means of Grace 173
    C. Cautions about the Means of Grace 179
    D. Discussion Questions 181

Chapter 7. The Sacraments 183
   A. Christian Baptism. 183
   B. The Lord's Supper 206
   C. Discussion Questions 225

Part Four: Toward a Uniquely Wesleyan Paradigm of Ministry

Chapter 8. Characteristics of a Wesleyan Life and Ministry 229
   A. The Unique Shape of Wesleyan Theology 230
   B. The Unique Shape of Wesleyan Practice 240

Chapter 9. Conclusion 271

Appendix

The Cultural Context of Wesley's England and Early Methodism's
    Response. 275

Index 291

ILLUSTRATIONS

FIGURES

2.1 Rescue of Young John Wesley from the Burning Parsonage 21
2.2 John Wesley and Companions at a Meeting of the "Holy Club". . . 23
2.3 John Wesley Preaching from His Father's Tombstone 28
2.4 John Wesley's Newcastle Orphan House 30
2.5 Frontispiece of John Wesley's *Primitive Physic* 31
2.6 First Methodist Conference, 1744 39
2.7 John Wesley Preaching in City Chapel 40
3.1 Humanity in the Image of God 46
3.2 Original Sin 58
3.3 The Goal of Salvation 60
3.4 Humanity in Bondage to Sin 62
3.5 God's Initiative through Prevenient Grace 76
4.1 Justifying Grace in Wesley's "House of Religion" 86
4.2 Imperfect Attempts to Bridge the Gap 100
4.3 Justification: Spiritual Bridge Built by Jesus 101
4.4 New Birth: Our First Step on the Bridge 103
5.1 A Reformed / Calvinist Understanding of Salvation 109
5.2 Wesleyan Sanctification: Traversing the Bridge 111
5.3 Sanctifying Grace in Wesley's "House of Religion" 112
5.4 Linear Understanding of Salvation, Conceptual 112
5.5 Linear Understanding of Salvation, Actual 113
5.6 Cross of Faith 115
5.7 The Sanctification "Spiral" 117
6.1 Early Methodist Society Structure 174
7.1 Christian Baptism: Our Part, God's Part 198

WESLEY'S SERMONS REFERENCED

"On God's Vineyard"

"Original Sin"

"The Scripture Way of Salvation"

"Justification by Faith"

"Christian Perfection"

"The Means of Grace"

"A Treatise on Baptism"

"The Duty of Constant Communion"

"Catholic Spirit"

INTRODUCTION

In today's world, fewer and fewer people are being raised as active members of a local Christian church. Those who are do not always learn the dynamics of what being a person of faith means and are also not usually exposed to the unique aspects of their particular Christian faith tradition or denomination until later in life—if at all.

I certainly fell into this latter category. While raised in a traditional United Methodist congregation and taught the basics of Protestant Christianity in my childhood and youth Sunday school classes and experiences, I do not ever remember a specific sermon or teaching on what being a "United Methodist Christian" was all about. While this may have been shared at some point by a pastor or Sunday school teacher (perhaps in my youth confirmation class), I have no recollection of this. In fact, it wasn't until experiences in my late teen and early adult years that I began to take an active interest in both the history and beliefs of my own Methodist Christian tradition.

Of course, since then I have come to understand that even when one does not (as in my case) remember anything specific from his or her years growing up in a particular Christian faith tradition, that person was still being exposed to—and influenced and shaped by—that view and practice of Christian faith. In my case, it was the unique view and practice of what we call Methodist, or "Wesleyan," Christianity. This exposure was subtle and indirect, but real, nevertheless, and it probably explains why these beliefs and practices later resonated with me once I was formally exposed to them.

You may be like me: you grew up in a traditional United Methodist church but only have a vague idea of what that meant. Or, you may have been raised in another Christian faith tradition—Baptist, Roman Catholic, Episcopalian, Lutheran, Presbyterian, Church of God, nondenominational, or something else. Perhaps you did not come to Christian faith until later in life. Or you may be reading either as a member of another world religion, or of none at all, yet seeking to understand what may be unique about the nature and practice of faith in Wesleyan Christianity.

Regardless of *why* you're reading, it's my belief that one doesn't need to be a Methodist/Wesleyan Christian to appreciate the great impact and influence of John Wesley and Methodism upon Christianity. Instead, it's my hope that regardless of your starting point, by the time you complete this book, you will be better equipped to understand what it means both to be and to live as a Wesleyan Christian in today's world. My goal, after all, is not to make you into a "good little Methodist" but merely to help you better understand what it means to be a great *Christian* who chooses to live out your Christianity in a uniquely *Wesleyan* way.

In this sense, the term "Wesleyan" is merely an adjective that describes what *kind* of Christian one is (hence, the title of the book). As much as the terms "Baptist," "Roman Catholic," and so on, describe other *types* of Christianity, it's my contention that "Wesleyan" or "Methodist" merely articulates both the beliefs and practices of a particular *kind* of Christian. My hope is that by exploring the history, the writings, and the beliefs (what's called "theology") of John Wesley and the Methodist movement that he founded, we'll better understand what's so special about a uniquely Wesleyan way of believing and practicing Christianity, and what Wesley's life and ministry can teach us about the living of a faithful Christian life today.

One thing you may have noticed already is that both historically and in many contemporary resources, the words "Methodist" and "Wesleyan" are often used interchangeably. However, while "Methodist" is obviously associated with specific Christian denominations that include that term (such as The United Methodist Church, the African Methodist Episcopal Church, the Christian Methodist Church, and others), "Wesleyan" is a broader term that is inclusive of the many other Christian faith traditions—and even independent churches—whose theology and practice are also associated with John Wesley but who do not use "Methodist" in their names (such as the Church of the Nazarene, the Salvation Army, and the Church of God–Cleveland, Tennessee). What's more, the term "Wesleyan," I believe, also signifies the presence of theology, concepts, and spiritual practices that transcend any specific "Methodist" doctrinal tradition. They simply derive from the life and ministry of John Wesley and his early Methodist movement (for example, Wesley's "way of salvation," the practice of the "means of grace," and Wesley's balance between personal and social piety). For these reasons, within this book I will most often use the term "Wesleyan," as I believe it contains a broader meaning within today's culture.

Before we continue, let me offer a few words about the nature, structure, and content of the book. First, while I hope the resources found herein will prove useful in a variety of settings by a variety of different readers, my primary target audience is clergy and laity who are seeking a compact overview of the history, theology, and practice of historic Wesleyan Christianity, with specific focus on part-time and full-time local pastors in the United Methodist tradition who are progressing through our denomination's Course of Study program. To this end, I have intentionally tried to combine primary source writings, interpretive subjective discussion, and essential history in a way that helps to walk readers through the heart of the context, history, theology, and practices of the ministry of John Wesley and the early Methodists, and then—along the way—to suggest practical implications for how these can be lived out in today's world.

I have chosen this integrative approach in the hopes that it will make the primary themes of Wesleyan theology and practice more readily accessible, both intellectually and practically. There are certainly many excellent primary source texts that reproduce Wesley's sermons and other writings, but most of them offer little or no interpretation. There are other texts that offer excellent interpretation *about* Wesley's writings, but only contain sample, illustrative quotes to reinforce a point or theme here or there. Finally, still other texts focus solely on the history and sociological context for Wesley's ministry and writings but do not explain the impact of that history on Wesley's theology. What this book seeks to share within this *one* resource is the relationship between (and integrative nature of) *all of the above:* select primary sources, essential interpretation, *and* historical context materials.

Let me also offer a brief general comment about John Wesley's sermons and other primary source writings in this book. As you read these, they may come across to contemporary ears as dry, antiseptic, and uninteresting. However, the diaries, journals, and other writings of many who heard Wesley preach in person often speak about how eloquent and gifted a speaker he was. So, why don't his sermons read that way today? Two reasons have been suggested: first, contemporaries of Wesley may have been looking to hear different theological emphases and themes than what we are used to today; and second, many scholars believe that Wesley's sermons as we have them today were meant merely to be sermon "skeletons" upon which Wesley would later add (in impromptu fashion) his own unique humor and personal illustrations—things *not* captured in his published writings. Therefore, please bear this in mind as you read these, and think of them more as sermon outlines to which were added Wesley's own individual flavor and personality.

INTRODUCTION

In addition, you will note throughout this book that I have tried not to alter original sermons and/or primary source writings in any way, so that they convey to you as closely as possible the texts as originally written by Wesley. Among other things, that means that these writings are usually lacking in what we today call gender-inclusive language. For example, you'll find in Wesley's original writings references to "man," "men," and "mankind" instead of to "people," "human," "humankind," and uses of "him" and "he" rather than inclusive ways of referring to God without masculine pronouns. Please understand that I utilize this approach not out of a lack of respect or appreciation for the need of such inclusivity in today's cultural context but in honor of and out of respect for the original language that Wesley used, dated as it is. To alter these in this context would be historically inappropriate because it would superimpose my own inclusive bias upon the original texts, creating presumption about a text's meaning. So, rather than altering these non-inclusive primary source texts, I have chosen to keep them intact, allowing my subsequent words of interpretation to reveal the inclusive bias that I believe Wesley's language would have originally conveyed in his day and time.

Furthermore, as you're reading, be aware that I delineate the beginning and ending of Wesley's sermons with a solid line across the page, and if there is any original content in these that I have omitted, I designate those with three successive asterisks (* * *). Finally, both to foster dialogue and to supply resources for readers to share this material with others, I have provided throughout the book the following tools: end-of-chapter discussion questions to spark both personal reflection and interactive group dialogue; periodic "focus" boxes with key Wesleyan terms, to highlight what I feel to be essential theology and practices of Wesleyan ministry; and instructive diagrams, to bring some of the theological concepts to life more visually. My hope is that all of these tools will help make this material more accessible in contexts such as Sunday school and "Methodism 101"–type small groups, confirmation classes, sermons, and other settings.

May you be blessed and enlightened as you read and learn about the fascinating history, theology, and ministry practices of Methodist/Wesleyan Christianity, and how it can make a difference in our lives today.

| Part One |

Introduction to Early Methodism

CHAPTER 1

THE SPIRITUAL CONTEXT OF WESLEY'S ENGLAND

Before we can truly appreciate the unique aspects of Wesleyan theology and practice, we need to remember that John Wesley did not create or form his Methodist movement out of the blue, so to speak. Instead, like our own, his theology and practice of ministry were shaped by the variety of influences (what we call his "context") in both his early life and throughout his lifetime. In the appendix, I share a few insights about how the sociological and cultural context of Wesley's England both impacted and was impacted by his ministry. However, since this book is oriented around Christian theology and practice, we begin by focusing on the *spiritual* context of Wesley's England. Specifically, I want us briefly to take time to remember several key seventeenth- and eighteenth-century Christian spiritual influences and practices that later helped to shape John Wesley's own theology and practice of ministry.

Martin Luther and Lutheranism

First, we must remember that Wesley himself was an inheritor of many of the emphases and ministry practices of certain branches of the Protestant Reformation. In 1517, when Martin Luther nailed his Ninety-Five Theses to the church door in Wittenberg (in present-day Germany), he set in motion an expression of Christian faith that, among other things, emphasized three major areas of focus:

- **primacy of scripture**—that a Christian's primary source of authority should be the Bible, rather than the history and tradition of the church

- **the doctrine of *sola fide***—that Christians are justified through faith alone (*sola fide*, "only faith"), rather than through righteous works and behaviors

- **the "priesthood of believers"**—that *all* of God's people (rather than just the clergy/those ordained and set apart by the church) have equal access to the grace and ministry of God (highlighting the importance of the partnership between laity and clergy in the work of ministry)

As we will see in later chapters, all three of these areas became essential components of Wesley's theology and practice of ministry, even though his emphasis on the priority of grace made his use and application of these different from Luther and other theologians.

For example, while Wesley referred to himself as *homo unius libri* ("a man of one book," meaning *the* book, the Bible), both his theology and practice of ministry consistently called upon other resources for ministry rationale and authority, including the various components of what we today call the Wesleyan Quadrilateral (scripture, church tradition, personal experience, and "faith that makes sense"/reason). As a result, while his ministry was clearly centered around scripture, he was not a biblical exclusivist—besides the Bible, he also invoked other sources of authority when he felt they were needed. In his practice of ministry, while these others could never contradict scripture, they nevertheless helped one to better understand it. Hence, while Wesley may have been "a man of one book," he was not a man of *only* one book—the Bible was certainly his primary, but not his only, source of authority.

Likewise, as with Luther and other Protestant Reformers, Wesley affirmed the traditional doctrine of *sola fide*—that Christians are saved through faith alone, apart from good works/deeds. Yet, in spite of this affirmation, Wesley's actual *practice* of ministry also included a variety of works/activities that he felt were important for Christians to some degree to exercise in order for salvation to be perceived and effectual. He called them "means of grace," and while we'll learn more about them in chapter 6, my point here is that—unlike Luther's and other Protestant Reformers'—Wesley's practice revealed a place for and the necessity of "works" in the work of salvation. For him, they were both the fruit of salvation and a means by which God works to bring about that salvation. Consequently, instead of pure salvation *sola fide* ("through faith alone"), Wesley in effect practiced salvation "through faith," but *not* "alone." This was his way of living out the words of James 2:17: "faith by itself, if it has no works, is dead" (NRSV).

Finally, while Wesley also followed the traditional Protestant practice of the "priesthood of believers" (based on 1 Peter 2:9) in affirming the important role that laity (i.e., non-clergy) play in the work and activity of God's church, he radically expanded what Luther and other Reformers both meant and practiced. We see this in Wesley's extensive use of lay preachers, lay leaders for his classes and bands (we'll learn more about these in later chapters), and his affirmation of the need for each person to read and interpret scripture for themselves. However, even here, there were a few practices—such as administration of the sacraments—that Wesley continued to reserve as the work and responsibility of clergy alone. For him, while all Christians are called to (and responsible for engaging in) servant ministry, not all Christians are called to ecclesial authority within the Church.

Philipp Jakob Spener and Pietism

One hundred fifty years after the founding of Protestantism, Christians in southern Germany (specifically, Bavaria and Moravia) began to believe that Lutheranism had grown morally and spiritually stale, no longer representing or practicing true (Protestant) Christian faith. Consequently, **Philipp Jakob Spener** led followers to form their own Lutheran renewal movement, which became known as **Pietism** because of their emphasis on personal religious piety (focused reverence for God) and the living of an intentional holy life.[1] In addition, Pietism also introduced Wesley to the use of small groups, such as Spener's *collegia pietatis* ("schools of piety") and his use of *ecclesiola in ekklesia* (church within Church). Both of these consisted essentially of groups of laypersons who gathered together regularly in homes for prayer, Bible study, and personal accountability. All of these practices (piety, holy living, and small group ministry) later became hallmarks of early Methodism.

Yet, Wesley was influenced not only by the writings and spiritual practices of this movement, but also by his personal connections and relationships with those within it. For instance, early in his ministry, Wesley became acquainted with the writings and ministry of Pietist leader Count Nikolaus von Zinzendorf, and in August 1738, he traveled to his retreat center in Moravia (in present-day Germany) called **Herrnhut**. There, Wesley learned many of the Pietists' spiritual practices, including Zinzendorf's use of "bands" for personal accountability and spiritual growth. Consequently, it is often said that Wesley based much of the structure of early Methodism's small group ministry (i.e., what became its **societies**, **classes**, and **bands**) on what he learned from Pietists such as Spener and Zinzendorf.

---

1 Spener outlined his program of personal and religious reform in a book titled *Pia Desideria* ("Pious Wishes"), and it became a source that led to religious revival throughout the Church and society in many fifteenth-century German states.

CHAPTER 1

In addition, Wesley was also personally influenced by a group of Zinzendorf Pietists living in England, known as **Moravians**.

> **Moravians**: members of a German Lutheran Pietist reform movement that influenced Wesley both theologically and personally to understand Christian faith as heartfelt trust rather than mere mental assent.

His first encounter with them occurred as he traveled to America as a missionary in 1736. While his ship, the *Simmonds*, passed through a terrible storm, the native English passengers feared for their lives, but a group of Moravian Christians held hands and sang hymns of praise to God. This simple faith and trust in God impressed the twenty-three-year-old Wesley, and upon returning to England two years later, he befriended several of their leaders to learn all he could about their religious faith and fervor. It was from what was learned in these friendships that several important elements of what became backbones of Wesleyan theology were probably derived—namely, Wesley's comprehension of the purpose and importance of "assurance/witness of the Spirit," and his understanding of Christian faith as heartfelt *trust* in God (rather than mere mental assent).

John Calvin, Ulrich Zwingli, and "Reformed" Christianity

One Christian tradition that Wesley did *not* follow, either in his theology or his practice of ministry, was **Reformed** Christianity—a tradition centered around the "sovereignty of God" that would form the theological foundations for most Presbyterian, Congregational, and Baptist churches of today. These themes originated from the teachings of two Protestant Reformers: Ulrich Zwingli and John Calvin. Hence, this is sometimes called the "Calvinist" tradition and its theology referred to as "Calvinism."

While Wesley was friends with a number of Anglican clergymen (such as George Whitefield) who practiced Reformed theology within the Church of England, in the end he rejected two of the main theological tenets of this tradition: the absolute nature in their understanding of the **"sovereignty of God"** (that God controls and is absolutely in charge of all things); and the related corollary doctrine known as **"predestination"** (that God chooses, "elects," or "predestines" some people to be saved and not others). In both of these theological concepts, human free will is severely de-emphasized, often to the point of nonexistence.

To be fair, Wesley did believe that both of these had a biblical basis, which may explain why he believed that the "truth of the gospel" lies "within a hair's breadth" of Calvinism.[2] Yet, his reframing of both his understanding and practice of these concepts was significant enough that, functionally, they no longer meant precisely what Reformed theologians meant. In the case of the former, while Reformed/Calvinist theology then tended (and still does) to view the sovereignty of God in terms of divine *control* (to the extreme of micromanagement), Wesley instead understood that phrase in terms of divine *empowerment* (to equip followers to live lives of faith). Similarly, for Wesley, "predestination" was merely the Bible's way of describing the fact that God—by default—"elects" or "predestines" for salvation *all* people (not just some, as proposed by Reformed theologians), but that, empowered by grace, we must then *choose* to accept and live into that salvation ourselves (in practice, focusing more on grace-empowered human free will than on divine-only sovereignty).

These distinctions are important today when attempting to understand how and why Wesleyan theology and practice rejects most contemporary Reformed concepts of divine sovereignty, such as "once saved, always saved," "divine election," and the absolute nature of the power and providence of God.

Jacob Arminius and "Arminian" Christianity

In its place, when seeking to understand the relationship between divine sovereignty and human free will, Wesleyan theology and practice follows a different branch of Protestantism (of which Lutheranism is a part) called **Arminianism**.

> **Arminian theology**—a theological perspective originating with Dutch clergyman Jacob Arminius

---

[2] While this phrase appears in numerous places throughout Wesley's writings, two prime examples are found in "Minutes of Some Late Conversations Between the Rev. Mr. Wesley and Others," August 2, 1745, Question 22, in *The Works of John Wesley* (3rd ed.), vol. 8, *Addresses, Essays, Letters*, ed. Thomas Jackson (Grand Rapids: Baker Book House, 1979), 284; and Wesley's "Letter to John Newton," May 14, 1765, in *The Bicentennial Edition of the Works of John Wesley*, vol. 27, *Letters III (1756–1765)*, ed. Ted A. Campbell (Nashville: Abingdon Press, 2015), 427.

> (1560–1609) asserting that humans have been gifted by God with *free will* both in their relationship with God, and in God's offer of salvation to us.

Based on the theological work of sixteenth-century Dutch clergyman Jacob Armimius, this tradition rejected the Reformed understanding of predestination as unbiblical and instead held that while God may have *foreknowledge* about our salvation, God does not *preordain it*—meaning that we human beings are not puppets, but instead can choose to exercise **free will** when it comes to matters of spirituality and faith. Granted, Wesley was clear that this is not inherently "natural" (in the sense that we are born with it). Instead, he insisted that even free will is supernaturally gifted to us by and through God's grace before we are ever aware of it.[3] Yet, even while empowered by *grace*, it is nevertheless still our choice. Consequently, this emphasis on the nature and importance of free will was essential to Wesley and his understanding of salvation, making Wesleyan/Methodist theology—at its heart—an Arminian, rather than a Calvinist/Reformed, Christian tradition.

The Church of England's "*Via Media* / Middle Way"

The spiritual tradition that, by far, had the greatest influence on shaping Wesley's theology and practice of ministry was, of course, the one in which he was raised: the Church of England, also known as the **Anglican** tradition. Even if one is not extremely familiar with church history, one may at least remember that the reason the Church of England broke away from Roman Catholicism in 1532 had little to do with theology, but instead with politics: the pope refused to annul King Henry VIII's marriage, so Henry pulled out of Roman Catholicism and created his own Church of England, with himself as the spiritual head.

Yet, even though Anglicanism was originally born out of politics, over a period of years it eventually did undergo a theological reformation of its own, which eventually was articulated through a variety of resources, including Thomas Cranmer's *Book of Homilies*, his Forty-two Articles, and the Anglican Book of Common Prayer (a version of which is still in use by

---

3   As we'll learn in chapter 3, free will is actually one of the manifestations and/or characteristics of what Wesley called the "preventing" (or prevenient) grace of God.

the Episcopal/Anglican Church today). These resources essentially spelled out an Anglican theological stance that became known as the **Via media (middle way)** because it charted a careful balance between the practices of radical Protestantism (as found, for instance, in the Puritan, Congregationalist, Anabaptist, and Quaker movements of the day) and those of Roman Catholicism.

> *Via media*: "middle way"; a theological perspective originating with the sixteenth-century Church of England that seeks to steer a middle course between the beliefs and practices of radical Protestantism and Roman Catholicism.

Examples of this balance include how the Church of England, on the one hand, retained the Roman Catholic offices of bishop and archbishop, the practice of "high" liturgy, the "mystery/paradox" of the Eucharist, and the practice of infant baptism (christening), while at the same time adopting traditionally Protestant theological doctrines such as sola fide (faith alone) and the "priesthood of believers."

Although this via media balance between Protestant and Roman Catholic theology and practice was severely tested numerous times in sixteenth-century England (such as through the English Civil Wars, and later through King James II's attempt to reestablish Roman Catholicism as England's official state religion), it nevertheless became a hallmark of the Anglican tradition. And it was into this understanding and practice of Christian faith that John Wesley was born, reared, influenced, and shaped as a Christian.

It's not surprising, then, that a thorough review of Wesley's mature theology and practice of ministry will note at least four major ways that Anglicanism influenced him:

- by instilling in him the importance of "balance" in the Christian life (e.g., avoiding extremes)
- by providing his essential understanding and practice of Christian worship and the sacraments (baptism and Holy Communion, which we'll learn about in chapter 7)
- by providing for him three of the four sources of authority that we today call the Wesleyan Quadrilateral (Anglicanism set forth a trilateral

of scripture, tradition, and reason, to which Wesley would later add a fourth: personal experience)

- by providing a further example of small group ministry practice—like the early church and the Pietist movement, the Church of England also developed small groups called **religious societies.** The most famous of these was the SPCK: Society for Promoting Christian Knowledge (originally formed in 1698), in which Wesley's father, Samuel Sr., was actively involved, and in which John himself became a member in 1732. And even though the main purpose of these groups was primarily to disseminate intellectual information (versus the personal accountability of Pietism's *collegia pietatis*), nevertheless Wesley saw firsthand yet another example of the value of small group ministry.

Puritanism (Nonconformist / Dissenter Tradition)

Despite the "proper" upbringing of John and his fellow siblings as staunch Anglicans, he was also influenced and shaped by the theology and ministry practices of various **Nonconformist/Dissenter** traditions within England—so called because, though they did not conform to establishment Church of England theology or ecclesiology, their "dissenting" views were allowed to exist in English society under the 1689 "Act of Toleration" as long as they met and followed certain conditions.[4] In the early 1700s, there were numerous Nonconformist/Dissenter traditions, but the one that influenced and shaped Wesley the most was **Puritanism**.

We Americans are familiar with at least one segment of the Puritan faith: the Pilgrims were the Protestant group who left England in 1620 to establish a settlement in what became Plymouth, Massachusetts. Later that century, Puritans under Oliver Cromwell led a failed uprising to overthrow the English monarchy—a crisis that later became known as the English Civil Wars. Consequently, by the time of Wesley's birth (1703), while the Puritans'

---

4 Among others, these conditions included: (1) Dissenter meeting houses (they couldn't be called "churches") must be registered with the government; (2) Dissenting preachers must be licensed; (3) Dissenter worship services must be held in the registered meeting houses, not in open arenas or private homes; (4) Roman Catholics and Unitarians were not defined as "Dissenters," and their practices were technically illegal, even though authorities in many cases turned a blind eye to some of these.

presence was legal in English culture, they were nonetheless considered theologically and politically incorrect.

Wesley's parents had a long lineage of Puritan involvement: Wesley's grandfather and great-grandfather on both sides were all registered Nonconformists, and were even ejected from their parishes for refusing to sign the 1662 Act of Uniformity—meaning that his mother and father both were raised in strict Puritan homes as children of Puritan clergy. To the dismay of both families, both later converted to establishment Anglicanism.

Yet, even if their parents were now faithful Anglicans, John, Charles, and their siblings spent many nights being read to from Puritan authors during family devotional time—many of whose writings remained dear to John the rest of his life. And while there were some characteristics of Puritan belief and practice that Wesley and early English Methodism did *not* later follow (such as their more Reformed understanding of the sovereignty of God and their devotion to simple styles of dress and architecture), several attributes later did become hallmarks of the Wesleyan revival. Among others, these included:

- The Puritan emphasis upon some sort of experience of **personal conversion**—the Puritans were the first large Christian movement to emphasize conversion as a specific event.

- The articulation of an ***ordo salutis*** (order of salvation)—specific steps/stages of faith development that one normally progresses through in Christian experience. As described more in chapter 3, the "order" for which Wesley would later be known (i.e., prevenient, then justifying, and finally, sanctifying grace) was not the same as what is found in the Puritan tradition and is also understood by many today (including me) to actually be a *via* salutis ("*way* of salvation") rather than a *ordo* salutis. Yet, by whatever phrase one uses to describe it, Wesley learned from the Puritans that such a process could, in fact, be articulated and followed.

> ***Ordo salutis***: order of salvation; a theological concept articulated by the Puritan tradition asserting that there are specific stages of faith development that one normally progresses through in his or her Christian development. This concept is also often articulated as a ***via salutis*** (way of salvation).

- The puritan focus on **"back to the basics" faith**—the idea that "primitive religion/Christianity" is the purest and best, leading to a desire to try and re-create the "primitive church." As a result, much of Wesley's practice of ministry focused on returning Christian community and practice to what he felt must have existed in the early church. Examples of these included his emphasis on the important role of laity, small group ministry, being a prophetic voice for social justice within society, and others.

- There was also a homiletical emphasis on **"plain-style preaching"**—the notion that the sermon should be an intentionally accessible focus of worship (i.e., not overly eloquent). Wesley later affirmed this emphasis when he wrote that he desired "plain truth for plain people," meaning that the more extemporaneous a sermon was, the better it would be. For him, this did *not* mean that sermons should never be written or well-thought-out. To the contrary: Wesley's sermons are remarkable in their use of logic and intellect for the purpose of persuasion. But he also did not believe one should use such sermons to talk over the heads of one's audience.[5]

Roman Catholic Mysticism

Despite the fact that the practice of Roman Catholicism was technically illegal in Wesley's day,[6] the reading of Catholic writings was not. So, while attending Oxford University, the young Wesley read—in addition to the writings of Puritan authors—works written by Roman Catholic figures, such as François Fenelon, John of Ávila, Brother Lawrence, and Miguel de Molinos. Most of these were part of a spiritual movement within both Roman Catholicism (and Eastern Orthodoxy) dating all the way back to the patristic period. Called **"mysticism,"** it emphasized the maturing of one's inner walk

---

5 This emphasis should in no way be taken to imply that Wesley valued preaching over the practice of The Lord's Supper. He valued both equally, as his Methodist revival movement was as much a sacramental awakening as an awakening of homiletics.

6 During this period (late 1600s–early 1800s), the civil rights of Roman Catholics in England were severely truncated. For example, they had only limited right to own property or inherit land; they were taxed with special taxes; they were forbidden to send children abroad for Catholic education; they could not vote; and practicing priests were subject to potential imprisonment.

with God, and many of its teachings influenced and shaped Wesley's later theology and practice of ministry.

Of all the authors Wesley read from this movement, probably the most influential was Thomas À Kempis. His work *The Imitation of Christ* convinced Wesley that the primary goal of all Christians should be to strive for "perfection" in God's love—a goal that later became a hallmark of Methodism/Wesleyan Christianity in the form of Wesley's concept of "Christian perfection" (discussed in more depth in chapter 5). Even though Wesley later rejected Thomas's notion of *how* to achieve it (e.g., through the doing of good works), nevertheless after reading this work at Oxford in 1725, Wesley continually affirmed that there *was* a goal in the first place—for all Christians to learn how "to love as God loves."[7] Because of the strong influence that many of these authors had on Wesley, he himself (along with his writings) was often accused of being a "papist" (i.e., Roman Catholic).

Early Church (Patristic) Authors

One final spiritual tradition that should be highlighted as having an important influence, at least on Wesley's articulation of theology and practice of ministry, are the writings of various early Christian church leaders, known as "**patristic literature**."[8] As Ted A. Campbell notes in *John Wesley and Christian Antiquity*:

> Over one hundred and fifty references to early Christian works can be found in Wesley's writings after 1737, including references to all of the following ancient Christian authors or writings: Arnobius, Augustine, the Athanasian Creed, Athanasius, Athenagoras, Basil, Chrysostom, Clement of Alexandria, Clement of Rome, Cyprian, Dionysius of Alexandria, Dionysius the Pseudo-Areopagite, Ephraem Syrus, Epiphanius, Eusebius, Ignatius of Antioch, Jerome,

---

7 This is the title of an excellent 1987 book by Roberta Bondi, outlining the importance of "perfected love" as advocated by leaders of the early Christian church. See Roberta C. Bondi, *To Love as God Loves: Conversations with the Early Church* (Minneapolis: Fortress, 1987).

8 While "patristic literature" literally refers to the writings of the early church "fathers," today the term is acknowledged also to include the writings of numerous early church "mothers," as well.

CHAPTER 1

> Justin Martyr, Macarius of Egypt, Origen, Polycarp, Tertullian, and Theophilus of Antioch.[9]

While Campbell goes on to acknowledge that there are numerous critical challenges in attempting to trace Wesley's theology and ministry practice directly back to any single patristic author (partly because of the many *other* sources from which Wesley's views can realistically be derived), the fact that Wesley cited these authors at all is significant—at the very least, he used them as theological support for his own views and ministry work.

Of special note here are the works of various Eastern patristic authors,[10] such as Macarius of Egypt (c. 295–392) and Ephraem Syrus (c. 306–373), whose writings convinced Wesley that biblical sanctification (growth in faith) should be primarily understood as a process, rather than as a completed state—that Christian salvation is best understood as a journey, rather than as a onetime event/destination. As Albert Outler notes, upon reading these, "the ancient and eastern tradition of holiness as disciplined love became fused in Wesley's mind with his own Anglican tradition of holiness as aspiring love, and thereafter was developed in what he regarded to the end as his own most distinctive doctrinal contribution" (i.e., Christian perfection).[11] In this Eastern patristic view of salvation, while there are always specific events and experiences that mark turning points in our spiritual walk, these are also best understood within the context of the overall *process* of our faith development.[12] As we'll learn later, this view became a defining characteristic of Wesleyan/Methodist Christianity.

There were certainly more spiritual traditions in the seventeenth and eighteenth centuries than these eight. However, this brief overview should be sufficient for one to see and understand the role that these played in helping

---

9 Ted A. Campbell, *John Wesley and Christian Antiquity: Religious Vision and Cultural Change* (Nashville: Kingswood Books, 1991), 41.

10 "Eastern" here refers to first-millennium Christian patristic authors who lived and ministered in the eastern parts of the late and post-Roman Empire, rather than to authors from the Eastern Orthodox Christian tradition, which was not even designated as a separate branch of Christianity until the Great Schism of 1066, at the beginning of the second millennium of Christianity.

11 Albert Outler, ed., *John Wesley* (New York: Oxford University Press, 1964, 1980), 10.

12 See generally, Outler, 9–10.

both to influence and shape several key components and themes later found in Wesleyan/Methodist theology and practice of ministry.

Discussion Questions

1. What spiritual traditions have helped to shape and influence your spiritual life? Name a few and describe how they have done so.

2. Are there traditions that—like the Reformed/Calvinist tradition of Wesley's life—have influenced and shaped your spiritual life by providing theological and practical concepts that you have rejected? If so, what are they, and how are you who you are today due to your rejection of them?

3. In general, what role and influence have small groups (such as Sunday school classes, Bible study groups, accountability groups, etc.) played in the formation and shaping of your spiritual life?

4. From Wesley's experiences of being read religious devotions as a young boy, what do you believe to be the role of religious education (formal or informal) in one's spiritual shaping?

5. Based on what you have read in this chapter, what would you say is the importance of spiritual context in the influencing and shaping of one's spiritual life? What role does it play, and how does it influence and shape us?

CHAPTER 2

THE LIFE AND LEGACY OF JOHN WESLEY AND THE EARLY METHODISTS

Now that we've highlighted essentials of the spiritual context of Wesley's England, let's turn to a brief exploration of the life and legacy of John Wesley the man, and to a simple overview of the rise and development of early Methodism in England.

Early Life (1703–25)

John Benjamin Wesley was born June 28, 1703, in Epworth, Lincolnshire, England (about 150 miles north of London). His father, Samuel—an ordained priest in the Church of England—and his mother, Susanna, raised John and his eighteen brothers and sisters (of which he was the fifteenth) with great discipline and strictness. In fact, it has been argued that John's superb organizational ability—a skill that proved so useful in structuring the early Methodist revival—was more than likely a product of the discipline and organization that he learned at home. This was, of course, in addition to the subtle influences of Puritanism from both parents' history that we discussed in the previous chapter.

Figure 2.1. Rescue of young John Wesley from the burning parsonage at Epworth, Lincolnshire. Mezzotint by S. W. Reynolds after H. P. Parker. Photograph courtesy of Wellcome Collection. Reproduced by permission.

CHAPTER 2

One famous story from John's early life is especially telling. On February 9, 1709, at age five, he narrowly escaped death when his house—the rectory of the Epworth church where his father Samuel was priest—caught on fire. As the story is told, the rest of the family had escaped from the house safely when they realized that little John had accidentally been left behind. Believing that he must have perished in the flames, Samuel began to pray and commend his soul to God. However, just then, John was heard crying for help from a second-floor window. The Wesleys' neighbors formed a human ladder, and the neighbor at the top reached up to the window and pulled John away—in true Hollywood fashion—just as the roof caved in. After this incident, John's mother, Susanna, remarked that she believed God had spared John from the flame for some great purpose—that he was (in words John later recorded in his diary) "a brand plucked from the burning"—a reference to Zechariah 3:2.

In 1714, at age eleven, John was sent to Charterhouse School in London, where he learned to read English, Latin, and Greek. Six years later, he went for more schooling at Christ Church College, where he excelled in foreign languages and theology.

Oxford and the "Holy Club" (1725–35)

At age twenty-three (1725), Wesley became a fellow of Lincoln College of Oxford University. Three years later, with little fanfare, following in the footsteps of his father, he was ordained a priest in the Church of England. While at Lincoln, however, he experienced what we today might call an "intellectual conversion" through his interaction with a movement known as the "holy living tradition." His reading of works such as Thomas À Kempis's *The Imitation of Christ* and Jeremy Taylor's *The Rule and Exercises of Holy Living* in 1725, and William Law's *A Serious Call to a Devout and Holy Life* in 1730, convinced him that the best way to achieve the goal of the Christian life (the "perfect love" talked about by Roman Catholic mystics) was through the doing of good deeds to and for others.

This led the young Wesley to begin seeking out opportunities to earn God's grace and "perfect love" through acts of mercy and service to/with others. At first, this took the form of his returning to Epworth to work as his father's curate (a type of associate minister) in the Epworth parish. However, when his responsibilities at Oxford forced him to choose where best to grow in faith, he eventually relinquished his Epworth work and returned to Oxford to pursue holiness through his religious studies. There, in keeping with his desire to do good deeds, he joined and eventually became leader of a religious society dedicated to personal devotion and service to the poor, initially begun by his younger brother Charles and other Oxford students, called the **Holy Club**.[1] Wesley created a structure for the Holy Club's methods and habits of prayer, discussion, and social work to give discipline to their devotional and service time.

Figure 2.2. John Wesley and his companions at a meeting of "the Holy Club" at Oxford, where the idea of Methodism was conceived. 1729. Photograph courtesy of Chronicle / Alamy Stock. Reproduced by permission.

The Holy Club: a religious organization formed in 1729 at Oxford University that would eventually include John and Charles Wesley, George Whitefield, and others for the purpose of prayer, Bible study,

---

1 As you might guess, this group was modeled after the basic structure of the Anglican religious societies that we learned about in the previous chapter. However, while the focus in most Anglican societies was on intellectual spiritual development and learning, the focus of this Oxford club was personal piety and service to the poor.

social works for the poor, and religious discipline. It was this group that was first called "Methodist."

According to Charles's account, other students laughed at the Holy Club's religious enthusiasm, and derisively called them "enthusiasts," "Bible moths" (because they were so pious in the reading and study of scripture), and "Sacramentarians" (because they received Communion every Sunday even though devout Anglicans of the time were only required to receive it three times per year). Furthermore, because they were so orderly, precise, and *methodical* about everything they did, they were also laughingly called **Method-ists.** While the actual origin of this title is more complex than this, nevertheless the term *Methodist* was eventually adopted as a badge of honor and has been used ever since as a designation for those who follow the teachings and practices of John Wesley.[2]

The Search for More: Georgia and the Moravians (1735–38)

In spite of his discipline, holy lifestyle, and good works, Wesley still did not feel satisfied with his own Christianity. So, upon the death of his father in 1735, he agreed to serve as missionary chaplain for General George Oglethorpe in his founding of a new colony in America—a colony to be populated by those who were imprisoned in England for failure to pay their debts. That colony was named "Georgia" after their king, George II. John's goal as part of Oglethorpe's team was not only to be chaplain to the colonists, but a missionary to the Native Americans in the region.

His two years in America, however, were a disaster. He preached both to the natives and the colonists with little effect and tried unsuccessfully to impose his sense of strict religious discipline and organization on both. While the Native Americans listened politely but were unconvinced by Wesley's pleadings, the rough and tough colonists had little use for the rigid religion that he tried to impose on them. In fact, convinced that Wesley was a Papist, one of the colonists later complained that "to make our Subjection the more compleat [sic], a new kind of Tyranny was this Summer begun to be imposed

---

[2] For a more detailed description of the origins of the term *Methodist* as it relates to the followers of John Wesley, see generally Richard P. Heitzenrater, *Wesley and the People Called Methodists* (Nashville: Abingdon Press, 1995), 45–46.

upon us; for Mr. John Wesley who had come over and receiv'd by us as a Clergyman of the *Church of England*, soon discovered that his Aim was to enslave our Minds, as a necessary Preparative for enslaving our Bodies."[3]

While in Georgia, Wesley also began courting a young woman named Sophie Hopkey, but unskilled as he was in romantic relationships, his inexperienced advances—mixed with his own indecision about whether he should pursue undistracted holiness or marriage—more often left young Sophie confused. Consequently, after growing tired of trying to figure him out, in 1737 she decided to marry another. But when the new couple did not announce their wedding ahead of time as required by the Church of England, John—as colony chaplain—eventually barred both of them from receiving the Lord's Supper. This defamation of character so infuriated Sophie's uncle and guardian that he formed a rigged grand jury, which indicted Wesley on a range of charges related to his having "deviated from the principles and regulations of the Established Church, in many particulars inconsistent with the happiness and prosperity of this Colony."[4] Before the charges were brought to trial, however, Wesley slipped across the Savannah River one night and journeyed for several days through the Low Country swamps of South Carolina to Charleston.[5] There, he boarded a boat and returned to England feeling lost, dejected, and close to what today we might call a nervous breakdown. In his *Journal*, he recorded, "I went to America, to convert the Indians; but oh! who shall convert me? who, what is He that will deliver me from this evil heart of mischief? I have a fair summer religion."[6]

---

3   Pat Tailfer, Hugh Anderson, Da. Douglas, et al., *A True and Historical Narrative of the Colony of Georgia* . . . (Charles Town, SC, 1741), 29–30 (emphasis and capitalization in original), in Spencer Bidwell King Jr., ed., *Georgia Voices: A Documentary History to 1872* (Athens: University of Georgia Press, 1966), 19.

4   Grand Jury Indictment against John Wesley, in Heitzenrater, 70.

5   It was during his short stay in Charleston, waiting on his boat back to England, that Wesley saw firsthand the brutal work of American slavery. He saw slaves being whipped, beaten, and sold at market, and made a point to remember this experience after he returned to England. Based on these memories, he became a vocal opponent of the English slave trade, and his advocacy on this subject went on to inspire younger contemporaries to get the slave trade abolished in March 1807 with the Abolition of the Slave Trade Act.

6   John Wesley, *Journal* (January 24, 1738), in *The Bicentennial Edition of the Works of John Wesley*, vol. 18, *Journals and Diaries I*, ed. W. Reginald Ward and Richard Heitzenrater *(1735–1738)* (Nashville: Abingdon Press, 1988), 211.

CHAPTER 2

However, you may remember from the previous chapter that on his way to America from England, he had been impressed by the vital and fervent Christianity of a group of German Pietists known as **Moravians** on board his ship, the *Simmonds*. As mentioned earlier, during a great storm, the ship was tossed about fiercely, causing the English passengers to fear for their lives. All the while, however, the Moravians stood on deck, holding hands, singing songs of praise to God. This simple trust in God at once fascinated and baffled Wesley, and both during his sojourn in Georgia and back in England, he sought out some of these Moravians to inquire about their living faith.

Two Moravians in particular became good friends and influences to Wesley: Augustus Spangenberg and Peter Böhler. Both led him to consider the notion that Christian faith involved more than simply good works and/or strict discipline. While still in Georgia, Spangenberg famously questioned Wesley about his own personal faith:

> "My brother, I must first ask you one or two questions. Have you the witness within yourself? Does the Spirit of God bear witness with your spirit that you are a child of God?" I was surprised, and knew not what to answer. He observed it and asked, "Do you know Jesus Christ?" I paused and said, "I know He is the Saviour of the world." "True," replied he; "but do you know He has saved you?" I answered, "I hope He has died to save me." He only added, "Do you know yourself?" I said, "I do." But I fear they were vain words.[7]

After returning to London, it was Böhler who then encouraged Wesley to consider that mature Christian faith, or "perfect love" (first considered by Wesley in his intellectual interaction with Roman Catholic mysticism) is founded not in good works or mental assent, but in one's heart through personal trust in the atonement of Jesus Christ.

Aldersgate: A Turning Point (1738)

From this point, Wesley began seeking this kind of faith for himself—to experience what he called a new "vital piety." This search led him to a small

---

7 Wesley, *Journal* (February 7, 1736), in Ward and Heitzenrater, 18:146.

prayer meeting in London on May 24, 1738. There, he had a deep and meaningful encounter with Christ. In his *Journal* for that day, Wesley wrote these now-famous words:

> In the evening I went very unwillingly to a society on Aldersgate Street, where one was reading Luther's preface to the epistle to the Romans. About a quarter before nine, while he was describing the change which God works in the heart through faith in Christ, I felt my heart strangely warmed. I felt I did trust in Christ—Christ alone for my salvation; and an assurance was given me that He had taken away *my* sins, even *mine*, and saved *me* from the law of sin & death.[8]

In other words, for the first time in Wesley's life, Christian faith became personal—more than a series of disciplines to be followed or good deeds to be achieved.

> **Aldersgate**: a reference to John Wesley's pivotal life experience of May 24, 1738, at a prayer meeting on Aldersgate Street (London) in which he felt his heart "strangely warmed" through personal faith in Christ.

As a result, this "Aldersgate experience," as it is known today, has been identified as everything from Wesley's conversion, to the "assurance" of his salvation, to merely one of many turning points in his life. Yet, no matter how one perceives this experience in Wesley's life, it is pivotal in our contemporary understanding of him and his ministry. After all, many things began to change in Wesley's practice of ministry after his Aldersgate experience that eventually became hallmarks of the Wesleyan movement.

Unorthodox Evangelism: Field Preaching (1739)

One of these was his introduction to and eventual adoption of a new, unorthodox form of preaching. Following Aldersgate, Wesley tried to preach his new, personal faith in Christ in the local Anglican churches. Unfortunately, the establishment wasn't interested in this brand of Christianity, and

---

8 Wesley, *Journal* (May 24, 1738), in Ward and Heitzenrater, 18:249–50 (emphasis in original).

many Anglican churches started banning him from their pulpits. About this same time, Wesley renewed his friendship with an old colleague from the Oxford Holy Club, named **George Whitefield**, who invited Wesley to join him in ministry.

Figure 2.3. John Wesley preaching from his father's tombstone at Epworth Church. Photograph courtesy of www .victorianpicturelibrary.com. Reproduced by permission.

What was initially troublesome about this request was that Whitefield's ministry had taken up the Nonconformist/Dissenter practice of preaching to crowds in the outdoors—a practice that, while not illegal in that day, was certainly irregular and uncouth for a "proper" Anglican priest. Nevertheless, on April 2, 1739, Wesley reluctantly agreed to try Whitefield's preaching form, writing in his *Journal* that day: "At four in the afternoon I submitted to be more vile, and proclaimed in the highways the glad tidings of salvation."[9] What's more, Wesley seemed to have a knack for this type of preaching, eventually attracting and preaching to crowds as large as twenty thousand or more—all in the days before microphones and electronic amplification. This unorthodox style of evangelism became known as **field preaching**, as it involved Wesley preaching *wherever* he could gather a crowd and to *whomever* would listen: in open country fields; in city streets and squares; in parlors of private homes; in coal mines and factories.

---

9 Wesley, *Journal* (April 2, 1739), in Ward and Heitzenrater, 19:46.

> **Field preaching**: a form of evangelism used by Wesley and the early Methodists in which the gospel was preached from unorthodox places, such as open country fields, city squares, streets, factories, mines, or private home parlors.

On one famous occasion, when Wesley was banned from his own father's church in Epworth, he preached from the only place that the church didn't legally own—his father's tombstone. When the educated clergy and sophisticated Anglican laity wouldn't listen, Wesley took his message of personal faith in Christ to the poor of Britain's slums, factories, and coal mines. And since Wesley had no congregation/parish of his own, in June 1739 he famously wrote in his *Journal*, "I look upon all the world as my parish."[10]

Wesley and the Poor: Social Holiness

Yet, Wesley was not only concerned about sharing the gospel verbally. From his days at Oxford University, he was also very active in social work—sharing the gospel through deeds of love and compassion. In today's culture, personal salvation (evangelism) and social salvation (social work and justice) are often viewed as opposites. For Wesley, however, the two went hand in hand—he did not believe in giving people *spiritual* nourishment without also trying to meet their *physical* needs, and vice versa. Nineteenth-century Methodist biographer Thomas Blanshard once shared a story to illustrate this point. Samuel Bradburn, a friend and itinerant of Wesley's, found himself in dire financial need. When Wesley discovered this, he wrote Bradburn the following letter, and enclosed several five-pound notes along with it: "Dear Sammy: Trust in the Lord, and do good; so shalt thou dwell in the land, and verily thou shalt be fed. Yours affectionately, John Wesley." Bradburn immediately responded, "Rev. and Dear Sir: I have often been struck with the beauty of the passage of scripture quoted in your letter, but I must confess that I never saw such useful expository notes on it before. I am, rev. [*sic*] and dear sir, your obedient and

---

10 Wesley, *Journal* (June 11, 1739), in Ward and Heitzenrater, 19:67.

CHAPTER 2

grateful servant, S. Bradburn."[11] Here we see an illustration of Wesley's belief that Christian action/deeds must always accompany our *words*.

Figure 2.4. John Wesley's Newcastle orphan house. Illustration courtesy of https://www.skyscrapercity.com/showthread.php?t=982536&page=182.

Several further examples may suffice to illustrate Wesley's focus on providing practical assistance and aid to the poor of society:

- At his direction and financing, early Methodists opened homes for widows and orphanages for children.
- From his Oxford days, Wesley encouraged his Methodists to make a regular practice of visiting those in jail and prison.

---

11 Thomas W. Blanshard, *The Life of Samuel Bradburn, the Methodist Demosthenes* (London: E. Stock, 1870), 52–53. Google Play eBook, https://play.google.com/store/books/details?id=iksBAAAAQAAJ&rdid=book-iksBAAAAQAAJ&rdot=1. Recall that in Wesley's day a "note" referenced a type of money.

- Wesley collected and disbursed money, clothing, and food for the needy, and opened several modest credit unions in which they could invest.
- He and his Methodists sponsored literacy classes and courses in small business skills for those who could not afford formal schooling.
- In a society in which working parents had neither the time nor the training for the homeschooling of their families, Wesley opened schools for children, giving impetus to the drive for popular education.
- He and his Methodists operated several free and low-cost medical clinics and pharmacies for those who couldn't afford high medical costs.

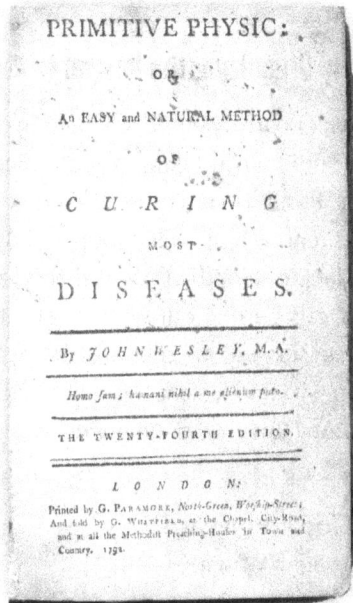

Figure 2.5. Frontispiece of John Wesley's Primitive Physic. Photograph courtesy of Wellcome Collection. Reproduced by permission.

- In addition to his religious writings, Wesley wrote numerous tracts on education, medical assistance, relaxation, and other topics to assist those who could not afford the expense of formal books or schooling. In fact, Wesley's most popular publication was neither religious nor theological in nature. Instead, *Primitive Physic: An Easy and Natural Method of Curing Most Diseases* (1747) was an inexpensive guide of home remedies, cures, and preventative medicines. While Wesley did believe strongly in the power of prayer and divine healing, he nevertheless also believed that such healing is brought about through medicine. Consequently,

Primitive Physic became a national best seller, and Wesley took its profits and invested them in the work of his Methodist ministry.[12]

> *Primitive Physick*: John Wesley's best-selling 1747 publication, written to share practical and inexpensive medical advice with those who could not afford private medical care.

It's no surprise, then, that to this day one of the hallmarks both of Wesleyan theology and practice has been its emphasis upon social work—attending to one's physical as well as spiritual needs.

The Development of Methodism: Organizing the Revival

As we consider the development of early Methodism, bear in mind that the Methodist revival was not the only revival taking place in England during Wesley's lifetime. Presbyterians, Puritans, and other Dissenter groups were also experiencing great religious renewals as well—former Holy Club member George Whitefield was, in fact, one of the great Calvinist evangelists of that day. Yet, most of these revivals burned out within a short span, while Methodism continued not only to survive but to flourish. Why? The answer lies in Methodism's organization. We find a clear sense of this focus in select portions of Wesley's 1788 sermon "On God's Vineyard."

On God's Vineyard[13]
by John Wesley

What could have been done more to my vineyard, that I have not done in it? wherefore, when I looked that it should bring forth grapes, brought it forth wild grapes? Isaiah 5:4

---

12 See generally, John Wesley, *Primitive Physic, or An Easy and Natural Method of Curing Most Diseases* (1747), in *The Bicentennial Edition of the Works of John Wesley*, vol. 32: *Medical and Health Writings*, ed. James G. Donat and Randy Maddox (Nashville: Abingdon Press, 2018), 110–266.

13 John Wesley, "On God's Vineyard" (Sermon 107), introduction, §§ 2, 3, and 5, ¶¶ 6–7, in *The Bicentennial Edition of the Works of John Wesley*, vol. 3, *Sermons III (71–114)*, ed. Albert C. Outler, (Nashville: Abingdon Press, 1988), 502–17.

The *vineyard of the Lord,* taking the word in its widest sense, may include the whole world. All the inhabitants of the earth may, in some sense, be called "the vineyard of the Lord;" "who hath made all nations of men, to dwell on all the face of the earth; that they might seek the Lord, if haply they may feel after him, and find him." But, in a narrower sense, the vineyard of the Lord may mean the Christian world; that is, all that name the name of Christ, and profess to obey his word. In a still narrower sense, it may be understood of what is termed the Reformed part of the Christian Church. In the narrowest of all, one may, by that phrase, "the vineyard of the Lord," mean, the body of people commonly called Methodists. In this sense I understand it now, meaning thereby that society only which began at Oxford in the year 1729, and remain united at this day. Understanding the word in this sense, I repeat the question which God proposes to the Prophet: "What could have been done more to my vineyard, that I have not done in it? wherefore, when I looked that it should bring forth grapes, brought it forth wild grapes?"

* * *

II.

Secondly, What could have been done which he hath not done in it, with regard to spiritual helps?

1. Let us consider this matter from the very beginning. Two young Clergymen, not very remarkable any way, of middle age, having a tolerable measure of health, though rather weak than strong, began, about fifty years ago, to call sinners to repentance. This they did, for a time, in many of the churches in and about London. But two difficulties arose: First. The churches were so crowded, that many of the parishioners could not get in. Secondly. They preached new doctrines,—that we are saved by faith, and that "without holiness no man could see the Lord." For one or other of these reasons, they were not long suffered to preach in the churches. They then preached in Moorfields, Kennington-Common, and in many other public places. The fruit of their preaching quickly appeared. Many sinners were changed both in heart and life. But it seemed this could not continue long; for every one clearly saw, these Preachers would quickly wear themselves out; and no Clergyman dared to assist them. But soon one and another, though not ordained,

offered to assist them. God gave a signal blessing to their word. Many sinners were thoroughly convinced of sin, and many truly converted to God. Their assistants increased, both in number, and in the success of their labours. Some of them were learned: some unlearned. Most of them were young; a few middle-aged: Some of them were weak; some, on the contrary, of remarkably strong understanding. But it pleased God to own them all; so that more and more brands were plucked out of the burning.

2. It may be observed, that these Clergymen, all this time, had no plan at all. They only went hither and thither, wherever they had a prospect of saving souls from death. But when more and more asked, "What must I do to be saved?" they were desired to meet all together. Twelve came the first Thursday night; forty the next; soon after, a hundred. And they continued to increase, till, three or four and twenty years ago, the London Society amounted to about 2,800.

3. "But how should this multitude of people be kept together? And how should it be known whether they walked worthy of their profession?" They were providentially led, when they were thinking on another thing, namely, paying the public debt, to divide all the people into little companies, or classes, according to their places of abode, and appoint one person in each class to see all the rest weekly. By this means it was quickly discovered if any of them lived in any known sin. If they did, they were first admonished; and, when judged incorrigible, excluded from the society.

4. This division of the people, and exclusion of those that walked disorderly, without any respect of persons, were helps which few other communities had. To these, as the societies increased, was soon added another. The stewards of the societies in each district were desired to meet the Preachers once a quarter, in some central place, to give an account of the spiritual and temporal state of their several societies. The use of these quarterly meetings was soon found to be exceeding great; in consideration of which, they were gradually spread to all the societies in the kingdom.

5. In order to increase the union between the Preachers, as well as that of the people, they were desired to meet all together in London; and, some time after, a select number of them. Afterwards, for more convenience, they met at London, Bristol, and

Leeds, alternately. They spent a few days together in this general Conference, in considering what might most conduce to the general good. The result was immediately signified to all their brethren. And they soon found, that what St. Paul observes of the whole Church, may be, in a measure, applied to every part of it: "The whole body being fitly framed together and compacted by that which every joint supplieth, maketh increase of the body to the edifying of itself in love." (Eph. 4:16)

6. That this may be the more effectually done, they have another excellent help, in the constant change of Preachers; it being their rule, that no Preacher shall remain in the same circuit more than two years together, and few of them more than one year. Some, indeed, have imagined that this was a hindrance to the work of God: But long experience, in every part of the kingdom, proves the contrary. This has always shown that the people profit less by any one person than by a variety of Preachers; while they

> Used the gifts on each bestow'd,
> Temper'd by the art of God.

7. Together with these helps, which are peculiar to their own society, they have all those which are enjoyed in common by the other members of the Church of England. Indeed, they have been long pressed to separate from it; to which they have had temptations of every kind. But they cannot, they dare not, they will not, separate from it, while they can remain therein with a clear conscience. It is true, if any sinful terms of communion were imposed upon them, then they would be constrained to separate; but as this is not the case at present, we rejoice to continue therein.

8. What then could God have done more for this his vineyard, which he hath not done in it, with regard to spiritual helps? He has hardly dealt so with any other people in the Christian world. If it be said, "He could have made them a separate people, like the Moravian Brethren;" I answer, This would have been a direct contradiction to his whole design in raising them up; namely, to spread scriptural religion throughout the land, among people of every denomination, leaving every one to hold his own opinions, and to follow his own mode of worship. This could only be done effectually, by leaving these things as they were, and endeavouring to leaven the whole nation with that "faith that worketh by love."

III.

1. Such are the spiritual helps which God has bestowed on this his vineyard with no sparing hand. Discipline might be inserted among these; but we may as well speak of it under a separate head. It is certain that, in this respect, the Methodists are a highly favoured people. Nothing can be more simple, nothing more rational, than the Methodist discipline: It is entirely founded on common sense, particularly applying the general rules of Scripture. Any person determined to save his soul may be united (this is the only condition required) with them. But this desire must be evidenced by three marks: Avoiding all known sin; doing good after his power; and, attending all the ordinances of God. He is then placed in such a class as is convenient for him, where he spends about an hour in a week. And, the next quarter, if nothing is objected to him, he is admitted into the society: And therein he may continue as long as he continues to meet his brethren, and walks according to his profession.

2. Their public service is at five in the morning, and six or seven in the evening, that their temporal business may not be hindered. Only on Sunday it begins between nine and ten, and concludes with the Lord's Supper. On Sunday evening the society meets; but care is taken to dismiss them early, that all the heads of families may have time to instruct their several households. Once a quarter, the principal Preacher in every circuit examines every member of the societies therein. By this means, if the behaviour of anyone is blameable, which is frequently to be expected in so numerous a body of people, it is easily discovered, and either the offence or the offender removed in time.

3. Whenever it is needful to exclude any disorderly member out of the society, it is done in the most quiet and inoffensive manner; only by not renewing his ticket at the quarterly visitation. But in some cases, where the offence is great, and there is danger of public scandal, it is judged necessary to declare, when all the members are present, "A. B. is no longer a member of our society." Now, what can be more rational or more scriptural than this simple discipline; attended, from the beginning to the end, with no trouble, expense, or delay?

* * *

V.

> 6. Was not another cause of it your despising that excellent help, union with a Christian society? Have you not read, "How can one be warm alone?" and, "Woe be unto him that is alone when he falleth?" But you have companions enough. Perhaps more than enough; more than are helpful to your soul. But have you enough that are athirst for God, and that labour to make you so? Have you companions enough that watch over your soul, as they that must give account; and that freely and faithfully warn you, if you take any false step, or are in danger of doing so? I fear you have few of these companions, or else you would bring forth better fruit!
>
> 7. If you are a member of the society, do you make a full use of your privilege? Do you never fail to meet your class; and that not as matter of form, but expecting that when you are met together in his name, your Lord will be in the midst of you? Are you truly thankful for the amazing liberty of conscience which is vouchsafed to you and your brethren; such as never was enjoyed before by persons in your circumstances? And are you thankful to the Giver of every good gift for the general spread of true religion? Surely, you can never praise God enough for all these blessings, so plentifully showered down upon you, till you praise him with angels and archangels, and all the company of heaven!

As Wesley wrote this sermon toward the end of his life, we can identify within it a few of the aspects of Methodist organization that he considered to be reasons for its success:

1) Laity-led small group ministry. As we learned in chapter 1, this approach to ministry was not original with the Wesleyan revival—the early church, Lutherans, Pietists, and Anglicans all utilized forms of small group ministry. However, Wesley's approach radically expounded the concepts found in these, grounding them in his via salutis and asking participants to be accountable to specific forms of Christian discipline (his "General Rules" of Methodism) in a way not usually asked.

> **Structure of early Methodism**: a reference to the societies, classes, and bands of early Methodism, in which seekers would explore and converts would mature in their faith in Christ. Methodist societies in a

> community were made up of required, coed "classes" of twelve, open to both seekers and converts. In addition, converts could also voluntarily participate in single-gender "bands" of five to eight people if they desired further growth in their faith.

In his case, as we read above, when those listening to his field preaching desired to grow further in faith, he organized them into small groups who would meet together for encouragement, prayer, study, service, and accountability.[14] These groups eventually formed the basis for the Methodist societies in every major city in Britain, and—unlike most of the Anglican religious societies—these were led primarily by committed laity (including, at times, even women—something unheard of in Wesley's day).

It has been estimated that approximately one out of every eight Methodists held significant leadership roles in the Wesleyan revival in England. And these were not the educated and wealthy patrons of society, who had a lot of time on their hands, but instead were the laboring men and women, who rarely had much education but were spiritually gifted and eager to serve. For that matter, even the majority of "clergy" in early Methodism were lay preachers—those who had not received formal education and ordination through the Church of England.

2) The itinerant system. As we also read in section 2, paragraph 6 of the sermon above, since few ordained Anglican clergy stepped in to assist Wesley in the spread of Methodism, he created an *itinerant* system whereby his preachers were sent to specific places of ministry (or "appointments") within a "circuit" (a rotation of ministry sites), and then moved/"reappointed" to a new place within that circuit after a period of time—a practice we Methodists still utilize today. By this means, Wesley felt that each preacher's gifts could be best matched with the needs of each ministry context, and—over time—each Methodist community would have the benefit of different pastoral skill sets to help them grow and mature in faith. Historian Abel Stevens once stated, "The itinerants were taught to manage difficulties in the societies, to face mobs, to brave any weather, to subsist without means, except such as might casually occur on their routes, to rise [and pray] at 4

---

14 Find these in Wesley's sermon "On God's Vineyard": § 2, ¶¶ 1–4; § 3, ¶¶ 1–3; and § 5, ¶¶ 6–7.

a.m. and preach at 5 a.m., to scatter books and tracts, to live by [the Methodist] rule, and to die without fear."[15]

3) Methodist conferences. Methodism grew so rapidly that Wesley soon found it impossible to visit each preacher as often as he desired. So, to keep connected with them (and them with each other), in 1744 he called together the first "Annual Conference"—an annual gathering of all his preachers for the purpose of worship and business regarding the work of the revival, a practice we continue today.[16]

Figure 2.6. First Methodist Conference, 1744. Image courtesy of the General Commission on Archives and History of The United Methodist Church, Madison, New Jersey. Reproduced by permission.

4) A renewal movement. Methodism has always been strongest when viewed as a renewal movement. As indicated in section 2, paragraphs 7–8 of the sermon above, Wesley never intended for his Methodists to separate from the Church of England, nor for his "societies" to become a new church. Instead, they were intended merely to be a source and instrument of renewal for and within his beloved Church of England. In emphasis of this point, he once famously wrote, "I declare once more, that I live and die a member of the Church of England, and that none who regard my judgment

---

15 Abel Stevens in Howard Snyder, *The Radical Wesley* (Downers Grove, IL: Francis Asbury Press, 1980), 63.

16 Wesley, "On God's Vineyard," § 2, ¶ 5.

or advice will ever separate from it."[17] Nevertheless, following America's independence from Britain, Wesley did help create the Methodist Episcopal Church in America, and following his death on March 2, 1791, Methodists in England eventually did form several new denominations there.

Growth and Legacy of the Movement

Like all new religious movements, Wesley and the early Methodists faced their fair share of controversy within British society. Yet, in spite of it all (and perhaps even because of it), Methodism spread and flourished. What began in 1743 as a single Methodist circuit in England with only a few members had by 1798 grown to a ministry of 149 circuits in England, Wales, Scotland, and Ireland, with nearly 102,000 members and an additional 50,000 Methodists in the United States, Nova Scotia, and the Caribbean Islands.

Figure 2.7. John Wesley preaching in City Chapel. Engraving by T. Blood, 1822. Illustration courtesy of Wellcome Collection. Reproduced by permission.

During his lifetime, Wesley had written, translated, and edited more than five hundred books and pamphlets, traveled more than 250,000 miles on horseback, and preached nearly forty-four thousand sermons! Today, the world Methodist family claims more than 40 million members, with nearly

---

17 John Wesley, "Farther Thoughts on Separation from the Church" (December 1789), published in F. O. Morris, "The Ghost of Wesley," *Arminian Magazine*, 1790, 52. Google Play eBook https://play.google.com/store/books/details?id=Z8MHAAAAQAAJ&rdid=book-Z8MHAAAAQAAJ&rdot=1.

20 million of those in North America, in more than twenty-five Methodist and/or Wesleyan-related denominations. In America, these include denominational traditions such as The United Methodist Church; the African Methodist Episcopal Church; African Methodist Episcopal Zion Church; the Christian Methodist Episcopal Church; the Wesleyan Church; the Church of the Nazarene; the Salvation Army; the Free Methodist Church; the Christian and Missionary Alliance; and the Church of God (Cleveland, Tennessee).

In the time since his death, Wesley has been called everything from a second-rate theologian, to a religious genius, to one whose movement prevented a bloody revolution in Britain similar to the one that occurred in France in the 1790s.[18] However, regardless of how one views Wesley the man, his understanding of theology and his practice of ministry have become irrefutable parts of contemporary Christian heritage. Therefore, we'll spend the rest of this book exploring the meaning and use of these in Christian faith as we know it today.

Discussion Questions

1. Based on what you read in this chapter, what is the importance of family in the nurturing, shaping, and development of Christian faith? What has been your experience of this?

2. In the preface to his book *Hymns and Sacred Poems*, Wesley insisted that "solitary religion is not to be found" in the Bible and that "the gospel of Christ knows of no religion, but social." Discuss how this proved to be true in the story of Wesley's own life (i.e., how who he became was shaped by those around him).

3. Based on the story of Wesley's life, what would you say is the importance of knowing and being able to articulate one's own personal narrative and testimony for Christian life and ministry? If you are a Christian, how have you carried this out in your own story?

---

18 This was first proposed in the early twentieth century by French historian Elie Halèvy (1870–1937) in his work *History of the English People*. Later historians and sociologists have subsequently refuted that claim, while still others (such as Bernard Semmel in his book *The Methodist Revolution*) have clarified it by saying that, far from *preventing* social revolution, Wesley's Methodism *was* the social revolution of England (albeit a nonviolent one).

4. Think about the story and development of your own spiritual life. If you were to share the story of the journey of your spiritual life with others, what would be the major events and/or themes that you would share? (Suggestion: make a time line tracing the major spiritual events and/or milestones of your own life to more easily see these).

5. From this chapter's story of the origins of early Methodism, discuss the essential need for and importance of organization and discipline in a movement of religious revival.

Part Two

The Christian Life and Wesley's "Way of Salvation"
(Via Salutis)

CHAPTER 3

TURNING TO GOD: THE WORK OF PREVENIENT GRACE

To understand how Wesley's theology and practice of ministry manifest themselves in today's cultural context, we first need to explore the heart of that theology in its mature form, beginning with a discussion of why he believed humanity needs salvation in the first place.

Humanity's "Original State" and the "*Imago Dei*"

For Wesley, this need is rooted in the fact that humanity did not start out needing it at all. Instead, Genesis 1:26 introduces what he called "that glorious image of God wherein man was originally created."[1]

> The "image of God": a term used to describe the nature and character of human beings as originally created in the spiritual likeness of God. Also referred to in Latin as the *imago Dei*.

For him, this *imago Dei* (Latin for "image of God") was the "original state" of humanity, and it included several important characteristics:

- **an inherent tendency toward love and goodness,** regarding humanity's relationship both with God and with our neighbors

- **a perfect union with God and God's nature**—i.e., that humanity was originally filled completely with divine love, containing no sin or brokenness whatsoever

- **an instinctive God-centeredness**—everything humanity said and did was always (instinctively) oriented around and within God's perfect will

---

[1] John Wesley, "Original Sin" (Sermon 44, printed below), introduction, ¶ 4, in *The Bicentennial Edition of the Works of John Wesley*, vol. 2, *Sermons II (34–70)*, ed. Albert C. Outler (Nashville: Abingdon Press, 1985), 173.

Let me illustrate this "original state" in two different ways (the latter of which I'll be referencing in other places throughout this book).

First, think of this in terms of a circle in which humanity in the imago Dei shares a "oneness" with God, who created it (fig. 3.1).

A second way to illustrate this is to picture a podium that represents God, and yourself as a symbolic representation of humanity. Now, extend your arms around that podium, giving it a big "hug," so to speak. That "oneness" with the podium represents the way God created humanity, according to what we find in Genesis 1–2. Yet, most of us know that what I've just described is *not* reflective of the general nature and state of humanity today. So, what happened?

Figure 3.1

Humanity's Natural State and Original Sin

To appreciate Wesley's understanding of the answer to this, it will be helpful to start by reading his 1759 sermon "Original Sin."

Original Sin[2]
by John Wesley

And God saw that the wickedness of man was great in the earth, and that every imagination of the thoughts of his heart was only evil continually. Genesis 6:5

1. How widely different is this from the fair pictures of human nature which men have drawn in all ages! The writings of many of the ancients abound with gay descriptions of the dignity of man; whom some of them paint as having all virtue and happiness in his composition, or, at least, entirely in his power, without being beholden to any other being; yea, as self-sufficient, able to live on his own stock, and little inferior to God himself.

---

2   John Wesley, "Original Sin," in Outler, 2:170–85.

2. Nor have Heathens alone, men who are guided in their researches by little more than the dim light of reason, but many likewise of them that bear the name of Christ, and to whom are entrusted the oracles of God, spoken as magnificently concerning the nature of man, as if it were all innocence and perfection. Accounts of this kind have particularly abounded in the present century; and perhaps in no part of the world more than in our own country. Here not a few persons of strong understanding, as well as extensive learning, have employed their utmost abilities to show, what they termed, "the fair side of human nature." And it must he acknowledged, that, if their accounts of him be just, man is still but "a little lower than the angels;" or, as the words may be more literally rendered, "a little less than God."

3. Is it any wonder, that these accounts are very readily received by the generality of men? For who is not easily persuaded to think favourably of himself? Accordingly, writers of this kind are most universally read, admired, applauded. And innumerable are the converts they have made, not only in the gay, but the learned world. So that it is now quite unfashionable to talk otherwise, to say any thing to the disparagement of human nature; which is generally allowed, notwithstanding a few infirmities, to be very innocent, and wise, and virtuous!

4. But, in the mean time, what must we do with our Bibles?—for they will never agree with this. These accounts, however pleasing to flesh and blood, are utterly irreconcilable with the scriptural. The Scripture avers, that "by one man's disobedience all men were constituted sinners;" that "in Adam all died," spiritually died, lost the life and the image of God; that fallen, sinful Adam then "begat a son in his own likeness;"—nor was it possible he should beget him in any other; for "who can bring a clean thing out of an unclean?"—that consequently we, as well as other men, were by nature "dead in trespasses and sins," "without hope, without God in the world," and therefore "children of wrath;" that every man may say, "I was shapen in wickedness, and in sin did my mother conceive me;" that "there is no difference," in that "all have sinned and come short of the glory of God," of that glorious image of God wherein man was originally created. And hence, when "the Lord looked down from heaven upon the children of men, he saw they were all gone out of the way; they

CHAPTER 3

were altogether become abominable, there was none righteous, no, not one," none that truly sought after God: Just agreeable this, to what is declared by the Holy Ghost in the words above recited, "God saw," when he looked down from heaven before, "that the wickedness of man was great in the earth;" so great, that "every imagination of the thoughts of his heart was only evil continually."

This is God's account of man: From which I shall take occasion,

I. First, to show what men were before the flood:
II. Secondly, to inquire, whether they are not the same now: And,
III. Thirdly, to add some inferences.

I.

1. I am, First, by opening the words of the text, to show what men were before the flood. And we may fully depend on the account here given: For God saw it, and he cannot be deceived. He "saw that the wickedness of man was great:"—Not of this or that man; not of a few men only; not barely of the greater part, but of man in general; of men universally. The word includes the whole human race, every partaker of human nature. And it is not easy for us to compute their numbers, to tell how many thousands and millions they were. The earth then retained much of its primeval beauty and original fruitfulness. The face of the globe was not rent and torn as it is now; and spring and summer went hand in hand. It is therefore probable, it afforded sustenance for far more inhabitants than it is now capable of sustaining; and these must be immensely multiplied, while men begat sons and daughters for seven or eight hundred years together. Yet, among all this inconceivable number, only "Noah found favour with God." He alone (perhaps including part of his household) was an exception from the universal wickedness, which, by the just judgment of God, in a short time after brought on universal destruction. All the rest were partakers in the same guilt, as they were in the same punishment.

2. "God saw all the imaginations of the thoughts of his heart;"—of his soul, his inward man, the spirit within him, the principle of all his inward and outward motions. He "saw all the imaginations:" It is not possible to find a word of a more extensive

signification. It includes whatever is formed, made, fabricated within; all that is or passes in the soul; every inclination, affection, passion, appetite; every temper, design, thought. It must of consequence include every word and action, as naturally flowing from these fountains, and being either good or evil according to the fountain from which they severally flow.

3. Now God saw that all this, the whole thereof, was evil;—contrary to moral rectitude; contrary to the nature of God, which necessarily includes all good; contrary to the divine will, the eternal standard of good and evil; contrary to the pure, holy image of God, wherein man was originally created, and wherein he stood when God, surveying the works of his hands, saw them all to be very good; contrary to justice, mercy, and truth, and to the essential relations which each man bore to his Creator and his fellow-creatures.

4. But was there not good mingled with the evil? Was there not light intermixed with the darkness? No; none at all: "God saw that the whole imagination of the heart of man was only evil." It cannot indeed be denied, but many of them, perhaps all, had good motions put into their hearts; for the Spirit of God did then also "strive with man," if haply he might repent, more especially during that gracious reprieve, the hundred and twenty years, while the ark was preparing. But still "in his flesh dwelt no good thing;" all his nature was purely evil: It was wholly consistent with itself, and unmixed with anything of an opposite nature.

5. However, it may still be matter of inquiry, "Was there no intermission of this evil? Were there no lucid intervals, wherein something good might be found in the heart of man?" We are not here to consider, what the grace of God might occasionally work in his soul; and, abstracted from this, we have no reason to believe, there was any intermission of that evil. For God, who "saw the whole imagination of the thoughts of his heart to be *only* evil," saw likewise, that it was always the same, that it "was only evil *continually*;" every year, every day, every hour, every moment. He never deviated into good.

II.

Such is the authentic account of the whole race of mankind which He who knoweth what is in man, who searcheth the heart and trieth the reins, hath left upon record for our instruction.

Such were all men before God brought the flood upon the earth. We are, Secondly, to inquire, whether they are the same now.

1. And this is certain, the Scripture gives us no reason to think any otherwise of them. On the contrary, all the above cited passages of Scripture refer to those who lived after the flood. It was above a thousand years after, that God declared by David concerning the children of men, "They are all gone out of the way, of truth and holiness; there is none righteous, no, not one." And to this bear all the Prophets witness, in their several generations. So Isaiah, concerning God's peculiar people, (and certainly the Heathens were in no better condition) "The whole head is sick, and the whole heart faint. From the sole of the foot even unto the head there is no soundness; but wounds, and bruises, and putrefying sores." The same account is given by all the Apostles, yea, by the whole tenor of the oracles of God. From all these we learn, concerning man in his natural state, unassisted by the grace of God, that "every imagination of the thoughts of his heart is" still "evil, only evil," and that "continually."

2. And this account of the present state of man is confirmed by daily experience. It is true, the natural man discerns it not: And this is not to be wondered at. So long as a man born blind continues so, he is scarce sensible of his want: Much less, could we suppose a place where all were born without sight, would they be sensible of the want of it. In like manner, so long as men remain in their natural blindness of understanding, they are not sensible of their spiritual wants, and of this in particular. But as soon as God opens the eyes of their understanding, they see the state they were in before; they are then deeply convinced, that "every man living," themselves especially, are, by nature, "altogether vanity;" that is, folly and ignorance, sin and wickedness.

3. We see, when God opens our eyes, that we were before *aqeoi en tv kosmv*—without God, or, rather, *Atheists, in the world*. We had, by nature, no knowledge of God, no acquaintance with him. It is true, as soon as we came to the use of reason, we learned "the invisible things of God, even his eternal power and Godhead, from the things that are made." From the things that are seen we inferred the existence of an eternal, powerful Being, that is not seen. But still, although we acknowledged his being we had no acquaintance with him. As we know there is

an Emperor of China, whom yet we do not know; so we knew there was a King of all the earth, yet we knew him not. Indeed we could not by any of our natural faculties. By none of these could we attain the knowledge of God. We could no more perceive him by our natural understanding, than we could see him with our eyes. For "no one knoweth the Father but the Son, and he to whom the Son willeth to reveal him. And no one knoweth the Son but the Father, and he to whom the Father revealeth him."

4. We read of an ancient king, who, being desirous to know what was the *natural language* of men, in order to bring the matter to a certain issue, made the following experiment: He ordered two infants, as soon as they were born, to be conveyed to a place prepared for them, where they were brought up without any instruction at all, and without ever hearing a human voice. And what was the event? Why that when they were at length brought out of their confinement, they spoke no language at all; they uttered only inarticulate sounds, like those of other animals. Were two infants in like manner to be brought up from the womb without being instructed in any religion, there is little room to doubt but (unless the grace of God interposed) the event would be just the same. They would have no religion at all: They would have no more knowledge of God than the beasts of the field, than the wild ass's colt. Such is natural religion, abstracted from traditional, and from the influences of God's Spirit!

5. And having no knowledge, we can have no love of God: We cannot love him we know not. Most men *talk* indeed of loving God, and perhaps imagine they do; at least, few will acknowledge they do not love him: But the fact is too plain to be denied. No man loves God by nature, any more than he does a stone, or the earth he treads upon. What we love we delight in: But no man has naturally any delight in God. In our natural state we cannot conceive how any one should delight in him. We take no pleasure in him at all; he is utterly tasteless to us. To love God! It is far above, out of our sight. We cannot, naturally, attain unto it.

6. We have by nature, not only no love, but no fear of God. It is allowed, indeed, that most men have, sooner or later, a kind of senseless, irrational fear, properly called superstition; though the blundering Epicureans gave it the name of religion. Yet even this is not natural, but acquired; chiefly by conversation or from

example. By nature "God is not in all our thoughts:" We leave him to manage his own affairs, to sit quietly, as we imagine, in heaven, and leave us on earth to manage ours; so that we have no more of the fear of God before our eyes, than of the love of God in our hearts.

7. Thus are all men "Atheists in the world." But Atheism itself does not screen us from idolatry. In his natural state, every man born into the world is a rank idolater. Perhaps, indeed, we may not be such in the vulgar sense of the word. We do not, like the idolatrous Heathens, worship molten or graven images. We do not bow down to the stock of a tree, to the work of our own hands. We do not pray to the angels or saints in heaven, any more than to the saints that are upon the earth. But what then? We have set up our idols in our hearts; and to these we bow down and worship them: We worship ourselves, when we pay that honour to ourselves which is due to God only. Therefore all pride is idolatry; it is ascribing to ourselves what is due to God alone. And although pride was not made for man, yet where is the man that is born without it? But hereby we rob God of his unalienable right, and idolatrously usurp his glory.

8. But pride is not the only sort of idolatry which we are all by nature guilty of. Satan has stamped his own image on our heart in self-will also. "I will," said he, before he was cast out of heaven, "I will sit upon the sides of the north;" I will do my own will and pleasure, independently on that of my Creator. The same does every man born into the world say, and that in a thousand instances; nay, and avow it too, without ever blushing upon the account, without either fear or shame. Ask the man, "Why did you do this?" He answers, "Because I had a mind to it." What is this but, "Because it was my will;" that is, in effect, because the devil and I agreed; because Satan and I govern our actions by one and the same principle. The will of God, mean time, is not in his thoughts, is not considered in the least degree; although it be the supreme rule of every intelligent creature, whether in heaven or earth, resulting from the essential, unalterable relation which all creatures bear to their Creator.

9. So far we bear the image of the devil, and tread in his steps. But at the next step we leave Satan behind; we run into an idolatry whereof he is not guilty: I mean love of the world;

which is now as natural to every man, as to love his own will. What is more natural to us than to seek happiness in the creature, instead of the Creator?—to seek that satisfaction in the works of his hands, which can be found in God only? What more natural than "the desire of the flesh?" That is, of the pleasure of sense in every kind? Men indeed talk magnificently of despising these low pleasures, particularly men of learning and education. They affect to sit loose to the gratification of these appetites wherein they stand on a level with the beasts that perish. But it is mere affectation; for every man is conscious to himself, that in this respect he is, by nature, a very beast. Sensual appetites, even those of the lowest kind, have, more or less, the dominion over him. They lead him captive; they drag him to and fro, in spite of his boasted reason. The man, with all his good breeding, and other accomplishments, has no pre-eminence over the goat: Nay, it is much to be doubted, whether the beast has not the pre-eminence over him. Certainly he has, if we may hearken to one of their modern oracles, who very decently tells us,

> *Once in a season beasts too taste of love;*
> *Only the beast of reason is its slave,*
> *And in that folly drudges all the year.*

A considerable difference indeed, it must be allowed, there is between man and man, arising (beside that wrought by preventing grace) from difference of constitution and of education. But, notwithstanding this, who, that is not utterly ignorant of himself, can here cast the first stone at another? Who can abide the test of our blessed Lord's comment on the Seventh Commandment: "He that looketh on a woman to lust after her hath committed adultery with her already in his heart?" So that one knows not which to wonder at most, the ignorance or the insolence of those men who speak with such disdain of them that are overcome by desires which every man has felt in his own breast; the desire of every pleasure of sense, innocent or not, being natural to every child of man.

10. And so is "the desire of the eye;" the desire of the pleasures of the imagination. These arise either from great, or beautiful, or uncommon objects;—if the two former do not coincide with the latter; for perhaps it would appear, upon a diligent inquiry, that neither grand nor beautiful objects please any longer

than they are new; that when the novelty of them is over, the greatest part, at least, of the pleasure they give is over; and in the same proportion as they become familiar, they become flat and insipid. But let us experience this ever so often, the same desire will remain still. The inbred thirst continues fixed in the soul; nay, the more it is indulged, the more it increases, and incites us to follow after another, and yet another object; although we leave every one with an abortive hope, and a deluded expectation. Yea,

> *The hoary fool, who many days*
> *Has struggled with continued sorrow,*
> *Renews his hope, and fondly lays*
> *The desperate bet upon tomorrow!*
> *To-morrow comes! 'Tis noon! 'Tis night!*
> *This day, like all the former, flies:*
> *Yet on he goes, to seek delight*
> *To-morrow, till to-night he dies!*

11. A third symptom of this fatal disease, the love of the world, which is so deeply rooted in our nature, is "the pride of life;" the desire of praise, of the honour that cometh of men. This the greatest admirers of human nature allow to be strictly natural; as natural as the sight, or hearing, or any other of the external senses. And are they ashamed of it, even men of letters, men of refined and improved understanding? So far from it that they glory therein! They applaud themselves for their love of applause! Yea, eminent Christians, so called, make no difficulty of adopting the saying of the old, vain Heathen, Animi dissoluti est et nequam negligere quid de se homines sentiant: "Not to regard what men think of us is the mark of a wicked and abandoned mind." So that to go calm and unmoved through honour and dishonour, through evil report and good report, is with them a sign of one that is, indeed, not fit to live: "Away with such a flow from the earth!" But would one imagine that these men had ever heard of Jesus Christ or his Apostles; or that they knew who it was that said, "How can ye believe who receive honour one of another, and seek not the honour which cometh of God only?" But if this is really so, if it be impossible to believe, and consequently to please God, so long as we receive or seek honour one of another, and seek not the honour which cometh of God only; then in what a condition are all mankind! The Christians as well as Heathens! Since they

all seek honour one of another! since it is as natural for them so to do, themselves being the judges, as it is to see the light which strikes upon their eye, or to hear the sound which enters their ear; yea, since they account it a sign of a virtuous mind, to seek the praise of men, and of a vicious one, to be content with the honour that cometh of God only!

III.

1. I proceed to draw a few inferences from what has been said. And, First, from hence we may learn one grand fundamental difference between Christianity, considered as a system of doctrines, and the most refined Heathenism. Many of the ancient Heathens have largely described the vices of particular men. They have spoken much against their covetousness, or cruelty; their luxury, or prodigality. Some have dared to say that "no man is born without vices of one kind or another." But still as none of them were apprized of the fall of man, so none of them knew of his total corruption. They knew not that all men were empty of all good, and filled with all manner of evil. They were wholly ignorant of the entire depravation of the whole human nature, of every man born into the world, in every faculty of his soul, not so much by those particular vices which reign in particular persons, as by the general flood of Atheism and idolatry, of pride, self-will, and love of the world. This, therefore, is the first grand distinguishing point between Heathenism and Christianity. The one acknowledges that many men are infected with many vices, and even born with a proneness to them; but supposes withal, that in some the natural good much over-balances the evil: The other declares that all men are conceived in sin," and "shapen in wickedness;"—that hence there is in every man a "carnal mind, which is enmity against God, which is not, cannot be, subject to" his "law;" and which so infects the whole soul, that "there dwelleth in" him, "in his flesh," in his natural state, "no good thing;" but "every imagination of the thoughts of his heart is evil," only evil, and that "continually."

2. Hence we may, Secondly, learn, that all who deny this, call it original sin, or by any other title, are but Heathens still, in the fundamental point which differences Heathenism from Christianity. They may, indeed, allow, that men have many vices; that some are born with us; and that, consequently, we are not

born altogether so wise or so virtuous as we should be; there being few that will roundly affirm, "We are born with as much propensity to good as to evil, and that every man is, by nature, as virtuous and wise as Adam was at his creation." But here is the *shibboleth:* Is man by nature filled with all manner of evil? Is he void of all good? Is he wholly fallen? Is his soul totally corrupted? Or, to come back to the text, is "every imagination of the thoughts of his heart only evil continually?" Allow this, and you are so far a Christian. Deny it, and you are but an Heathen still.

3. We may learn from hence, in the Third place, what is the proper nature of religion, of the religion of Jesus Christ. It is *qerapeia yuchs*, God's method of *healing a soul* which is thus diseased. Hereby the great Physician of souls applies medicines to heal this sickness; to restore human nature, totally corrupted in all its faculties. God heals all our Atheism by the knowledge of Himself, and of Jesus Christ whom he hath sent; by giving us faith, a divine evidence and conviction of God, and of the things of God,—in particular, of this important truth, "Christ loved *me*—and gave himself for *me.*" By repentance and lowliness of heart, the deadly disease of pride is healed; that of self-will by resignation, a meek and thankful submission to the will of God; and for the love of the world in all its branches, the love of God is the sovereign remedy. Now, this is properly religion, "faith" thus "working by love;" working the genuine meek humility, entire deadness to the world, with a loving, thankful acquiescence in, and conformity to, the whole will and word of God.

4. Indeed, if man were not thus fallen, there would be no need of all this. There would be no occasion for this work in the heart, this renewal in the spirit of our mind. The superfluity of godliness would then be a more proper expression than the "superfluity of naughtiness." For an outside religion, without any godliness at all, would suffice to all rational intents and purposes. It does, accordingly, suffice, in the judgment of those who deny this corruption of our nature. They make very little more of religion than the famous Mr. Hobbes did of reason. According to him, reason is only "a well-ordered train of words:" According to them, religion is only a well-ordered train of words and actions. And they speak consistently with themselves; for if the inside be not full of wickedness, if this be clean already, what remains, but

to "cleanse the outside of the cup?" Outward reformation, if their supposition be just, is indeed the one thing needful.

5. But ye have not so learned the oracles of God. Ye know, that He who seeth what is in man gives a far different account both of nature and grace, of our fall and our recovery. Ye know that the great end of religion is, to renew our hearts in the image of God, to repair that total loss of righteousness and true holiness which we sustained by the sin of our first parent. Ye know that all religion which does not answer this end, all that stops short of this, the renewal of our soul in the image of God, after the likeness of Him that created it, is no other than a poor farce, and a mere mockery of God, to the destruction of our own soul. O beware of all those teachers of lies, who would palm this upon you for Christianity! Regard them not, although they should come unto you with all the deceivableness of unrighteousness; with all smoothness of language, all decency, yea, beauty and elegance of expression, all professions of earnest good will to you, and reverence for the Holy Scriptures. Keep to the plain, old faith, "once delivered to the saints," and delivered by the Spirit of God to our hearts. Know your disease! Know your cure! Ye were born in sin: Therefore, "ye must be born again," born of God. By nature ye are wholly corrupted. By grace ye shall be wholly renewed. In Adam ye all died: In the second Adam, in Christ, ye all are made alive. "You that were dead in sins hath he quickened:" He hath already given you a principle of life, even faith in him who loved you and gave himself for you! Now, "go on from faith to faith," until your whole sickness be healed; and all that "mind be in you which was also in Christ Jesus!"

Here, we read Wesley's understanding of what he calls the "natural state" of humanity,[3] or *"original sin,"* first identified in Genesis 3 with the fall of Adam and Eve. Let's return to our two illustrations to talk about what this means. First, the completed circle illustration (fig. 3.2) now shows three things: (1) one broken half circle representing God and the image of God that we

---

3 To be clear, Wesley uses the phrase "natural state" in two ways: (1) to reference the *speculative* state of corporate humanity devoid of God's grace (as here); but also (2) the *actual* state of an individual person who has not yet experienced Regeneration/New Birth (described in chapter 4).

humans were created to have/be in; (2) the other broken half circle representing *fallen* humanity, devoid of God's grace; and (3) a large gap separating the two, known in theological circles as "original sin."

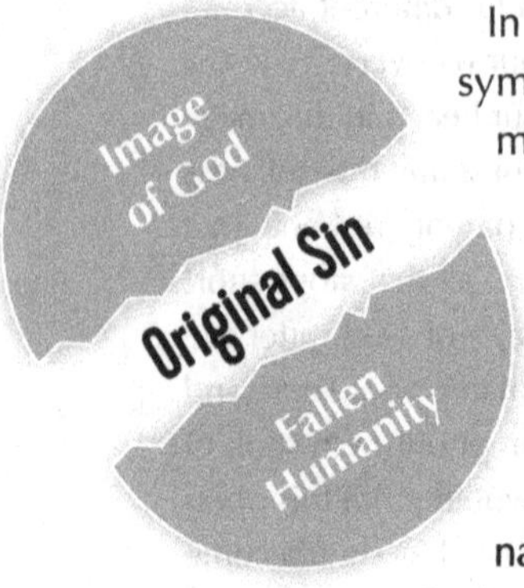

In our second illustration ("hugging" the podium, symbolizing the oneness between God and humanity in the "original state"), picture yourself walking and facing away from that podium, so that there is now a gap of ten feet or more between you and it. The podium still represents God and how we were created to be in God's image. However, one's distance from that podium now represents the fallen/broken nature of humanity, who has walked away from God, with the gap between representing "original sin."

Figure 3.2

> **Original sin:** A term used to describe the state of inherent brokenness caused by the spiritual "fall" of Adam and Eve (Genesis 3) in our "natural" state (i.e., apart from God). All sinful actions and behaviors today result from this brokenness.

According to Wesley, this "natural state" of humanity is characterized by the following effects:

- Humanity's original inherent tendency to love and do good *devolved* into an **inherent tendency to sin and do evil**. Verse 2 of the famous Wesley hymn "Love Divine, All Loves Excelling" refers to this as our "bent to sinning."[4]

- Humanity's instinctive God-centeredness turned into an **instinctive self-centeredness**—meaning that our inherent focus is no longer on God or the things of God, but upon ourselves. Humans experience this today in our infatuation with self: from "self-help" books, to our societal focus on consumerism and marketing, and even to the naming of many of our culture's iconic products (like the **i**Phone and **i**Pad).

---

4 Charles Wesley, "Love Divine, All Love's Excelling" (1747) in *The United Methodist Hymnal* (Nashville: The United Methodist Publishing House, 1989), verse 2, 384.

- As human beings, we **do not care if there is sin or brokenness** in our lives—instead, we possess a general *apathy* about things spiritual and/or divine. Our spiritual eyes, so to speak, have either unconsciously or willfully (or both) turned away from God and God's image within us, so that they are fixed on things other than God. In our "separated" state in the podium example, this can be illustrated by us turning our bodies and eyes completely *away from* the podium, so that our focus is elsewhere.

- A separation/gap now exists between God and us, and between who we are and who we want and were created to be. This separation is so great that in our own strength it is impossible for us to respond to or care about God's love at all. Hence, *no response* toward God is possible. Indeed, in this state, our disposition, motivations, and passions are so bound by original sin that there is no desire to respond to or care about God in the first place! The reason for this is that while Wesley used the phrase "original sin" to refer to our inherent human *tendency* toward sin, he also used the phrase "actual sin" to refer to specific *acts* of sin (of which there was "inward sin," referencing our inward *passions* and dispositions of our *heart*, and "outward sin," referencing our outward *actions* and *behaviors*). However, Wesley believed that it was not our "actual sin" (the bad things that we *do*) that keeps us separated from God, but our inherent "brokenness" (i.e., original sin) in the first place. As perhaps you've heard it popularly said before, "We are not sinners because we commit acts of sin. Instead, we commit acts of sin because we are sinners." So, in our "natural state" without God, we exist as broken beings. This brokenness, consequently, is why humanity needs saving/salvation in the first place.

The Goal / Purpose of Salvation: Restoration of the Image of God

Wesley believed that God offers salvation to overcome the dilemma of this human reality. In section 3 of the sermon you just read, he wrote, "The great end of religion is, to renew our hearts in the image of God, to repair that total loss of righteousness and true holiness which we sustained by the sin of our first parent."[5] For him, that means that the purpose and goal of

---

5 Wesley, "Original Sin," § 3, ¶ 5, in Outler, 2:185.

salvation, in effect, is the reunion of humanity with God again—the restoration of the imago Dei in our lives.

In terms of our two illustrations, our first example can be represented once again as a completed, restored circle (fig. 3.3).

Regarding the podium illustration, picture one's separated self walking back to the podium and hugging it once again. That represents the restoration of the imago Dei in one's life—that we and God are now once again "one" in heart and spirit.

In fact, the biblical terms that translate into English as "salvation" and "saved" carry this same sense. In the Old Testament, the Hebrew word is *shalom*, and while we commonly think of this as "peace," the literal meaning is "completeness, wellness, soundness, health, welfare"[6]—as used, for example, in the final phrase of the famous priestly blessing from Numbers 6:24-26. Likewise, in the New Testament, the Greek word is *sozo*, which literally means "to heal, preserve, be made whole"[7]—as used in Jesus's final phrase from John 3:16-17.

An important digression to make here is that "salvation" in these contexts does not simply mean going to heaven (as is often implied in today's pop-culture Christianity), but instead is about having the imago Dei restored to our lives—of receiving God's wholeness, completeness, healing, and peace for our minds, bodies, souls, and spirits. As we'll read below again in its entirety, in his sermon "The Scripture Way of Salvation," Wesley wrote:

> Salvation . . . is not what is frequently understood by that word, the going to heaven, eternal happiness. It is not the soul's going to paradise, . . . not a blessing which lies on the other side death. . . . It is not something at a distance: it is a present thing;

Figure 3.3

The Way We Were

Humanity in the Image of God

The Goal of Salvation

---

6 Olive Tree Bible Software. "Enhanced Strong's Dictionary," Strong's Number h7965, Version 7.5.5, Build 1562 (July 2, 2019).

7 Olive Tree Bible Software. "Enhanced Strong's Dictionary," Strong's Number g4982.

a blessing which, through the free mercy of God, ye are now in possession of.[8]

In other words, for Wesley, the reality was that "going to heaven" (what Wesley called "going to paradise") is merely one manifestation of salvation/being saved. For him, "paradise" (where we go after we die) along with "heaven" (God's coming kingdom) are both vital and important consequences of salvation. But the heart of its meaning lies in understanding, claiming, and living in God's *wholeness*—a wholeness that begins now, but transcends death.

When I am teaching a class on this topic, at this point I often remind students of the famous children's nursery rhyme "Humpty Dumpty":

> Humpty Dumpty sat on a wall;
> Humpty Dumpty had a great fall;
> All the King's horses and all the King's men
>   couldn't put Humpty back together again.

I then explain that the Christian version (which I invented) has an altogether different outcome that's possible:

> Humpty Dumpty [representing humanity] sat on a wall [representing life itself];
> Humpty Dumpty had a great fall [a metaphor for the spiritual fall of humanity described in Genesis 3, and for the brokenness that has plagued all human lives since]
> But the King [here a metaphor for God], through the faith community of men, women, angels, and principalities [God's people] CAN put Humpty back together again!

A number of years ago, a television commercial for an electronic safety alert device pictured an older adult who had fallen on the floor, calling out "Help! I've fallen and I can't get up!" That is an accurate metaphor for our human condition without God. Still, the good news of salvation is that while we may have "fallen" (i.e., are broken by sin), we can "get up" and find wholeness and completeness in our lives because of God's gift of Jesus.

---

8 John Wesley, "The Scripture Way of Salvation" (Sermon 43) § 1, ¶ 1, in Outler, ed., *The Bicentennial Edition of the Works of John Wesley*, 2:156 (see chap. 3, n. 1).

CHAPTER 3

That is the purpose and goal of salvation/being saved from a Wesleyan theological perspective.

Nevertheless, while that may be the goal, the problem remains that—without God in our lives—we humans remain broken by sin. In the podium illustration, once again picture one facing and walking away from the podium, separated from the wholeness/completeness that they were created to have. So, how could anything we ever hope to do restore the image of God in our lives? Is there anything we can do to close the gap, repair the break caused by original sin, and bring us back into the original close, holistic relationship with God? In many ways, the Bible is the story of one attempt after another to try to do this: the Tower of Babel; the Ten Commandments; Old Testament animal sacrifices; the Hebrew monarchy (Saul, David, Solomon); and so on. But every one of these attempts to reach back to God ultimately failed. One could illustrate this in the following way (fig. 3.4):

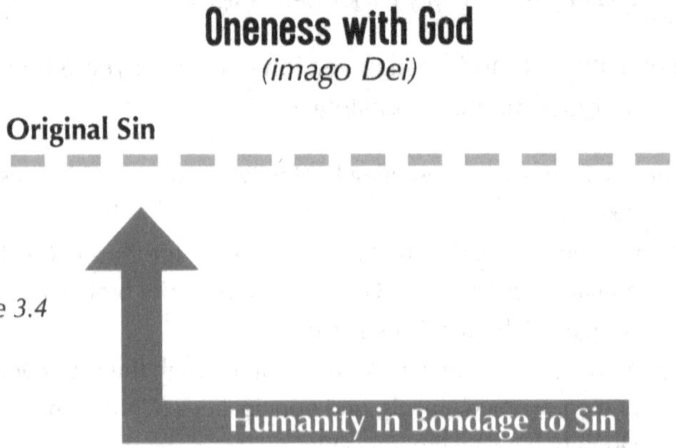

Oneness with God
(imago Dei)

Original Sin

- - - - - - - - - - - - - - -

Figure 3.4

Humanity in Bondage to Sin

Some people have called Christianity a "crutch for weak people." Wesley would, in fact, agree, because *all people* are "weak," in the sense that we are *all* spiritually broken and cannot save ourselves. We therefore *all* need a savior—we need a way out of our human dilemma.

In 1765, Wesley wrote his sermon "The Scripture Way of Salvation," offering an excellent overview of his understanding of God's ultimate answer to the human condition of original sin. In it, he explored the meaning of salvation, how one can enter into it, and also offers some thoughts on the nature of the Christian life itself.

The Scripture Way of Salvation[9]
by John Wesley

Ye are saved through faith. Ephesians 2:8

1. Nothing can be more intricate, complex, and hard to be understood, than religion, as it has been often described. And this is not only true concerning the religion of the Heathens, even many of the wisest of them, but concerning the religion of those also who were, in some sense, Christians; yea, and men of great name in the Christian world; men who seemed to be pillars thereof. Yet how easy to be understood, how plain and simple a thing, is the genuine religion of Jesus Christ; provided only that we take it in its native form, just as it is described in the oracles of God! It is exactly suited, by the wise Creator and Governor of the world, to the weak understanding and narrow capacity of man in his present state. How observable is this, both with regard to the end it proposes, and the means to attain that end! The end is, in one word, salvation; the means to attain it, faith.

2. It is easily discerned, that these two little words, I mean faith and salvation, include the substance of all the Bible, the marrow, as it were, of the whole Scripture. So much the more should we take all possible care to avoid all mistake concerning them, and to form a true and accurate judgement concerning both the one and the other.

3. Let us then seriously inquire,

   I. What is Salvation?
   II. What is that faith whereby we are saved? And,
   III. How are we saved by it?

I.

1. And, first, let us inquire, What is salvation? The salvation which is here spoken of is not what is frequently understood by that word, the going to heaven, eternal happiness. It is not the soul's going to paradise, termed by our Lord, "Abraham's bosom." It is not a blessing which lies on the other side death; or, as we usually speak, in the other world. The very words of the text itself

---

9 Wesley, in Outler, 2:153–69.

put this beyond all question: "Ye are saved." It is not something at a distance: it is a present thing; a blessing which, through the free mercy of God, ye are now in possession of. Nay, the words may be rendered, and that with equal propriety, "Ye have been saved": so that the salvation which is here spoken of might be extended to the entire work of God, from the first dawning of grace in the soul, till it is consummated in glory.

2. If we take this in its utmost extent, it will include all that is wrought in the soul by what is frequently termed "natural conscience," but more properly, "preventing grace";—all the drawings of the Father; the desires after God, which, if we yield to them, increase more and more;—all that light wherewith the Son of God "enlighteneth every one that cometh into the world;" showing every man "to do justly, to love mercy, and to walk humbly with his God";—all the convictions which His Spirit, from time to time, works in every child of man—although it is true, the generality of men stifle them as soon as possible, and after a while forget, or at least deny, that they ever had them at all.

3. But we are at present concerned only with that salvation which the Apostle is directly speaking of. And this consists of two general parts, justification and sanctification.

Justification is another word for pardon. It is the forgiveness of all our sins; and, what is necessarily implied therein, our acceptance with God. The price whereby this hath been procured for us (commonly termed "the meritorious cause of our justification"), is the blood and righteousness of Christ; or, to express it a little more clearly, all that Christ hath done and suffered for us, till He "poured out His soul for the transgressors." The immediate effects of justification are, the peace of God, a "peace that passeth all understanding," and a "rejoicing in hope of the glory of God" "with joy unspeakable and full of glory."

4. And at the same time that we are justified, yea, in that very moment, sanctification begins. In that instant we are born again, born from above, born of the Spirit: there is a *real* as well as a *relative* change. We are inwardly renewed by the power of God. We feel "the love of God shed abroad in our heart by the Holy Ghost which is given unto us"; producing love to all mankind, and more especially to the children of God; expelling the love of the world, the love of pleasure, of ease, of honour, of

money, together with pride, anger, self-will, and every other evil temper; in a word, changing the earthly, sensual, devilish mind, into "the mind which was in Christ Jesus."

5. How naturally do those who experience such a change imagine that all sin is gone; that it is utterly rooted out of their heart, and has no more any place therein! How easily do they draw that inference, "I *feel* no sin; therefore, I *have* none: it does not *stir*; therefore it does not *exist*: it has no *motion*; therefore, it has no *being*!"

6. But it is seldom long before they are undeceived, finding sin was only suspended, not destroyed. Temptations return, and sin revives; showing it was but stunned before, not dead. They now feel two principles in themselves, plainly contrary to each other; "the flesh lusting against the Spirit"; nature opposing the grace of God. They cannot deny, that although they still feel power to believe in Christ, and to love God; and although His "Spirit" still "witnesses with their spirits, that they are children of God"; yet they feel in themselves sometimes pride or self-will, sometimes anger or unbelief. They find one or more of these frequently *stirring* in their heart, though not *conquering*; yea, perhaps, "thrusting sore at them that they may fall"; but the Lord is their help.

7. How exactly did Macarius, fourteen hundred years ago, describe the present experience of the children of God: "The unskilful," or unexperienced, "when grace operates, presently imagine they have no more sin. Whereas they that have discretion cannot deny, that even we who have the grace of God may be molested again. For we have often had instances of some among the brethren, who have experienced such grace as to affirm that they had no sin in them; and yet, after all, when they thought themselves entirely freed from it, the corruption that lurked within was stirred up anew, and they were wellnigh burned up."

8. From the time of our being born again, the gradual work of sanctification takes place. We are enabled "by the Spirit" to "mortify the deeds of the body," of our evil nature; and as we are more and more dead to sin, we are more and more alive to God. We go on from grace to grace, while we are careful to "abstain from all appearance of evil," and are "zealous of good works," as we have opportunity, doing good to all men; while we walk in all

His ordinances blameless, therein worshipping Him in spirit and in truth; while we take up our cross, and deny ourselves every pleasure that does not lead us to God.

9. It is thus that we wait for entire sanctification; for a full salvation from all our sins,—from pride, self-will, anger, unbelief; or, as the Apostle expresses it, "go unto perfection." But what is perfection? The word has various senses: here it means perfect love. It is love excluding sin; love filling the heart, taking up the whole capacity of the soul. It is love "rejoicing evermore, praying without ceasing, in everything giving thanks."

II.

But what is faith through which we are saved? This is the second point to be considered.

1. Faith, in general, is defined by the Apostle, *elegcos pragmatvn ou blepomenvn*. *An evidence*, a divine *evidence and conviction* (the word means both) *of things not seen;* not visible, not perceivable either by sight, or by any other of the external senses. It implies both a supernatural *evidence* of God, and of the things of God; a kind of spiritual *light* exhibited to the soul, and a supernatural *sight* or perception thereof. Accordingly, the Scripture speaks of God's giving sometimes light, sometimes a power of discerning it. So St. Paul: "God, who commanded light to shine out of darkness, hath shined in our hearts, to give us the light of the knowledge of the glory of God in the face of Jesus Christ." And elsewhere the same Apostle speaks of "the eyes of" our "understanding being opened." By this two-fold operation of the Holy Spirit, having the eyes of our soul both *opened* and *enlightened*, we see the things which the natural "eye hath not seen, neither the ear heard." We have a prospect of the invisible things of God; we see the *spiritual world*, which is all round about us, and yet no more discerned by our natural faculties than if it had no being. And we see the *eternal world*; piercing through the veil which hangs between time and eternity. Clouds and darkness then rest upon it no more, but we already see the glory which shall be revealed.

2. Taking the word in a more particular sense, faith is a divine *evidence* and *conviction* not only that "God was in Christ, reconciling the world unto Himself," but also that Christ loved *me*, and gave Himself for *me*. It is by this faith (whether we term

it the *essence*, or rather a *property* thereof) that we *receive Christ*; that we receive Him in all His offices, as our Prophet, Priest, and King. It is by this that He is "made of God unto us wisdom, and righteousness, and sanctification, and redemption."

3. "But is this the *faith of assurance*, or *faith of adherence*?" The Scripture mentions no such distinction. The Apostle says, "There is one faith, and one hope of our calling"; one Christian, saving faith; "as there is one Lord," in whom we believe, and "one God and Father of us all." And it is certain, this faith necessarily implies an *assurance* (which is here only another word for *evidence*, it being hard to tell the difference between them) that Christ loved me, and gave Himself for me. For "he that believeth" with the true living faith "hath the witness in himself": "the Spirit witnesseth with his spirit that he is a child of God." "Because he is a son, God hath sent forth the Spirit of His Son into his heart, crying, Abba, Father"; giving him an assurance that he is so, and a childlike confidence in Him. But let it be observed, that, in the very nature of the thing, the assurance goes before the confidence. For a man cannot have a childlike confidence in God till he knows he is a child of God. Therefore, confidence, trust, reliance, adherence, or whatever else it be called, is not the first, as some have supposed, but the second, branch or act of faith.

4. It is by this faith we are saved, justified, and sanctified; taking that word in its highest sense. But how are we justified and sanctified by faith? This is our third head of inquiry. And this being the main point in question, and a point of no ordinary importance, it will not be improper to give it a more distinct and particular consideration.

III.

1. And, first, how are we justified by faith? In what sense is this to be understood? I answer, Faith is the condition, and the only condition, of justification. It is the *condition*: none is justified but he that believes: without faith no man is justified. And it is the *only condition*: this alone is sufficient for justification. Every one that believes is justified, whatever else he has or has not. In other words: no man is justified till he believes; every man when he believes is justified.

2. "But does not God command us to repent also? Yea, and to 'bring forth fruits meet for repentance'—to cease, for instance,

from doing evil, and learn to do well? And is not both the one and the other of the utmost necessity, insomuch that if we willingly neglect either, we cannot reasonably expect to be justified at all? But if this be so, how can it be said that faith is the only condition of justification?" God does undoubtedly command us both to repent, and to bring forth fruits meet for repentance; which if we willingly neglect, we cannot reasonably expect to be justified at all: therefore both repentance, and fruits meet for repentance, are, in some sense, necessary to justification. But they are not necessary in the *same sense* with faith, nor in the *same degree*. Not in the *same degree*; for those fruits are only necessary *conditionally*; if there be time and opportunity for them. Otherwise a man may be justified without them, as was the *thief* upon the cross (if we may call him so; for a late writer has discovered that he was no thief, but a very honest and respectable person!) but he cannot be justified without faith; this is impossible. Likewise, let a man have ever so much repentance, or ever so many of the fruits meet for repentance, yet all this does not at all avail; he is not justified till he believes. But the moment he believes, with or without those fruits, yea, with more or less repentance, he is justified.—Not in the *same sense*; for repentance and its fruits are only *remotely* necessary; necessary in order to faith; whereas faith is *immediately* necessary to justification. It remains, that faith is the only condition, which is *immediately* and *proximately* necessary to justification.

3. "But do you believe we are sanctified by faith? We know you believe that we are justified by faith; but do not you believe, and accordingly teach, that we are sanctified by our works?" So it has been roundly and vehemently affirmed for these five-and-twenty years: but I have constantly declared just the contrary; and that in all manner of ways. I have continually testified in private and in public, that we are sanctified as well as justified by faith. And indeed the one of those great truths does exceedingly illustrate the other. Exactly as we are justified by faith, so are we sanctified by faith. Faith is the condition, and the only condition, of sanctification, exactly as it is of justification. It is the *condition*: none is sanctified but he that believes; without faith no man is sanctified. And it is the *only condition*: this alone is sufficient for sanctification. Every one that believes is sanctified, whatever

else he has or has not. In other words, no man is sanctified till he believes: every man when he believes is sanctified.

4. "But is there not a repentance consequent upon, as well as a repentance previous to, justification? And is it not incumbent on all that are justified to be 'zealous of good works'? Yea, are not these so necessary, that if a man willingly neglect them he cannot reasonably expect that he shall ever be sanctified in the full sense; that is, perfected in love? Nay, can he grow at all in grace, in the loving knowledge of our Lord Jesus Christ? Yea, can he retain the grace which God has already given him? Can he continue in the faith which he has received, or in the favour of God? Do not you yourself allow all this, and continually assert it? But, if this be so, how can it be said that faith is the only condition of sanctification?"

5. I do allow all this, and continually maintain it as the truth of God. I allow there is a repentance consequent upon, as well as a repentance previous to, justification. It is incumbent on all that are justified to be zealous of good works. And these are so necessary, that if a man willingly neglect them, he cannot reasonably expect that he shall ever be sanctified; he cannot grow in grace, in the image of God, the mind which was in Christ Jesus; nay, he cannot retain the grace he has received; he cannot continue in faith, or in the favour of God. What is the inference we must draw herefrom? Why, that both repentance, rightly understood, and the practice of all good works,—works of piety, as well as works of mercy (now properly so called, since they spring from faith), are, in some sense, necessary to sanctification.

6. I say, "repentance rightly understood"; for this must not be confounded with the former repentance. The repentance consequent upon justification is widely different from that which is antecedent to it. This implies no guilt, no sense of condemnation, no consciousness of the wrath of God. It does not suppose any doubt of the favour of God, or any "fear that hath torment." It is properly a conviction, wrought by the Holy Ghost, of the *sin* which still *remains* in our heart; of the *jronhma sarkos, the carnal mind,* which "does still *remain*" (as our Church speaks) "even in them that are regenerate"; although it does no longer *reign*; it has not now dominion over them. It is a conviction of our proneness to evil, of an heart bent to backsliding, of the still

continuing tendency of the flesh to lust against the spirit. Sometimes, unless we continually watch and pray, it lusteth to pride, sometimes to anger, sometimes to love of the world, love of ease, love of honour, or love of pleasure more than of God. It is a conviction of the tendency of our heart to self-will, to Atheism, or idolatry; and above all, to unbelief; whereby, in a thousand ways, and under a thousand pretenses, we are ever departing, more or less, from the living God.

7. With this conviction of the sin remaining in our hearts, there is joined a clear conviction of the sin remaining in our lives; still *cleaving* to all our words and actions. In the best of these we now discern a mixture of evil, either in the spirit, the matter, or the manner of them; something that could not endure the righteous judgement of God, were He extreme to mark what is done amiss. Where we least suspected it, we find a taint of pride or self-will, of unbelief or idolatry; so that we are now more ashamed of our best duties than formerly of our worst sins: and hence we cannot but feel that these are so far from having anything meritorious in them, yea, so far from being able to stand in sight of the divine justice, that for those also we should be guilty before God, were it not for the blood of the covenant.

8. Experience shows that, together with this conviction of sin *remaining* in our hearts, and *cleaving* to all our words and actions; as well as the guilt which on account thereof we should incur, were we not continually sprinkled with the atoning blood; one thing more is implied in this repentance; namely, a conviction of our helplessness, of our utter inability to think one good thought, or to form one good desire; and much more to speak one word aright, or to perform one good action, but through His free, almighty grace, first preventing us, and then accompanying us every moment.

9. "But what good works are those, the practice of which you affirm to be necessary to sanctification?" First, all works of piety; such as public prayer, family prayer, and praying in our closet; receiving the supper of the Lord; searching the Scriptures, by hearing, reading, meditating; and using such a measure of fasting or abstinence as our bodily health allows.

10. Secondly, all works of mercy; whether they relate to the bodies or souls of men; such as feeding the hungry, clothing the

naked, entertaining the stranger, visiting those that are in prison, or sick, or variously afflicted; such as the endeavouring to instruct the ignorant, to awaken the stupid sinner, to quicken the lukewarm, to confirm the wavering, to comfort the feeble-minded, to succour the tempted, or contribute in any manner to the saving of souls from death. This is the repentance, and these the "fruits meet for repentance," which are necessary to full sanctification. This is the way wherein God hath appointed His children to wait for complete salvation.

11. Hence may appear the extreme mischievousness of that seemingly innocent opinion, that there is no sin in a believer; that all sin is destroyed, root and branch, the moment a man is justified. By totally preventing that repentance, it quite blocks up the way to sanctification. There is no place for repentance in him who believes there is no sin either in his life or heart: consequently, there is no place for his being perfected in love, to which that repentance is indispensably necessary.

12. Hence it may likewise appear, that there is no possible danger in *thus* expecting full salvation. For suppose we were mistaken, suppose no such blessing ever was or can be attained, yet we lose nothing: nay, that very expectation quickens us in using all the talents which God has given us; yea, in improving them all; so that when our Lord cometh, He will receive His own with increase.

13. But to return. though it be allowed, that both this repentance and its fruits are necessary to full salvation; yet they are not necessary either in the same sense with faith, or in the same degree:—Not in the *same degree*; for these fruits are only necessary *conditionally*, if there be time and opportunity for them; otherwise a man may be sanctified without them. But he cannot be sanctified without faith. likewise, let a man have ever so much of this repentance, or ever so many good works, yet all this does not at all avail: he is not sanctified till he believes. But the moment he believes, with or without those fruits, yea, with more or less of this repentance, he is sanctified.—Not in the *same sense*; for this repentance and these fruits are only *remotely* necessary,—necessary in order to the continuance of his faith, as well as the increase of it; whereas faith is *immediately* and *directly* necessary to sanctification. It remains, that faith is the

only condition which is *immediately* and *proximately* necessary to sanctification.

14. "But what is that faith whereby we are sanctified,—saved from sin, and perfected in love?" It is a divine evidence and conviction, first, that God hath promised it in the holy Scripture. Till we are thoroughly satisfied of this, there is no moving one step further. And one would imagine there needed not one word more to satisfy a reasonable man of this, than the ancient promise, "Then will I circumcise thy heart, and the heart of thy seed, to love the Lord thy God with all thy heart, and with all thy soul, and with all thy mind." How clearly does this express the being perfected in love!—how strongly imply the being saved from all sin! For as long as love takes up the whole heart, what room is there for sin therein?

15. It is a divine evidence and conviction, secondly, that what God hath promised He is able to perform. Admitting, therefore, that "with men it is impossible" to "bring a clean thing out of an unclean," to purify the heart from all sin, and to till it with all holiness; yet this creates no difficulty in the case, seeing "with God all things are possible." And surely no one ever imagined it was possible to any power less than that of the Almighty! But if God speaks, it shall be done. God saith, "Let there be light; and there" is "light"!

16. It is, thirdly, a divine evidence and conviction that He is able and willing to do it now. And why not? Is not a moment to Him the same as a thousand years? He cannot want more time to accomplish whatever is His will. And He cannot want or stay for any more *worthiness* or *fitness* in the persons He is pleased to honour. We may therefore boldly say, at any point of time, "Now is the day of salvation!" "To-day, if ye will hear His voice, harden not your hearts!" "Behold, all things are now ready; come unto the marriage!"

17. To this confidence, that God is both able and willing to sanctify us now, there needs to be added one thing more,—a divine evidence and conviction that He doeth it. In that hour it is done: God says to the inmost soul, "According to thy faith be it unto thee!" Then the soul is pure from every spot of sin; it is clean "from all unrighteousness." The believer then experiences the deep meaning of those solemn words, "If we walk in the

light as He is in the light, we have fellowship one with another, and the blood of Jesus Christ His Son cleanseth us from all sin."

18. "But does God work this great work in the soul gradually or instantaneously?" Perhaps it may be gradually wrought in some; I mean in this sense,—they do not advert to the particular moment wherein sin ceases to be. But it is infinitely desirable, were it the will of God, that it should be done instantaneously; that the Lord should destroy sin "by the breath of His mouth," in a moment, in the twinkling of an eye. And so He generally does; a plain fact, of which there is evidence enough to satisfy any unprejudiced person. *Thou* therefore look for it every moment! Look for it in the way above described; in all those *good works* whereunto thou art "created anew in Christ Jesus." There is then no danger: you can be no worse, if you are no better, for that expectation. For were you to be disappointed of your hope, still you lose nothing. But you shall not be disappointed of your hope: it will come, and will not tarry. Look for it then every day, every hour, every moment! Why not this hour, this moment? Certainly you may look for it *now*, if you believe it is by faith. And by this token you may surely know whether you seek it by faith or by works. If by works, you want something to be done *first, before* you are sanctified. You think, I must first *be* or *do* thus or thus. Then you are seeking it by works unto this day. If you seek it by faith, you may expect it *as you are*; and expect it *now*. It is of importance to observe, that there is an inseparable connexion between these three points,—expect it *by faith*; expect it *as you are*; and expect it *now*! To deny one of them, is to deny them all; to allow one, is to allow them all. Do *you* believe we are sanctified by faith? Be true then to your principle; and look for this blessing just as you are, neither better nor worse; as a poor sinner that has still nothing to pay, nothing to plead, but "Christ *died.*" And if you look for it as you are, then expect it *now*. Stay for nothing: why should you? Christ is ready; and He is all you want. He is waiting for you: He is at the door! Let your inmost soul cry out,

> *Come in, come in, thou heavenly Guest!*
> *Nor hence again remove;*
> *But sup with me, and let the feast*
> *Be everlasting love.*

CHAPTER 3

Here we find Wesley describing the beginning of the Christian life—what it means to turn to God and begin the process of becoming a Christian. Section 1 in particular outlines Wesley's process of salvation that I believe is best understood as his "via salutis" (way of salvation) because it outlines a series of conceptual and practical stages that humans experience in the journey (called "salvation") toward a reestablished relationship with God.

While many Christian traditions—and some within the Wesleyan tradition itself—reference an *"ordo* salutis" (*order* of salvation), I believe that the most accurate way to articulate Wesley's theology is as a *"via* salutis" (*way* of salvation).

> **Via salutis (way of salvation):** a series of conceptual and practical stages that humans experience in the journey (called "salvation") toward a reestablished relationship with God. The primary stages of this "way" are prevenient grace, justifying grace, and sanctifying grace, which Wesley seems to understand best as a "way" because it is more organic and processive than the transactional and static concepts of a traditional ordo salutis (order of salvation).

The distinction may seem trivial, but it is significant: an *order* of salvation conceptualizes salvation as a series of compartmentalized, individual steps, and/or concepts that need to be appropriated one at a time, leaving behind the previous step(s) or concept(s) once the next one is achieved or adopted; a *way* of salvation, on the other hand, conceptualizes salvation as a progression of stages along a fluid and organic journey that never fully leaves previous stages behind, but merely builds on them—in musical terms, each stage is essentially merely a "movement" within the larger "symphony" of salvation. This way of thinking about salvation is unique because, unlike the more forensic view espoused by Calvin, Zwingli, and others in the Reformed Protestant tradition (and also fashionable in pop Christianity today), I view the Wesleyan understanding of how one experiences salvation as more therapeutic. That is, it views salvation primarily as a dynamic process, rather than a static state—as an organic journey that one takes with God, rather than an inanimate transaction. Hence, I believe this process to be best characterized as a *via* ("way"), rather than as an *ordo* ("order").[10] With this distinction in mind, then, let's proceed to explore the specific stages or "movements" of Wesley's "symphony" of salvation.

Prevenient Grace

The first thing to notice in Wesley's "The Scripture Way of Salvation" is his acknowledgment that since we humans can do absolutely nothing to save ourselves, God takes the first step toward solving the "human dilemma" of original sin by giving *Godself* in the form of Jesus, God's Son. As read in section 1, paragraph 2 of the sermon above, Wesley had a particular name for this act of God: **"preventing"** (or **"prevenient"**) **grace**—from the Latin terms *pre* (meaning "before") and *veneri* (meaning "to come").

> **Prevenient grace:** the grace of God active in our lives before any conscious, personal awareness of it, overcoming the brokenness of original sin and wooing us back to a relationship with God. It is God's *initiating love* reaching toward us before we deserve, desire, or are even aware of it. Human conscience is the indication of its presence in and for all people.

This is, quite literally, "grace which comes before" any conscious personal experience with God. While the term itself does not appear in scripture, Wesley believes that its concept can be found in numerous locations, including the key text of Romans 5:8, "God proves his love for us in that while we were still sinners, Christ died for us" (NRSV). For Wesley, prevenient grace is the grace of God offered to us "while we were yet sinners"—that is, before we knew it or were aware of it.

The concept refers to the fact that it is God (not humanity) who takes the initiative—the first step to break through the barrier of original sin to redeem humanity and create the conditions whereby humanity can once again have a right relationship with the Divine. Biblically, we find examples of this in the actions of the main characters of Jesus's parables in Luke 15:

---

10 For a more extensive discussion of the debate over whether Wesley's theology espouses a via salutis versus an ordo salutis, see generally Randy Maddox, *Responsible Grace: John Wesley's Practical Theology* (Nashville: Kingswood Books, 1994), 157–58.

the shepherd who leaves the ninety-nine to rescue the one lost sheep; the woman who sweeps her house to find her lost coin; and the father who waits patiently but expectantly for his prodigal son to come home. The initiative of each of these persons exemplifies God's action in prevenient grace, which can also be illustrated in the following way (fig. 3.5):

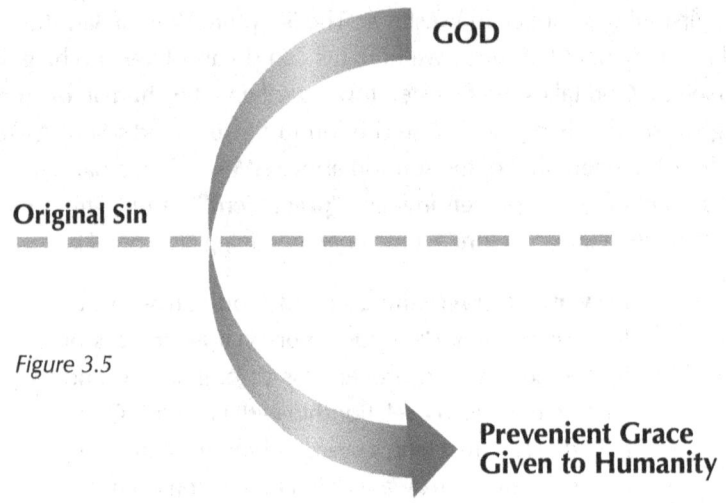

Figure 3.5

What, then, are some of its characteristics and effects? Let me discuss a few. First, prevenient grace is a *supernatural gift from God*—meaning that we cannot do anything to earn, merit, or create it. Instead, we are given this manifestation of grace as a gift, simply because of who and whose we are: created, loved, and redeemed by God. Think of prevenient grace as being like God "priming the pump" of our spiritual lives. Anyone who grew up on a farm fifty or sixty years ago may be familiar with this: before being able to draw water out of a dug well, one had to "prime the pump" with an external bucket of water. Once the primer water was poured down the pump, it created suction that enabled the pump to function properly, so that groundwater could actually be tapped. In the same way, Wesley believed that God supernaturally gifts us with "primer spirituality," if you will, to enable the "pump" of our spiritual lives to function properly, so that the "living water" of God's grace can actually be tapped. Another way of stating this is to say that, since we are spiritually dead in our natural state, through prevenient grace God actually provides the groundwater to be tapped in the first place!

Second, prevenient grace also gives us a *slight tendency to love*.

Remember that in our natural state, as humans we are inherently bent toward sin, evil, and selfishness, incapable of truly loving God or others. But with this infusion of God's prevenient grace, we now possess a small, incremental ability to fight these things and to begin to obey our spiritual conscience again. It is not yet full, complete, mature obedience, but we are now at least capable of offering some small degree of it by the way we live our lives.

A third effect of prevenient grace is that it gives human beings something that Steven Harper calls "response-ability"—an "ability to respond" to God's love that we would not have had otherwise.[11] Again, it is a "primer" of sorts for the "spiritual pump" of our lives—without this initiating grace, we *cannot* respond to God's offer of love; with it, we *can* respond. In one of his sermons, Wesley himself put it this way: "God worketh in you; therefore you can work. Otherwise it would be impossible."[12] Prevenient grace is therefore grace from God which both *enables* and *invites* our response, but which is not coercive. A number of years ago, I remember a travel commercial on television that urged viewers, "Come back to Jamaica! Come back to the way things used to be!" In a spiritual sense, this is what prevenient grace does: it invites and urges anyone willing to listen to its serenading call to "come back home to God"—to "come back to the way things used to be" (e.g., the sense of oneness with the imago Dei that God desires for every person to experience). Yet even here, as a consequence of God's supernatural gift of prevenient grace, humans nevertheless still possess the freedom and liberty to respond or not—we can turn down and walk away from grace. This then, by definition, is fundamentally different from the Reformed/Calvinist notion of "predestination" or "divine election."

Finally, since Wesley believed that Jesus died for all people (so that all—not merely some—may be saved), he therefore also believed that prevenient grace is *given by God to all people*. He based this not only on scripture but also on pure observation. Wesley noticed that most people had at least some degree of *human conscience* (a sense of "right and wrong"), and therefore believed that that conscience is a sign of prevenient grace. In one of his sermons, he once wrote, "There is no man . . . that is wholly void of the grace

---

11 Steven Harper, *John Wesley's Message for Today* (Grand Rapids: Francis Asbury Press, 1983), 44.

12 Wesley, "On Working Out Our Own Salvation" (Sermon 85) §III, ¶ 3, in Outler, ed., *The Bicentennial Edition of the Works of John Wesley*, 3:206.

of God. No man living is entirely destitute of what is vulgarly called 'natural conscience.' . . . But this is not natural: it is more properly termed 'preventing [or prevenient] grace.' Every man has a greater or less measure of this."[13]

For Wesley, then, prevenient grace is *not* merely given to church members, or those who've been baptized or confirmed in a particular Christian tradition, or even (for that matter) only to confessing Christians. Instead, it is for *everyone*—again, making it different from the Reformed/Calvinist doctrine of predestination/divine election.[14] This is precisely why Wesley invited non-Christians and children to Holy Communion—a practice we continue still today. It's also one reason that Wesley baptized infants—because it recognizes that even before the child is old enough to make a decision to accept Jesus Christ, Christ already died for them. So, it is accurate to say that in the Wesleyan Christian tradition, both Holy Communion and Christian baptism (baptism of infants, in particular) are acknowledgments and signs of God's prevenient grace, which is given that all might be saved, *if* they claim and live into God's invitational covenant (more about this in chapter 7).

Bear in mind that while, for Wesley, God's offer of prevenient grace is a necessary *first* step in the process of human redemption, it is *not* full or total salvation. Again, it merely gets the process going by giving us an ability to respond. The next steps, however, are up to us.

The Legal State: Conviction and Repentance

Because they have to do with the "moral law"—obedience to God motivated by a sense of duty and fear of judgment—Wesley called these next two steps the "legal state" of Christianity: **conviction of sin**, and **repentance**. And even though his writings treat these two concepts as synonyms, for purposes of discussion I am describing them separately here.

First, remember that in our purely natural state, we as humans are separated from God and completely apathetic about that reality. Yet, because of love, God preveniently reaches out to us, seeking and inviting us back

---

13 Wesley, in Outler, 3:207.

14 In fact, it has been fairly noted that Wesley, in fact, did believe in predestination/divine election. However, how he interpreted it was very un-Calvinistic essentially by saying that *all* people (not merely some) are "preveniently" predestined by God, even though one must choose their own election (through new birth).

to a vital relationship. We may experience this as an awareness that God exists, or that God wants a relationship with us. We may hear about God's "moral law" through our reading of the Ten Commandments, or of "dos and don'ts" that we find in scripture, and we begin to realize how futile are our own efforts to bridge the gap between us and God. Wesley calls this experience **conviction of sin**—a self-awareness of how our sin separates us from God, and of how utterly helpless we are to reunite our lives with God by our own strength and efforts.

Today, we don't usually like to talk about conviction. Perhaps it conjures up negative memories of pulpit-pounding televangelists, "hellfire and damnation" preachers, or of someone casting judgment on us. Yet, as uncomfortable as it might appear, Wesley believed that conviction was altogether necessary for us to experience in order for true Christianity to take root. He once wrote that despite its negative appearance, it is actually

> the spirit of love which, by this painful means, tears away our confidence in the flesh, which leaves us no broken reed whereon to trust, and so constrains the sinner, stripped of all, to cry out in the bitterness of his soul, or groan in the depth of his heart, I give up every plea beside,—Lord, I am damn'd; but Thou hast died.[15]

In other words, while it may be painful to face our own sin, it is necessary, for until we acknowledge and face our own brokenness, we can never truly appreciate the meaning and value of Christ's sacrifice for us.

Consider an illustration from our own bodies. When we cut ourselves, it usually hurts. But what would happen if it didn't hurt? In extreme cases, we might bleed to death. Even if not, we would at least be neglecting to attend a wound that needs attention. So, the question could be asked: What is the purpose of pain in the human body? Answer: To let us know that something is not right; that something needs to be fixed. Conviction of sin functions spiritually much the same way as physical pain—it is the warning light of the soul, letting us know that all is not well, and that something (i.e., our hearts and souls) needs fixing.

It could, in fact, be said that conviction of sin (i.e., feeling under God's judgment) after encountering a scriptural "law" of obedience (found in

---

15 John Wesley "Original, Nature, Properties, and Use of the Law" (Sermon 34) § 4, ¶ 2, in Outler, ed., *The Bicentennial Edition of the Works of John Wesley*, 2:16 (chap. 3, n. 1).

both Testaments of the Bible) is actually a fifth effect of prevenient grace. Indeed, another way Wesley describes this is to refer to it synonymously as **repentance**. In his sermon "The Lord Our Righteousness" (1765), Wesley explains it this way:

> Must not we put off the filthy rags of our own righteousness, before we can put on the spotless righteousness of Christ? Certainly we must; that is, in plain terms, we must *repent,* before we can believe the gospel. We must be cut off from dependence upon ourselves, before we can truly depend upon *Christ.* We must cast away all confidence in our own righteousness, or we cannot have a true confidence in his. Till we are delivered from trusting in anything that *we* do, we cannot thoroughly trust in what *he* has done and suffered. First, we receive the sentence of death in ourselves: Then, we trust in *Him* that lived and died for us.[16]

For Wesley, this small yet vital human response means nothing more than for one to turn *away from sin* and turn *toward God*.

In our podium illustration, consider putting yourself again in the natural state, where you are separated and facing away from the God-podium. Now picture yourself doing an about-face, facing the podium once again, but without physically moving any closer toward it. *That* is repentance: literally a reorienting of our focus *away from* our spiritual apathy and the "things of the world," and *toward* God and the things of God.

> **Repentance**: the human act of turning *away* from sin and *toward* God by consciously and intentionally choosing to believe (i.e., have a heartfelt trust in) the gospel of Jesus Christ. It is a "low species" of faith and is observable by outward "fruits" in our words and behaviors.

We may still be in bondage to our brokenness and sin, but now we understand the direction and source from which our redemption and saving will ultimately come, and consequently have reoriented the focus of our lives

---

16 John Wesley, "The Lord Our Righteousness," (Sermon 20) § 2, ¶ 11, in *The Bicentennial Edition of the Works of John Wesley*, vol. 1, *Sermons I*, ed. Albert C. Outler (1–33) (Nashville: Abingdon Press, 1984), 1:458; emphasis added.

toward that. Of course, even this reorientation is made possible only by the enabling power of God's grace. As Wesley explains in "Predestination Calmly Considered":

> "Natural free-will," in the present state of mankind, I do not understand. I only assert that there is a measure of free-will supernaturally restored to every man, together with that supernatural light which "enlightens every man that cometh into the world."[17]

So then, even this first response of faith is made possible *by* God's grace granted through our belief in the gospel.

This "belief," however, is not merely *mental assent*—not simply agreeing with a doctrinal creed or rational statement of faith; nor is it simply us saying things like "I believe in the Bible" or "I believe that Jesus is God's Son" (Wesley said that even the devil could make such statements). Instead, as we read in Wesley's quote above, for him "belief" means having a heartfelt, true confidence and trust in Jesus Christ—or in other words, faith, which he described as "a sure trust and confidence that Christ died for *my* sins, that he loved *me* and gave himself for *me*."[18] For the mature Wesley, then, faith (for which repentance is the first step) is a very personal, subjective thing, rather than something to be inspected and scrutinized rationally and objectively. It results in various "fruits of repentance," which are changes (however small) in our words and behaviors that are outwardly observable and which indicate that God is working within us to begin a process of transformation.

Before concluding this chapter, let me point out that Wesley differentiated between what he called the "faith of servant" and "faith of a son." A servant obeys his master either because he fears punishment if he doesn't or desires the *rewards* of obedience (or both). So, the "faith of a servant" is faith that is motivated either by fear of consequences (such as divine judgment, "going to hell," etc.) and/or by a desire to receive God's blessings and the benefits of salvation (such as good health, earthly success, and/or

---

17 John Wesley, "Predestination Calmly Considered," ¶ 46, in, *The Bicentennial Edition of the Works of John Wesley*, vol. 13, *Doctrinal and Controversial Treatises II*, ed. Paul Wesley Chilcote and Kenneth J. Collins (Nashville: Abingdon Press, 2013), 287.

18 John Wesley, "Justification by Faith" (Sermon 5), § 4, ¶ 2, in Outler, ed., *The Bicentennial Edition of the Works of John Wesley*, 1:194; emphasis added.

getting into heaven after we die). On the other hand, a son (or daughter) is one who obeys and follows the parents not out of fear of the consequences of disobedience, or merely the desire for the rewards of obedience, but simply because of that child's love for them. The "faith of a son," therefore, is Christian faith that obeys and follows God simply out of love for God as our divine Parent, and a conscious desire to do God's will—it is love for love's own sake, rather than for the sake of anything else.[19]

For Wesley, while one who has repented is manifesting the "faith of a servant," he nevertheless urged his followers not to remain content at this level. Speaking of those stuck there, in his sermon "On the Discoveries of Faith," Wesley urged:

> Exhort him to press on by all possible means, till he passes "from faith to faith"; from the faith of a servant to the faith of a son; from the spirit of bondage unto fear, to the spirit of childlike love. He will then have "Christ revealed in his heart."[20]

So, as with prevenient grace, conviction and repentance are not to be understood as full salvation. Nevertheless, they do demonstrate what Wesley called a "low species of faith,"[21] and open the door to the higher and purer forms and processes of faith, which is the subject of the next two chapters.

Discussion Questions

1. Describe a time in your own life when you felt separated from the presence of God.
2. Name some ways that you have experienced God's prevenient grace in your life—specific things or people that helped you to experience God's love and presence perhaps before you even knew it was God.

---

19 For more information about this differentiation, see generally, John Wesley, "On the Discoveries of Faith" (Sermon 117), ¶¶ 12–14, in *The Bicentennial Edition of the Works of John Wesley*, vol. 4, *Sermons IV* (115–51), ed. Albert C. Outler (Nashville: Abingdon Press, 1987), 34–36.

20 Wesley, in Outler, 4:35.

21 Read more in John Wesley "On Faith" (Sermon 106), intro, ¶ 1; §1, ¶¶ 11–13; and §2, ¶ 5, in Outler, ed., *The Bicentennial Edition of the Works of John Wesley*, 1:492, 497–98, 500–501.

3. How have you experienced feelings of "conviction of sin" in your own life? How did you respond to those feelings? What did you do?

4. Think about your general understanding of Christian "salvation" both *before* reading this chapter and *after*. Did the reading of this chapter change that understanding in any way? Was your understanding reaffirmed? Challenged? What new insights did this chapter raise regarding that understanding?

5. If you had to identify which type of Christian "faith" you possess—"faith of a servant" or "faith of a son"—which would it be at present, and why?

CHAPTER 4

BECOMING A CHRISTIAN: THE WORK OF JUSTIFYING GRACE

To briefly recap Wesley's "way of salvation" to this point: (1) In our "original state," humans are created in the imago Dei (image of God); (2) in our "natural state," however, both original sin (our inherent human brokenness) and actual sin (the specific behaviors of sin that we commit) cause us to be separated from that image and from any kind of relationship with God; yet, since the goal of salvation is the restoration of that image in our lives, and since there is nothing we can do to accomplish that on our own, (3) God sends Jesus to earth as the foundation of all grace, and the Holy Spirit then "preveniently" invites and empowers us to begin to respond; (4) this response begins after we encounter and consciously acknowledge God's "law" in the "legal state" of Christianity, where—motivated primarily by fear of the consequences of *not* responding to God, and empowered by God's prevenient grace—we become convicted of our sin, we repent by "believing in the gospel," and begin to bear "fruits of our repentance." However, we ended chapter 3 by being reminded that there is much more to being a Christian than merely fearing God, and that the "legal state" is merely the *beginning* of our renewal in God's image.

Another way of describing this recap is found in a 1746 pamphlet that Wesley titled "The Principles of a Methodist Farther Explained," where he described the process of salvation using the metaphor of a house[1] (fig. 4.1). For him, conviction and repentance of sin are what he refers to as the "porch" of religion. Here, we recognize our utter inability to save ourselves (conviction), and therefore we turn from our sin and toward God (repentance). And while Wesley did not specifically identify where prevenient (or "preventing") grace fit in this metaphor, from the context, we can glean that

---

1 There, referring to Methodism, he explains that "our main doctrines, which include all the rest, are three, that of repentance, of faith, and of holiness. The first of these we account, as it were, the porch of religion; the next, the door; the third is religion itself." John Wesley, "The Principles of a Methodist Farther Explained," § 6, ¶ 4, in *The Bicentennial Edition of the Works of John Wesley*, vol. 9, *The Methodist Societies: History, Nature and Design*, ed. Rupert E. Davies (Nashville: Abingdon Press, 1989), 227.

he probably felt it to be implied in this first step.[2] It may help to think of prevenient grace as being like a loving parent standing on the front porch of the house, calling out or ringing a bell to invite their child(-ren) to come home—*that* is prevenient grace.

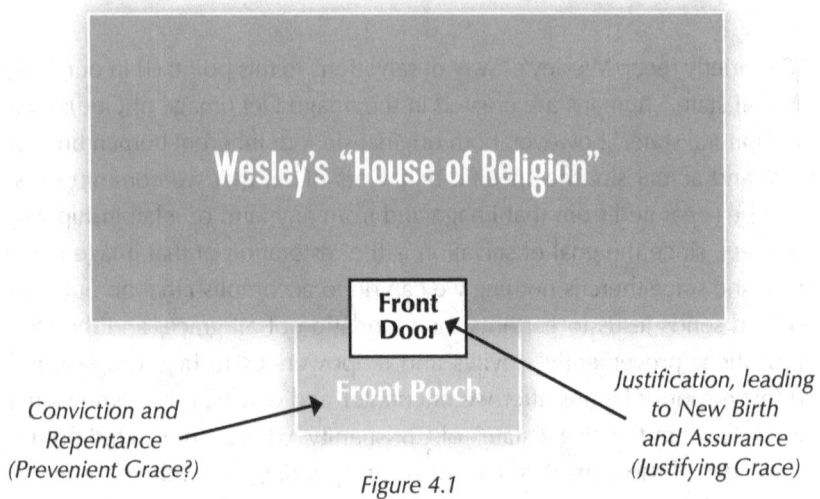

Figure 4.1

Simply being on the front porch, however, does not yet place us inside. To enter, one must pass through a front *door*. In his "house of religion" metaphor, Wesley refers to this entryway as "faith in God" through Jesus Christ, and it will be the focus of this chapter. In fact, in other Wesley writings, we find him describing this front door and its results essentially as a series of three theological concepts that he collectively refers to as the "evangelical state" of Christianity. Again, even though he used the word "state," remember that this is better understood as a stage or movement within the overall "symphony" of salvation.

Whereas in the prevenient grace stage/movement of salvation, recipients are invited and enabled to respond to God's initiative and begin to move toward a renewed relationship, in this second stage/movement—known as **justifying grace**—that relationship is reconstituted, and the image of God

---

2 In fact, in Wesley's later writings, he distinguishes between prevenient and Convicting (or convincing) Grace as two separate manifestations of Grace. In my analogy here, however, I am simplifying these to designate the work of Conviction/Convicting Grace merely as a sub-category of prevenient grace itself.

actually begins to be restored in our lives, even though it is not completed until a later stage, described in chapter 5.

> **Justifying grace:** the state (or movement) of God's grace in which God works both to make possible and to begin to bring about the restoration of the imago Dei in our souls.

In 1746, Wesley published a sermon called "Justification by Faith" in which he outlines his understanding of the purpose, nature and work of God's justifying grace within the "evangelical state" of his via salutis.

Justification by Faith[3]
by John Wesley

To him that worketh not, but believeth on him that justifieth the ungodly, his faith is counted for righteousness. Romans 4:5

1. How a sinner may be justified before God, the Lord and Judge of all, is a question of no common importance to every child of man. It contains the foundation of all our hope, inasmuch as while we are at enmity with God, there can be no true peace, no solid joy, either in time or in eternity. What peace can there be, while our own heart condemns us; and much more, He that is "greater than our heart, and knoweth all things?" What solid joy, either in this world or that to come, while "the wrath of God abideth on us?"

2. And yet how little hath this important question been understood! What confused notions have many had concerning it! Indeed, not only confused, but often utterly false; contrary to the truth, as light to darkness; notions absolutely inconsistent with the oracles of God, and with the whole analogy of faith. And hence, erring concerning the very foundation, they could not possibly build thereon; at least, not "gold, silver, or precious stones," which would endure when tried as by fire; but only "hay and stubble," neither acceptable to God, nor profitable to man.

---

3 John Wesley, "Justification by Faith" (Sermon 5), in Outler, ed., *The Bicentennial Edition of the Works of John Wesley*, 1:181–99 (see chap. 3, n. 16).

CHAPTER 4

3. In order to do justice, in far as in me lies, to the vast importance of the subject, to save those that seek the truth in sincerity from "vain jangling and strife of words," to clear the confusedness of thought into which so many have already been led thereby, and to give them true and just conceptions of this great mystery of godliness, I shall endeavour to show,

> First. What is the general ground of this whole doctrine of justification.
> Secondly. What justification is.
> Thirdly. Who they are that are justified. And,
> Fourthly. On what terms they are justified.

I

I am, First, to show, what is the general ground of this whole doctrine of justification.

1. In the image of God was man made, holy as he that created him is holy; merciful as the Author of all is merciful; perfect as his Father in heaven is perfect. As God is love, so man, dwelling in love, dwelt in God, and God in him. God made him to be an "image of his own eternity," an incorruptible picture of the God of glory. He was accordingly pure, as God is pure, from every spot of sin. He knew not evil in any kind or degree, but was inwardly and outwardly sinless and undefiled. He "loved the Lord his God with all his heart, and with all his mind, and soul, and strength."

2. To man thus upright and perfect, God gave a perfect law, to which he required full and perfect obedience. He required full obedience in every point, and this to be performed without any intermission, from the moment man became a living soul, till the time of his trial should be ended. No allowance was made for any falling short: As, indeed, there was no need of any; man being altogether equal to the task assigned, and thoroughly furnished for every good word and work.

3. To the entire law of love which was written in his heart, (against which, perhaps, he could not sin directly,) it seemed good to the sovereign wisdom of God to superadd one positive law: "Thou shalt not eat of the fruit of the tree that groweth in the midst of the garden;" annexing that penalty thereto, "In the day that thou eatest thereof, thou shalt surely die."

4. Such, then, was the state of man in Paradise. By the free, unmerited love of God, he was holy and happy: He knew, loved, enjoyed God, which is, in substance, life everlasting. And in this life of love, he was to continue for ever, if he continued to obey God in all things; but, if he disobeyed him in any, he was to forfeit all. "In that day," said God, "thou shalt surely die."

5. Man did disobey God. He "ate of the tree, of which God commanded him, saying, Thou shalt not eat of it." And in that day he was condemned by the righteous judgment of God. Then also the sentence whereof he was warned before, began to take place upon him. For the moment he tasted that fruit, he died. His soul died, was separated from God; separate from whom the soul has no more life than the body has when separate from the soul. His body, likewise, became corruptible and mortal; so that death then took hold on this also. And being already dead in spirit, dead to God, dead in sin, he hastened on to death everlasting; to the destruction both of body and soul, in the fire never to be quenched.

6. Thus "by one man sin entered into the world, and death by sin. And so death passed upon all men," as being contained in him who was the common father and representative of us all. Thus, "through the offence of one," all are dead, dead to God, dead in sin, dwelling in a corruptible, mortal body, shortly to be dissolved, and under the sentence of death eternal. For as, "by one man's disobedience," all "were made sinners;" so, by that offence of one, "judgment came upon all men to condemnation." (Romans v. 12, &c.)

7. In this state we were, even all mankind, when "God so loved the world, that he gave his only-begotten Son, to the end we might not perish, but have everlasting life." In the fullness of time he was made Man, another common Head of mankind, a second general Parent and Representative of the whole human race. And as such it was that "he bore our griefs," "the Lord laying upon him the iniquities of us all." Then was he "wounded for our transgressions, and bruised for our iniquities." "He made his soul an offering for sin:" He poured out his blood for the transgressors: He "bare our sins in his own body on the tree," that by his stripes we might be healed: And by that one oblation of himself, once offered, he hath redeemed me and all mankind; having thereby

"made a full, perfect, and sufficient sacrifice and satisfaction for the sins of the whole world."

8. In consideration of this, that the Son of God hath "tasted death for every man," God hath now "reconciled the world to himself, not imputing to them their" former "trespasses." And thus, "as by the offence of one judgment came upon all men to condemnation, even so by the righteousness of one the free gift came upon all men unto justification." So that, for the sake of his well-beloved Son, of what he hath done and suffered for us, God now vouchsafes, on one only condition, (which himself also enables us to perform,) both to remit the punishment due to our sins, to reinstate us in his favour, and to restore our dead souls to spiritual life, as the earnest of life eternal.

9. This, therefore, is the general ground of the whole doctrine of justification. By the sin of the first Adam, who was not only the father, but likewise the representative, of us all, we all fell short of the favour of God; we all became children of wrath; or, as the Apostle expresses it, "judgment came upon all men to condemnation." Even so, by the sacrifice for sin made by the Second Adam, as the Representative of us all, God is so far reconciled to all the world, that he hath given them a new covenant; the plain condition whereof being once fulfilled, "there is no more condemnation" for us, but "we are justified freely by his grace, through the redemption that is in Jesus Christ."

II

1. But what is it to be "justified?" What is "justification?" This was the Second thing which I proposed to show. And it is evident, from what has been already observed, that it is not the being made actually just and righteous. This is "sanctification;" which is, indeed, in some degree, the immediate fruit of justification, but, nevertheless, is a distinct gift of God, and of a totally different nature. The one implies what God does for us through his Son; the other, what he works in us by his Spirit. So that, although some rare instances may be found, wherein the term "justified" or "justification" is used in so wide a sense as to include "sanctification" also; yet, in general use, they are sufficiently distinguished from each other, both by St. Paul and the other inspired writers.

2. Neither is that far-fetched conceit, that justification is the clearing us from accusation, particularly that of Satan, easily provable from any clear text of holy writ. In the whole scriptural account of this matter, as above laid down, neither that accuser nor his accusation appears to be at all taken in. It can not indeed be denied, that he is the "accuser" of men, emphatically so called. But it does in nowise appear, that the great Apostle hath any reference to this, more or less, in all he hath written touching justification, either to the Romans or the Galatians.

3. It is also far easier to take for granted, than to prove from any clear scripture testimony, that justification is the clearing us from the accusation brought against us by the law: At least if this forced, unnatural way of speaking mean either more or less than this, that, whereas we have transgressed the law of God, and thereby deserved the damnation of hell, God does not inflict on those who are justified the punishment which they had deserved.

4. Least of all does justification imply, that God is deceived in those whom he justifies; that he thinks them to be what, in fact, they are not; that he accounts them to be otherwise than they are. It does by no means imply, that God judges concerning us contrary to the real nature of things; that he esteems us better than we really are, or believes us righteous when we are unrighteous. Surely no. The judgment of the all-wise God is always according to truth. Neither can it ever consist with his unerring wisdom, to think that I am innocent, to judge that I am righteous or holy, because another is so. He can no more, in this manner, confound me with Christ, than with David or Abraham. Let any man to whom God hath given understanding, weigh this without prejudice; and he cannot but perceive, that such a notion of justification is neither reconcilable to reason nor Scripture.

5. The plain scriptural notion of justification is pardon, the forgiveness of sins. It is that act of God the Father, hereby, for the sake of the propitiation made by the blood of his Son, he "showeth forth his righteousness (or mercy) by the remission of the sins that are past." This is the easy, natural account of it given by St. Paul, throughout this whole epistle. So he explains it himself, more particularly in this and in the following chapter. Thus, in the next verses but one to the text, "Blessed are they," saith he, "whose iniquities are forgiven, and whose sins are covered:

Blessed is the man to whom the Lord will not impute sin." To him that is justified or forgiven, God "will not impute sin" to his condemnation. He will not condemn him on that account, either in this world or in that which is to come. His sins, all his past sins, in thought, word, and deed, are covered, are blotted out, shall not be remembered or mentioned against him, any more than if they had not been. God will not inflict on that sinner what he deserved to suffer, because the Son of his love hath suffered for him. And from the time we are "accepted through the Beloved," "reconciled to God through his blood," he loves, and blesses, and watches over us for good, even as if we had never sinned.

Indeed the Apostle in one place seems to extend the meaning of the word much farther, where he says, "Not the hearers of the law, but the doers of the law, shall be justified." Here he appears to refer our justification to the sentence of the great day. And so our Lord himself unquestionably doth, when he says, "By thy words thou shalt be justified;" proving hereby, that "for every idle word men shall speak, they shall give an account in the day of judgment." But perhaps we can hardly produce another instance of St. Paul's using the word in that distant sense. In the general tenor of his writings, it is evident he doth not; and least of all in the text before us, which undeniably speaks, not of those who have already "finished their course," but of those who are now just "setting out," just beginning to "run the race which is set before them."

III

1. But this is the third thing which was to be considered, namely, Who are they that are justified? And the Apostle tells us expressly, the ungodly: "He (that is, God) justifieth the ungodly;" the ungodly of every kind and degree; and none but the ungodly. As "they that are righteous need no repentance," so they need no forgiveness. It is only sinners that have any occasion for pardon: It is sin alone which admits of being forgiven. Forgiveness, therefore, has an immediate reference to sin, and, in this respect, to nothing else. It is our "unrighteousness" to which the pardoning God is "merciful:" It is our "iniquity" which he "remembereth no more."

2. This seems not to be at all considered by those who so vehemently contend that a man must be sanctified, that is, holy,

before he can be justified; especially by such of them as affirm, that universal holiness or obedience must precede justification. (Unless they mean that justification at the last day, which is wholly out of the present question.) So far from it, that the very supposition is not only flatly impossible, (for where there is no love of God, there is no holiness, and there is no love of God but from a sense of his loving us,) but also grossly, intrinsically absurd, contradictory to itself. For it is not a saint but a sinner that is forgiven, and under the notion of a sinner. God justifieth not the godly, but the ungodly; not those that are holy already, but the unholy. Upon what condition he doeth this, will be considered quickly: but whatever it is, it cannot be holiness. To assert this, is to say the Lamb of God takes away only those sins which were taken away before.

3. Does then the good Shepherd seek and save only those that are found already? No: He seeks and saves that which is lost. He pardons those who need his pardoning mercy. He saves from the guilt of sin, (and, at the same time, from the power,) sinners of every kind, of every degree: men who, till then, were altogether ungodly; in whom the love of the Father was not; and, consequently, in whom dwelt no good thing, no good or truly Christian temper,—but all such as were evil and abominable,— pride, anger, love of the world,—the genuine fruits of that "carnal mind" which is "enmity against God."

4. These who are sick, the burden of whose sins is intolerable, are they that need a Physician; these who are guilty, who groan under the wrath of God, are they that need a pardon. These who are "condemned already," not only by God, but also by their own conscience, as by a thousand witnesses, of all their ungodliness, both in thought, and word, and work, cry aloud for Him that "justifieth the ungodly," through the redemption that is in Jesus;—the ungodly, and "him that worketh not;" that worketh not, before he is justified, anything that is good, that is truly virtuous or holy, but only evil continually. For his heart is necessarily, essentially evil, till the love of God is shed abroad therein. And while the tree is corrupt, so are the fruits; "for an evil tree cannot bring forth good fruit."

5. If it be objected, "Nay, but a man, before he is justified, may feed the hungry, or clothe the naked; and these are good

works;" the answer is easy: He may do these, even before he is justified; and these are, in one sense, "good works;" they are "good and profitable to men." But it does not follow, that they are, strictly speaking, good in themselves, or good in the sight of God. All truly "good works" (to use the words of our Church) "follow after justification;" and they are therefore good and "acceptable to God in Christ," because they "spring out of a true and living faith." By a parity of reason, all "works done before justification are not good," in the Christian sense, "forasmuch as they spring not of faith in Jesus Christ;" (though from some kind of faith in God they may spring;) "yea, rather, for that they are not done as God hath willed and commanded them to be done, we doubt not" (how strange soever it may appear to some) "but they have the nature of sin."

6. Perhaps those who doubt of this have not duly considered the weighty reason which is here assigned, why no works done before justification can be truly and properly good. The argument plainly runs thus:—No works are good, which are not done as God hath willed and commanded them to be done.

But no works done before justification are done as God hath willed and commanded them to be done:

Therefore, no works done before justification are good.

The first proposition is self-evident; and the second, that no works done before justification are done as God hath willed and commanded them to be done, will appear equally plain and undeniable, if we only consider, God hath willed and commanded that "all our works" should "be done in charity;" (*en agape*) in love, in that love to God which produces love to all mankind. But none of our works can be done in this love, while the love of the Father (of God as our Father) is not in us; and this love can not be in us till we receive the "Spirit of Adoption, crying in our hearts, Abba, Father." If, therefore, God doth not "justify the ungodly," and him that (in this sense) "worketh not," then hath Christ died in vain; then, notwithstanding his death, can no flesh living be justified.

IV

1. But on what terms, then, is he justified who is altogether "ungodly," and till that time "worketh not?" On one alone; which is faith: He "believeth in Him that justifieth the ungodly." And

"he that believeth is not condemned;" yea, he is "passed from death unto life." "For the righteousness (or mercy) of God is by faith of Jesus Christ unto all and upon all them that believe: — Whom God hath set forth for a propitiation, through faith in his blood; that he might be just, and" (consistently with his justice) "the Justifier of him which believeth in Jesus:" "Therefore we conclude that a man is justified by faith without the deeds of the law;" without previous obedience to the moral law, which, indeed, he could not, till now, perform. That it is the moral law, and that alone, which is here intended, appears evidently from the words that follow: "Do we then make void the law through faith? God forbid: Yea, we establish the law. What law do we establish by faith? Not the ritual law: Not the ceremonial law of Moses. In nowise; but the great, unchangeable law of love, the holy love of God and of our neighbour."

2. Faith in general is a divine, supernatural *"elegchos,"* "evidence" or "conviction," "of things not seen," not discoverable by our bodily senses, as being either past, future, or spiritual. Justifying faith implies, not only a divine evidence or conviction that "God was in Christ, reconciling the world unto himself;" but a sure trust and confidence that Christ died for "my" sins, that he loved "me," and gave himself for "me." And at what time soever a sinner thus believes, be it in early childhood, in the strength of his years, or when he is old and hoary-haired, God justifieth that ungodly one: God, for the sake of his Son, pardoneth and absolveth him, who had in him, till then, no good thing. Repentance, indeed, God had given him before; but that repentance was neither more nor less than a deep sense of the want of all good, and the presence of all evil. And whatever good he hath, or doeth, from that hour when he first believes in God through Christ, faith does not "find," but "bring." This is the fruit of faith. First the tree is good, and then the fruit is good also.

3. I cannot describe the nature of this faith better than in the words of our own Church: "The only instrument of salvation" (whereof justification is one branch) "is faith; that is, a sure trust and confidence that God both hath and will forgive our sins, that he hath accepted us again into His favour, for the merits of Christ's death and passion. —But here we must take heed that we do not halt with God, through an inconstant, wavering faith:

CHAPTER 4

Peter, coming to Christ upon the water, because he fainted in faith, was in danger of drowning; so we, if we begin to waver or doubt, it is to be feared that we shall sink as Peter did, not into the water, but into the bottomless pit of hell fire." ("Second Sermon on the Passion")

"Therefore, have a sure and constant faith, not only that the death of Christ is available for all the world, but that he hath made a full and sufficient sacrifice for "thee," a perfect cleansing of "thy" sins, so that thou mayest say, with the Apostle, he loved "thee," and gave himself for "thee." For this is to make Christ "thine own," and to apply his merits unto "thyself."" ("Sermon on the Sacrament, First Part").

4. By affirming that this faith is the term or "condition of justification," I mean, First, that there is no justification without it. "He that believeth not is condemned already;" and so long as he believeth not, that condemnation cannot be removed, but "the wrath of God abideth on him." As "there is no other name given under heaven," than that of Jesus of Nazareth, no other merit whereby a condemned sinner can ever be saved from the guilt of sin; so there is no other way of obtaining a share in his merit, than "by faith in his name." So that as long as we are without this faith, we are "strangers to the covenant of promise," we are "aliens from the commonwealth of Israel, and without God in the world." Whatsoever virtues (so called) a man may have, —I speak of those unto whom the gospel is preached; for "what have I to do to judge them that are without?"—whatsoever good works (so accounted) he may do, it profiteth not; he is still a "child of wrath," still under the curse, till he believes in Jesus.

5. Faith, therefore, is the "necessary" condition of justification; yea, and the "only necessary" condition thereof. This is the Second point carefully to be observed; that, the very moment God giveth faith (for "it is the gift of God") to the "ungodly" that "worketh not," that "faith is counted to him for righteousness." He hath no righteousness at all, antecedent to this, not so much as negative righteousness, or innocence. But "faith is imputed to him for righteousness," the very moment that he believeth. Not that God (as was observed before) thinketh him to be what he is not. But as "he made Christ to be sin for us," that is, treated

him as a sinner, punishing him for our sins; so he counteth us righteous, from the time we believe in him: That is, he doth not punish us for our sins; yea, treats us as though we are guiltless and righteous.

6. Surely the difficulty of assenting to this proposition, that "faith is the "only condition" of justification," must arise from not understanding it. We mean thereby thus much, that it is the only thing without which none is justified; the only thing that is immediately, indispensably, absolutely requisite in order to pardon. As, on the one hand, though a man should have every thing else without faith, yet he cannot be justified; so, on the other, though he be supposed to want everything else, yet if he hath faith, he cannot but be justified. For suppose a sinner of any kind or degree, in a full sense of his total ungodliness, of his utter inability to think, speak, or do good, and his absolute meetness for hell-fire; suppose, I say, this sinner, helpless and hopeless, casts himself wholly on the mercy of God in Christ, (which indeed he cannot do but by the grace of God,) who can doubt but he is forgiven in that moment? Who will affirm that any more is "indispensably required" before that sinner can be justified?

Now, if there ever was one such instance from the beginning of the world, (and have there not been, and are there not, ten thousand times ten thousand?) it plainly follows, that faith is, in the above sense, the sole condition of justification.

7. It does not become poor, guilty, sinful worms, who receive whatsoever blessings they enjoy, (from the least drop of water that cools our tongue, to the immense riches of glory in eternity,) of grace, of mere favour, and not of debt, to ask of God the reasons of his conduct. It is not meet for us to call Him in question "who giveth account to none of his ways;" to demand, "Why didst thou make faith the condition, the only condition, of justification? Wherefore didst thou decree, "He that believeth," and he only, "shall be saved?" This is the very point on which St. Paul so strongly insists in the ninth chapter of this Epistle, viz., That the terms of pardon and acceptance must depend, not on us, but "on him that calleth us;" that there is no "unrighteousness with God," in fixing his own terms, not according to ours, but his own good pleasure; who may justly say, "I will have mercy on whom I will have mercy;" namely, on

him who believeth in Jesus. "So then it is not of him that willeth, nor of him that runneth," to choose the condition on which he shall find acceptance; "but of God that showeth mercy;" that accepteth none at all, but of his own free love, his unmerited goodness. "Therefore hath he mercy on whom he will have mercy," viz., on those who believe on the Son of his love; "and whom he will," that is, those who believe not, "he hardeneth," leaves at last to the hardness of their hearts.

8. One reason, however, we may humbly conceive, of God's fixing this condition of justification, "If thou believest in the Lord Jesus Christ, thou shalt be saved," was to "hide pride from man." Pride had already destroyed the very angels of God, had cast down "a third part of the stars of heaven." It was likewise in great measure owing to this, when the tempter said, "Ye shall be as gods," that Adam fell from his own steadfastness, and brought sin and death into the world. It was therefore an instance of wisdom worthy of God, to appoint such a condition of reconciliation for him and all his posterity as might effectually humble, might abase them to the dust. And such is faith. It is peculiarly fitted for this end: For he that cometh unto God by this faith, must fix his eye singly on his own wickedness, on his guilt and helplessness, without having the least regard to any supposed good in himself, to any virtue or righteousness whatsoever. He must come as a "mere sinner," inwardly and outwardly, self-destroyed and self-condemned, bringing nothing to God but ungodliness only, pleading nothing of his own but sin and misery. Thus it is, and thus alone, when his "mouth is stopped," and he stands utterly "guilty before" God, that he can "look unto Jesus," as the whole and sole "Propitiation for his sins." Thus only can he be "found in him," and receive the "righteousness which is of God by faith."

9. Thou ungodly one, who hearest or readest these words! thou vile, helpless, miserable sinner! I charge thee before God, the Judge of all, go straight unto him, with all thy ungodliness. Take heed thou destroy not thy own soul by pleading thy righteousness, more or less. Go as altogether ungodly, guilty, lost, destroyed, deserving and dropping into hell; and thou shalt then find favour in his sight, and know that he justifieth the ungodly. As such thou shalt be brought unto the "blood of sprinkling,"

> as an undone, helpless, damned sinner. Thus "look unto Jesus!" There is "the Lamb of God," who "taketh away thy sins!" Plead thou no works, no righteousness of thine own! No humility, contrition, sincerity! In nowise. That were, in very deed, to deny the Lord that bought thee. No: Plead thou, singly, the blood of the covenant, the ransom paid for thy proud, stubborn, sinful soul. Who art thou, that now seest and feelest both thine inward and outward ungodliness? Thou art the man! I want thee for my Lord! I challenge "thee" for a child of God by faith! The Lord hath need of thee. Thou who feelest thou art just fit for hell, art just fit to advance his glory; the glory of his free grace, justifying the ungodly and him that worketh not. O come quickly! Believe in the Lord Jesus; and thou, even thou, art reconciled to God.

When Christians today think of the concept and practice of "conversion," "being saved," or "accepting Christ," we often think of it as one complete act or action. In this sermon, however, Wesley points out that—by whatever name we call it—this act/action of justifying grace consists of at least three distinct parts: **justification**; **new birth** (or regeneration); and **assurance** (or witness of the Spirit). Wesley believed that all three of these terms/concepts are related but quite different.

Justification

First, let's be reminded of what Wesley wrote about **justification** in his sermon above: "The plain scriptural notion of justification is pardon, the forgiveness of sins . . . To [one] that is justified or forgiven, . . . all his past sins, in thought, word, and deed, are covered, blotted out, shall not be remembered or mentioned against [them], any more than if they had not been."[4]

> **Justification**: the work of God's justifying grace for us, to forgive our original and actual sin and restore the possibility of a right relationship with God.

In this definition, we see at least two important things happening. In Justification **we are freed from the *guilt* of sin**. In this, God does not excuse our

---

4 Wesley, § 2, ¶ 5, in Outler, 1:189–90.

actual sin. Instead, he recognizes it, but then consciously chooses to ignore it. Perhaps you've heard the cliché that says that justification means "just as if I never sinned"—the phrase is even partially found in the letters of the word itself: **just-if-I**cation. In this case, the cliché is essentially correct. For Wesley, justification is akin to us standing before God in heaven's courtroom, where we are being judged and fined for our sin, and Jesus enters and pays the fine *for us.*

Before I entered the United Methodist ordained ministry, my career began in law school, and I vividly remember learning about an American legal practice in one of my classes, called "J.N.O.V.," which stands for *judgment non obstante verdict* (judgment "notwithstanding the verdict"). Essentially, it is a courtroom practice that allows a presiding judge in a civil trial to set aside the decision or verdict of a jury *if* certain legal conditions are met. That is essentially what happens in divine justification. In the "court" of spiritual judgment, the host of evil and even our own human peers find and declare us guilty because of our original and actual sin; yet, if we have met the condition of being a disciple of Christ, then his sacrifice on the cross pays the "debt" of our sin, and we are now freed from the guilt of that sin. It doesn't mean that we didn't commit the sin—we did! But because of Christ's sacrifice, we are no longer held accountable for its effects in our lives.

There is, however, a second action happening in Wesley's understanding of justification: in it, **our reconciliation with God is made possible.** You'll remember that because of our original and actual sin, we as human beings are separated from God. Even when we want to return, we find that even our best efforts fall far short in attempting to span the gap between us and God (fig. 4.2).

Figure 4.2

However, for Wesley, justification means that Jesus has bridged that gap for us—we have a way back home now—a bridge that spans the separation between us and God (fig. 4.3).

BECOMING A CHRISTIAN: THE WORK OF JUSTIFYING GRACE

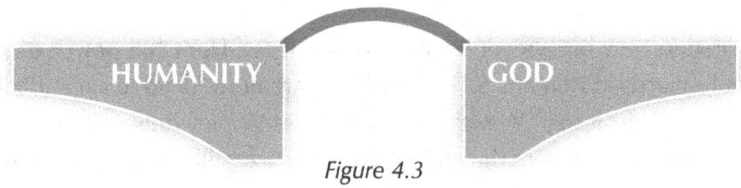

Figure 4.3

Bear in mind, of course, that while this spiritual bridge has now been built in *principle*, it does *not* mean that we have yet crossed it in *practice*—we are not yet fully reconciled to God; the way is simply now open and available for that to occur.

New Birth / Regeneration

So, if justification makes *possible* our reconciliation with God once again, the second component of justifying grace begins the actual process of reconciliation itself. Wesley called it **"new birth"** (or "Regeneration"), and in his 1760 sermon of the same name, he describes it in the following way:

> It is that great change which God works in the soul when he brings it into life; when he raises it from the death of sin to the life of righteousness. It is the change wrought in the whole soul by the almighty Spirit of God when it is "created anew in Christ Jesus;" when it is "renewed after the image of God, in righteousness and true holiness;" when the love of the world is changed into the love of God; pride into humility; passion into meekness; hatred, envy, malice, into a sincere, tender, disinterested love for all mankind. In a word, it is that change whereby the earthly, sensual, devilish mind is turned into the "mind which was in Christ Jesus."[5]

Once again here we see several actions of the Holy Spirit taking place all at once.

> **New birth/regeneration:** the work of God's justifying grace within us to remake and re-create our souls again, thereby beginning the process of actually restoring the image of God within us.

---

5 John Wesley, "The New Birth" (Sermon 45), § 2, ¶ 5, in Outler, ed., *The Bicentennial Edition of the Works of John Wesley*, 2:193–94 (see chap. 3, n. 1).

First, in new birth/regeneration, we are **freed from the *power* of sin**. In Paul's words in Romans 6:11 (NRSV), we are now "dead to sin and alive to God in Christ Jesus." We learned earlier that Wesley believed that while justification frees us from the *guilt* of sin, its *power* still remains. But in new birth, sin loses its actual power, as well. So, whereas in justification God *cancels sin* (yet its power remains), verse 4 of Charles Wesley's famous hymn "O for a Thousand Tongues to Sing" explains that in new birth, God "breaks the power of cancelled sin." Whereas in our "natural state" we are spiritually blind, deaf, and dumb (i.e., spiritually dead) because of sin, Wesley says that after new birth, our "whole soul is now sensible of God," with the "eyes of [our] understanding . . . now 'open.'"[6] In the words of verse 6 of that same hymn: "Hear him, ye deaf, His praise, ye dumb, Your loosened tongues employ. Ye blind behold, your Savior comes, and leap ye lame for joy!"

Therefore, one consequence of our new birth/regeneration in Christ is that we are now free not to commit known sin. First John 3:9 says: "Those who have been born of God do not sin, because God's seed abides in them; they cannot sin, because they have been born of God" (NRSV). Wesley explains it this way:

> "Whosoever is born of God," *while he abideth in faith and love, and in the spirit of prayer and thanksgiving*, not only doth not, but can not, thus commit sin. So long as he thus believeth in God through Christ, and loves Him, and is pouring out his heart before Him, he cannot voluntarily transgress any command of God.[7]

In other words, if we have been born anew, then for the first time in our lives, we can fight sin and conquer it *if we so choose*. However, the key to this is intentional choice. For Wesley, this is why "born again" Christians can still commit actual sin—not because their salvation is incomplete (which is the explanation given in some traditions for sinful behavior following conversion), but because they voluntarily choose not to *appropriate* the power to conquer sin that's now available.

In addition to freeing us from the power of sin, though, a second thing

---

6 John Wesley, "The Great Privilege of Those That Are Born of God" (Sermon 19), § 1, ¶¶ 8–9, in Outler, ed., *The Bicentennial Edition of the Works of John Wesley*, 1:434–35 (see chap. 3, n. 16).

7 Wesley, in Outler, 436, emphasis added.

that happens in new birth is that the **image of God actually begins to be restored** in us. Because our souls are now spiritually remade, or re-created, we begin a renewed, daily relationship with God. In the podium illustration that we introduced in the previous chapter, new birth means that we now take our first step toward the restoration of the imago Dei in our lives. That image is not yet fully restored, but we are on our way toward it. In the bridge metaphor introduced in this chapter, it means actually beginning to *cross* the spiritual bridge built by God's justification. Again, we have not yet arrived on the other side, but we have taken our *first step* onto the spiritual bridge (fig. 4.4).

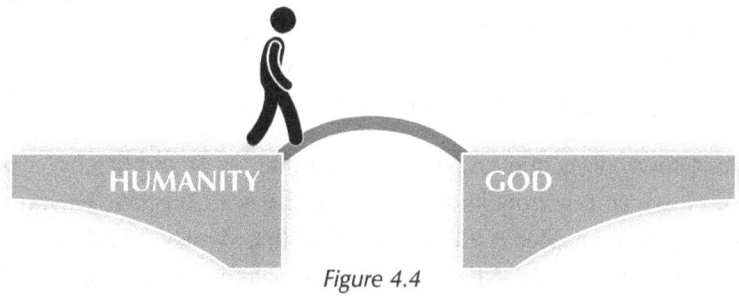

Figure 4.4

In thinking about the relationship between justification and new birth, it's important to remember that though these two occur at the same moment in one's life, they reference two distinctively different concepts within the work of justifying grace. They are, in effect, two sides of the same coin. In his sermon "The Great Privilege of Those That Are Born of God," Wesley explains it this way,

> Justification and the new birth are, in point of time, inseparable from each other, yet they are easily distinguished, as being . . . things of a widely different nature. Justification implies only a relative, the new birth a real, change. God in justifying us does something *for* us. In begetting us again, He does the work *in* us. The [former] is the taking away of the guilt [of sin, whereas the latter is] the taking away the power of sin.[8]

Here we learn that whereas justification is God's *forgiving* of us, new birth explains what happens when we allow that forgiveness to actually *work* in

---

8 Wesley, 1:431–32; emphasis in the original.

our lives—we become changed people. In one respect, we might refer to new birth as our soul's *response* to the forgiveness we receive in justification.

However, while new birth can be viewed as a result or consequence of justification, at the same time it is also the beginning (or first step) of the process of *sanctification* (which we'll discuss in the next chapter). In his sermon "The Scripture Way of Salvation," Wesley states that "at the same time that we are justified, yea, in that very moment, sanctification begins. In that instant we are born again, born from above, born of the Spirit: there is a *real* as well as a *relative* change"[9] In many ways, then, new birth is the hinge that connects the final two spiritual movements in Wesley's via salutis (justifying and sanctifying grace).

Assurance / Witness of the Spirit

So how, then, does one know for certain that he or she has been born again? How can one truly know that he or she is a Christian? As you may remember from chapter 2, this is a question that Wesley wrestled with for much of his life as well. Whatever his Aldersgate experience of May 1738 was, it was certainly at least an affirmation of his Christianity—that is, it gave him an *assurance* about his salvation; it enabled him to have certainty that he was a child of God.

Wesley later described this affirmation as a third dimension in the work of God's justifying grace and referred to it as the doctrine of **assurance**. In his sermon "Witness of the Spirit, Discourse II," he explains:

> By "testimony of the Spirit" I mean an inward impression on the soul, whereby the Spirit of God immediately and directly witnesses to my spirit, that I am a child of God; that "Jesus Christ hath loved me and given Himself for me"; that all my sins are blotted out, and I, even I, am reconciled to God.[10]

He based this on Romans 8:16, which affirms that God's "very Spirit [bears] witness with our spirit that we are children of God" (NRSV).

---

9 Wesley, "The Scripture Way of Salvation," § 1, ¶ 4 in Outler, ed., *Works*, 2:154; emphasis in the original.

10 John Wesley, "The Witness of the Spirit, Discourse I" (Sermon 10), § 1, ¶ 7, in Outler, ed., *The Bicentennial Edition of the Works of John Wesley*, 1:274 (see chap. 3, n. 16).

> **Assurance/witness of the Spirit**: one's personal awareness that he or she is loved, forgiven, accepted, and claimed as a child of God.

For him, this is God's assurance of love, an assurance of *present* pardon, and the certainty of God's presence in and with a believer in his or her life of faith. Assurance, for Wesley, was when someone can say for the first time in his or her own heart "I know that I know that I know that I am loved and accepted by God." And even though the famous hymn hadn't been written yet, it meant being able to sing in one's spirit, "Blessed assurance, Jesus is mine" and know that it was true!

As affirming as this doctrine was, Wesley nevertheless also offered some cautions about it. For one, he reminded his Methodists that assurance is *not an emotional feeling*. Feelings and emotions of forgiveness may come and go, but the *witness of God's Spirit* is more properly an *inner conviction* of our hearts and spirits of the truth and promise of the fact of God's forgiveness of us, and our reliance upon it.

Second, Wesley was clear to point out that assurance refers to the affirmation of our faith in the *present*, but that it is *not a guarantee for the future*. It is, therefore, not his version of the Reformed Christian doctrine of "once saved, always saved." One could still "backslide" and fall from God's grace (this will be discussed more in chapter 5). One should not presume to rest one's faith upon any particular spiritual experience or event from the *past*, but instead constantly inquire about the depth and fruits of one's salvation in the *present*. Its focus is on affirming one in his or her *present* faith situation and helping that person to have certainty of God's love for him or her in the present moment.

A third caution Wesley shared was that even though assurance was helpful in our Christian identity, nevertheless *it is not necessary for salvation*. In 1768, he wrote in one of his letters:

> I believe a consciousness of being in the favour of God [i.e., assurance] . . . is the common privilege of Christians fearing God and working righteousness. Yet I do not affirm that there are no exceptions to this general rule. Possibly some may be in the favour of God and yet go mourning all the day long. But I believe this is usually owing either to disorder of body or ignorance of the gospel promises. Therefore I have not for

many years thought a consciousness of pardon to be essential to justifying faith.[11]

What he was saying here is that there may be times when people who are actual Christians are not aware of their salvation and think themselves still apart from God (i.e., those who "go mourning all the day long") simply because they've never been taught that they *could* be aware of it—what Wesley calls "ignorance of the gospel promises."[12]

I have witnessed this reality of Wesley's firsthand. I was once working on an ecumenical Christian retreat where I was teaching my understanding of what it means to be converted (i.e., justified and born anew), and in passing I mentioned my belief (based on Wesley's here) that one does not need to be able to name the time and place of one's conversion in order for one truly to be a Christian. At that point, I remember noticing one retreat participant in the back of the room begin to weep profusely. At the time, I didn't know what it was about, but I completed my teaching and—as required by the retreat structure—left the conference room so the participants could discuss my teaching at their tables. A short while later, a retreat leader frantically came running to me, saying that I had to come back to the conference room quickly because one of the participants was very upset. I didn't know what I had said that would have been so offensive, but I went nevertheless.

As it turned out, it was the woman who had begun to cry during my teaching, so I sat down to talk with her privately. Evidently, she had been raised in a Christian tradition that teaches that if one cannot identify or name a specific date when he or she was converted or "saved," then he or she has not been pardoned or "saved" at all. During my teaching about the reality that such an identification is *not* actually necessary for salvation, that woman experienced great emotional and spiritual freedom and release. Here was someone who had experienced what Wesley called "ignorance of the gospel promises"—she was already a believer but did not yet know it due to the strictness of her upbringing. In this case, my words had enabled her instead to experience and claim for herself what Wesley would call assurance, or "witness of the Spirit." She now *knew* that she was a child of God—and

---

11 John Wesley, "Letter to Dr. Rutherforth" (March 28, 1768) in *The Letters of the Rev. John Wesley*, standard ed., ed. John Telford (London: Epworth Press, 1931), 5:358–59.

12 Wesley, 5:359.

had been for some time! There is power, you see, in the knowledge of one's assurance, but it is *not* a requirement for salvation.

So, thinking about the "House of Religion" metaphor introduced at the beginning of this chapter, we have discussed two stages, or movements, within Wesley's via salutis: on the "porch" of salvation, God works to overcome original sin through prevenient grace, conviction, and repentance to enable us to *turn from* a life of sin and *turn toward* God; within the "front door" of salvation, God works through justifying grace to begin the process of restoration of the imago Dei (both positionally and practically) through the Holy Spirit's activity of justification, which enables and leads both to new birth, and to assurance. Yet, while all of this enables us to begin a renewed life and renewed relationship with God through Christ, it is not the end of God's work of salvation. It is, instead, only the beginning of our Christian life. In the next chapter, we'll discuss what happens *after* we begin that new life. Specifically, how does one grow and develop in one's life of faith with God, so that he or she becomes more like Christ, and so that the imago Dei is spiritually restored in actuality in its fullness?

Discussion Questions

1. How have you experienced God's forgiveness and pardon in your life?
2. Describe someone you know whose life is different because of his or her faith in Jesus Christ.
3. Wesley says that the experience of "new birth" gives humans the ability to fight sin and win for the first time, *if they so choose.* Can you think of times in your life when you fell prey to temptation or the power of sin because you did not choose to fight it? Have you seen this happen to others? What do you see of the value and importance of *choice* in the Christian life?
4. Do you know anyone who seems to have experienced what Wesley called "ignorance of the gospel promises" in his or her spiritual life (i.e., someone who may have been a Christian but not known it)? What do you see as the value and importance of assurance in the Christian life?

CHAPTER 5

GROWING IN SALVATION: THE WORK OF SANCTIFYING GRACE

Sanctification

So, what happens in one's spiritual life after he or she metaphorically enters the "House of Religion" through the "front door" of justifying grace (i.e., justification, resulting in new birth and assurance)? At that point, isn't that person a completed Christian? What more is there to the Christian life and faith beyond that experience of what we today call "conversion"? Different Christian traditions answer these questions in different ways.

In the Reformed/Calvinist tradition (including Presbyterian and Baptist churches), the work of justifying grace can be understood to be a **single, instantaneous act** that makes the recipient *immediately* holy by taking on the full and complete righteousness of Christ (by which we are saved and eventually judged by God), with the rest of that person's life then being spent *living out* that imputed righteousness. While the imago Dei is not fully restored in practice in this instantaneous experience of "being saved" (as these traditions would call it), nevertheless the individual now stands before God in position in a *completed state* of righteousness (fig. 5.1).

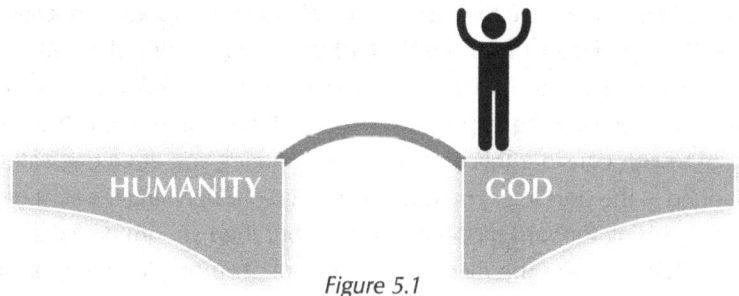

Figure 5.1

Considering that this is the essence of Christian life from God's perspective, there is certainly a truth to this view. After all, if we truly believe that God is omniscient (i.e., all-knowing due to an existence outside of the confines of time and space), then when we are converted, God already knows and sees the completed and perfected spiritual beings that we will become. What's more, even from a human perspective, justification (with its consequent results of new birth and assurance) *is* certainly something that we can experience at a definite point in time.

As one might guess, however, Wesley addressed this subject differently. While he acknowledged that from God's ideal perspective and **position**, conversion does bring about a sense of imputed completion to justification, he also argued that God does not see or view us from that *ideal* perspective, but from the reality of who we actually *are* and who we are *becoming* through the power of the Holy Spirit. In Romans 7:15-25, for example, even the apostle Paul talked about the inner spiritual conflict he experienced after his Damascus road conversion. For him, the Christian life obviously involved not just an *ideal* that we adopt, but also a process of reality that we *live into*.

Consider, for instance, the words of Hebrews 6:1, "Therefore let us go on toward perfection, leaving behind the basic teaching about Christ, and not laying again the foundation: repentance from dead works and faith toward God" (NRSV). This text indicates that for the author of Hebrews, Christianity does include a foundation and basic teaching that one needs to embrace, and which includes "repentance" and "faith toward God" (what Wesley would refer to as the legal and evangelical states of faith). But the first phrase ("let us go on . . .") also makes it clear that once we experience these, we are to *move beyond them* into something more.

A few chapters later, Hebrews 12:1-2 shares a helpful metaphor: "Let us run with perseverance the race that is set before us, looking to Jesus the pioneer and perfecter of our faith" (NRSV). Here, we find the author essentially saying that the Christian life on earth is like a track race to be run, rather than merely being a spectator's seat that we sit in to enjoy the show. For a moment, consider this metaphor by assuming you are a track athlete positioned at the start line. You hear the gun go off, signaling the start of the race. You spring forward past the start line, but then you immediately stop running. Did you win the race? Of course not! You only crossed the start line. To win, you have to continue running until the *finish* line!

In like fashion, conversion for Wesley is merely the *beginning* of the restoration of the imago Dei in our lives—it is merely the *start line* of our salvation, rather than its *end/goal*. Instead of focusing on God's ideal perspective and *position*, for him conversion focuses on our human perspective and **practice**. Thinking of both the bridge and podium metaphors from our previous two chapters, I reminded us that conversion is merely the *first step* in our journey back toward God (figure 4.4 in the previous chapter).[1]

For Wesley, the rest of those steps is the work of **sanctifying grace** (or **sanctification**)—the process *after* conversion whereby one is actually made holy (i.e., more and more Christlike) each and every day for the rest of one's life (fig. 5.2). In his sermon "The Scripture Way of Salvation," Wesley explains it this way: "From the time of our being born again, the gradual work of sanctification takes place."[2]

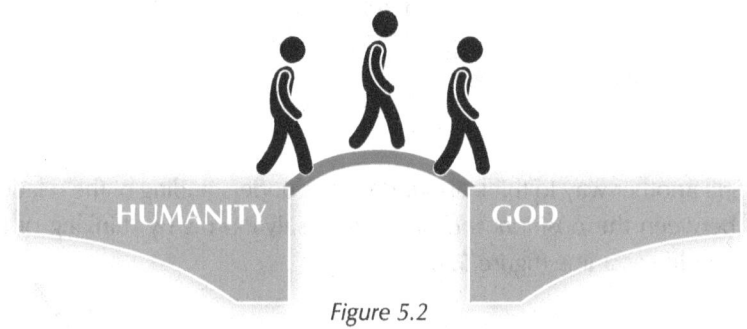

Figure 5.2

This is the third stage or "movement" of salvation, and through it, the gap in holiness between actual *practice* and imputed *position* is gradually decreased, to the point where the two become one once again (see fig. 3.3).

Do you remember our "House of Religion" metaphor from the previous chapter? If prevenient grace references the activity of God on the front porch of that house, and justifying grace references conversion as the work of both God and humanity to allow us to enter through the front door of the house, then think of sanctifying grace as one exploring and experiencing the *rest* of the house over the remainder of one's lifetime (figure 5.3).

---

1 The contrast between "positional" and "practical" holiness is sometimes also seen in a comparison between the experience of "dramatic" conversion (as found, for instance, in the life of the apostle Paul in Acts 9) and that of "gradual" conversion (as found, for instance, in the lives of the original twelve disciples). In the former, conversion seems to take the form of an instantaneous point in time (like a lightning bolt from the sky that one can see and identify precisely when it occurs). In the latter, conversion seems to take the form of a gradual experience that happens over time (like a sunrise that one can watch and not really know for sure when it occurred, but one knows that it happened). Yet, *both* of these forms are equally powerful and valid ways to be spiritually "reborn."

2 Wesley, "The Scripture Way of Salvation," § 1, ¶ 8, in Outler, ed., *Works*, 2:160 (see chap. 3, n. 1).

CHAPTER 5

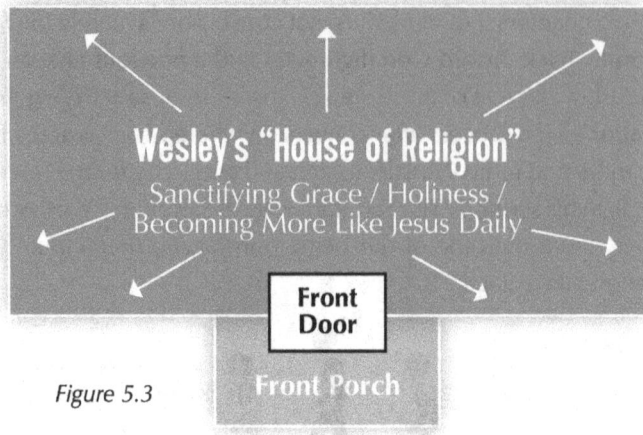

Figure 5.3

Still another way to think about Wesley's understanding of the relationship between the *position and practice* of salvation is by thinking of the Christian life as a line (figure 5.4).3

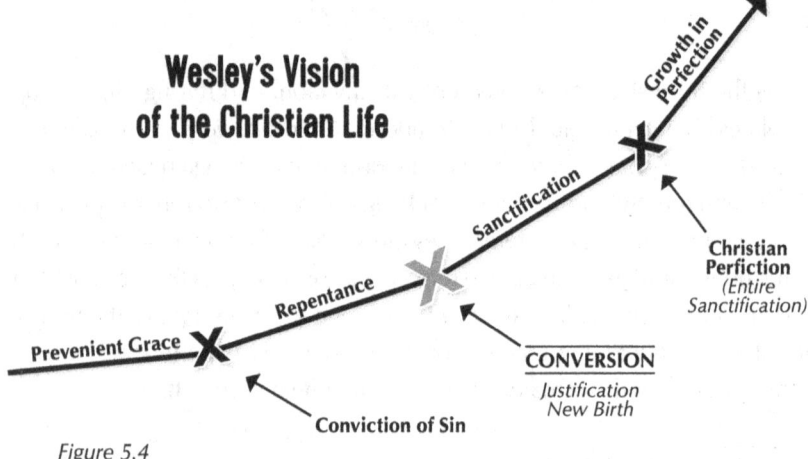

Figure 5.4

The x's above mark examples of *individual events* that one can experience instantaneously in the Christian life (such as conviction, justification, new birth). However, notice that these individual events are subsumed within the

---

3 This particular visual metaphor was first shared with me by my professor of Wesleyan theology, Henry H. Knight III, in one of my classes at Emory University's Candler School of Theology in 1991. Used with permission.

continuous upward line that represents the *gradual process* of growth back to, and renewal in, the image of God. While the imputed righteousness of Christ is given *instantly*, nevertheless the eradication of the root of sin within us occurs gradually over the rest of our lifetime.

> **Sanctifying grace/sanctification**: the grace of God continuing to work gradually in one's life after conversion (justification, new birth, and assurance) to enable, empower, and bring about growth in faith and more Christlike character over the course of one's lifetime, illustrated in Hebrews 12:1-2.

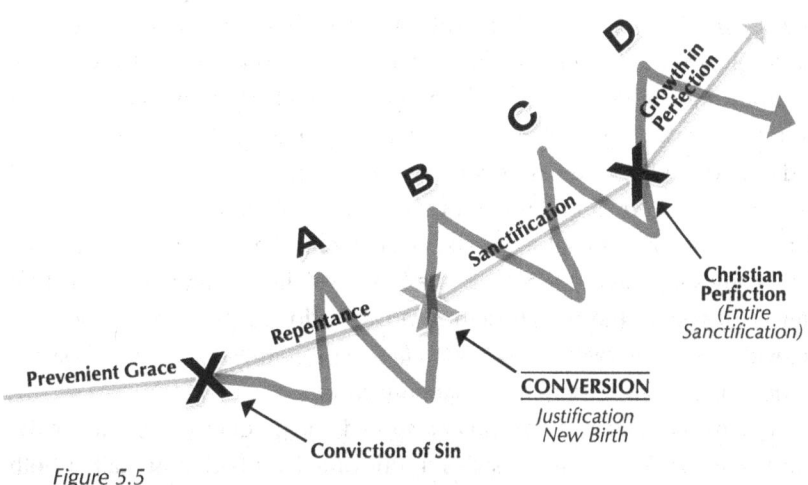

Figure 5.5

The reality of this work is not even as neat and orderly as figure 5.4 indicates. Instead, in this metaphor, Wesley's "gradual work of sanctification" looks more like figure 5.5 in *practice:* a series of fits and spurts in which there are "down" times when we either decline (or at least are not growing) in our walk with God; and "up" times when we are growing and advancing in our faith walk. What is important in this metaphor, however, is not the reality or degree of decline, but the *overall trajectory of our journey*. Are we growing or declining over the course of our lives as a whole? Are we closer to God at point D than at point C? Closer at point C than at point B? All of this explains why, in a Wesleyan view, it is technically incorrect to use the term "saved" merely to reference one's conversion (justification, new birth, and assurance). Instead, biblically speaking, "being saved" includes *all* of God's work in one's life—from prevenient grace, through justifying grace, to sanctifying grace.

Fruit of the Spirit

So, how will one know one is growing in faith through the process of sanctification? Of course, assurance (or witness of the Spirit) gives one confidence that he or she is presently on this path. However, for Wesley, another important way to identify the work of sanctifying grace in one's life was through the presence and operation of the **"fruit of the Spirit,"** which Paul lists in Galatians 5:22–23 as "love, joy, peace, patience, kindness, generosity, faithfulness, gentleness, and self-control" (NRSV). These, for Wesley, were the marks of a true Christian, and their presence and work in one's life is one of the truest indicators of genuine faith. It didn't matter how dramatically you claimed to have been converted, or that you prayed six hours every day, or had memorized a certain number of scripture verses. Instead, if one did not *show* one's faith by and through one's spiritual fruit (especially love),[4] then one's salvation may be false. Wesley once wrote, "Let none ever presume to rest in any supposed testimony of the Spirit which is separate from the fruit of it."[5] Of course, these fruits do not *earn* salvation for anyone, but they can be evidence of the reality of salvation (a sort of "witness of our *own* spirits," if you will) for one experiencing sanctification.

In what context(s), then, can and should one practice these fruits of the Spirit? For Wesley, the answer lies in our practice of what he called both "acts of piety" and "acts of mercy"—which I am collectively referencing here as the **"Cross of Faith"** (figure 5.6).

> **"Acts of piety"** and **"acts of mercy"**: two contexts in which the fruit of the Spirit (Galatians 5:22–23) manifest themselves in the life of a converted Christian. Together they form two essential dimensions/beams of the Cross of Faith: (1) "Acts of piety" reference acts/

---

[4] Wesley took this emphasis on *"love"* from Paul's words in 1 Corinthians 13:1-3.

[5] Wesley, "The Witness of the Spirit, Discourse II" (Sermon 11), § 5, ¶ 3, in Outler, ed., *The Bicentennial Edition of the Works of John Wesley*, 1:297 (see chap. 3, n. 16).

activities that enable one to connect with and grow (vertically) in one's relationship with God; (2) "acts of mercy" reference acts/activities that enable one to connect and interact with other fellow human beings and with the created order.

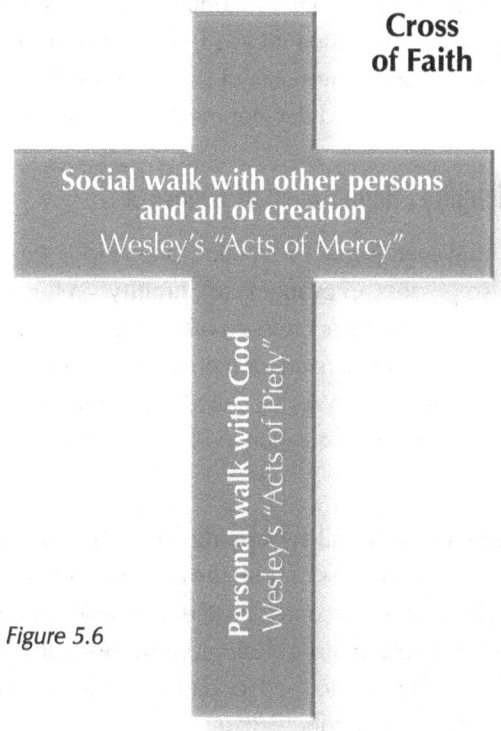

Figure 5.6

"Acts of piety" reference the vertical dimension/beam of faith—acts and/or activities one does that enable one to grow closer to God. These equip and empower one's *personal* walk with God, and include practices such as prayer, Bible reading, fellowship with other Christians, partaking of the sacraments, and others. "Acts of mercy," on the other hand, reference the horizontal dimension/beam of faith—acts and/or activities one does to interact with and make a difference not only in the lives of one's fellow humankind but also with and for the created order. These equip and empower one's *social* walk with others and with all of God's creation, and include practices such as feeding the hungry, clothing the naked, standing up for the rights of the oppressed, taking care of the environment, sharing the gospel, helping others grow in their Christian faith and life, and others. In the same way that a *literal* cross cannot exist without *both* beams, so Wesleyan Christianity affirms that biblical salvation does not exist without the consistent practice of *both* dimensions of faith: one's personal/vertical walk with God; and one's social/horizontal walk with others and creation. Consequently, through our identification of the fruit of the Spirit operating in one's life through both one's acts of piety and one's acts of mercy, one can be assured of growth and development in sanctification.

Evangelical Humility / Repentance of Believers

What's more, however, is that for Wesley, one who is experiencing sanctification will also possess an **evangelical humility**—a humble awareness of the sin still remaining in one's life even *after* being born anew, and thus an awareness of one's continual need for more grace from God. This awareness, in turn, leads one into what Wesley called the **repentance of believers**—a special type of repentance experienced by those who have already been converted.

> **Evangelical humility/repentance of believers**: the humble awareness of both the presence and activity of sin remaining in one's life after conversion (Romans 7:15-25), leading to a desire to turn more and more of one's life over to God for daily cleansing and continual sanctification.

In "The Scripture Way of Salvation," Wesley describes it like this:

> The repentance consequent upon justification is widely different from that which is antecedent to it. This implies no guilt, no sense of condemnation, no consciousness of the wrath of God. . . . It is properly a conviction, wrought by the Holy Ghost, of the "sin" which still "remains" in our heart . . . although it does no longer reign. . . . It is a conviction of our proneness to evil, of a heart bent to backsliding, of the still continuing tendency of the flesh to lust against the spirit. . . . It is a conviction of the tendency of our heart to self-will, atheism, idolatry, and, above

all, to unbelief, . . . a conviction of our helplessness, of our utter inability to think one good thought or to form one good desire, to speak one word aright, or to perform one good action, but through [God's] free, almighty grace.[6]

So then, the act of repentance is not merely confined to pre-conversion but is something we must also do continually *after* our conversion and throughout our sanctification.

This work essentially looks like a spiral in our lives of faith (fig. 5.7). After an experience of prevenient and justifying grace/conversion, we possess an evangelical humility in which we realize that the root of sin is still within us (remember Paul's lament about the remaining sin in his own life in Romans 7:15-25). God's sanctifying grace then gives us the power to continue to repent of the remaining sin still found within us ("repentance of believers"), with that same grace developing more fruits of the Spirit in our lives. Sanctifying grace, then, leads us to more humility, and empowers us

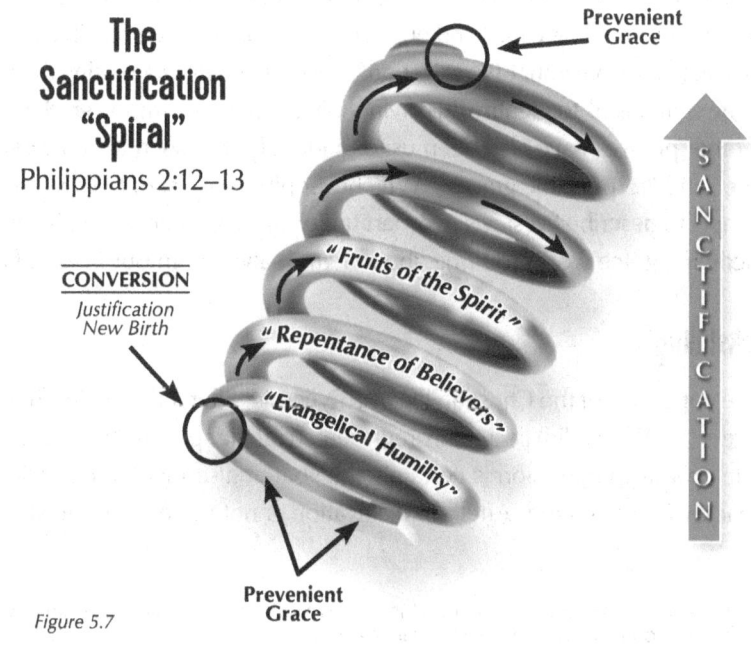

Figure 5.7

---

6 Wesley, "The Scripture Way of Salvation", § 3, ¶¶ 6 and 8, in Outler, ed., *Works*, 2:164–66.

toward even more believer's repentance, resulting in even more consistent spiritual fruit. The process then continually repeats itself for the rest of our lives until we experience Christian perfection. While not a phrase used by Wesley himself, in today's terminology, this cycle is often called "divine synergism," whereby: (1) God's grace works in human lives, and (2) enabled by that grace, we humans respond.[7]

> **Divine Synergism**: the repeating spiritual cycle throughout one's life with God whereby: (1) God's grace initiates and works in human lives; and (2) enabled by that grace, we humans respond. Identified by Paul in Philippians 2:12-13.

Paul actually identifies this cycle in Philippians 2:12-13, where he said we are to "work out [our] own salvation with fear and trembling; for it is God who is at work in you, enabling you both to will and to work for his good pleasure" (NRSV). Here we see both God's initiative ("God who is at work in you, enabling you.") and our human response, made possible by that initiative ("work out your own salvation"). Note that while I am using the term "divine synergism" to identify this divine-initiated, divine-empowered dialectic, other phrases have also been used to identify this, such as "co-operant grace" and "responsible grace."[8] Whichever phrase is used, however, each attempts to describe Wesley's two-part understanding of how sanctification/sanctifying grace works to bring about *actual* salvation in our lives of faith.

Backsliding

If one conceives of the Christian life as a dynamic, interactive divine-human process (as Wesley did) accurately represented by the spiral in figure 5.7, then while upward progression is certainly the goal, it also raises the possibility of backward regression. After all, if salvation is not merely a static state to

---

[7] I use this phrase here to reference what Randy Maddox identifies as "grace-empowered human-cooperation in salvation." Maddox, *Responsible Grace*, 91 (see chap. 3, n. 10). See Also Don Thorsen, *Calvin vs. Wesley: Bringing Belief in Line with Practice* (Nashville: Abingdon Press, 2013), 40–42.

[8] The debate over what this divine-human dialectic should properly be termed is discussed at length in Maddox, *Responsible Grace*, 91–92.

be achieved (as proposed in Reformed theology) but a processive journey (as in Wesleyan theology), then the lack of enough forward momentum may produce retrogression. Wesley called this **backsliding**, and he believed that it occurs when a converted Christian consistently rejects and/or ignores the empowering work of God's sanctifying grace.[9]

> **Backsliding:** the retrogression that occurs in faith when a converted Christian consistently rejects and/or ignores the empowering work of God's sanctifying grace through inattention, carelessness, and/or conscious denial. Continued spiritual regression can cause one to nullify or make ineffective one's *relationship* with God.

In his 1778 sermon "A Call to Backsliders," Wesley wrote:

> It is a common thing for those who are thus sanctified to believe they cannot fall . . . Nevertheless we have seen some of the strongest of them, after a time, moved from their steadfastness. Sometimes suddenly, but oftener by slow degrees, they have yielded to temptation; and pride, or anger, or foolish desires have again sprung up in their hearts. Nay, sometimes they have utterly lost the life of God, and sin hath regained dominion over them![10]

Consequently, since backsliding was, for Wesley, not merely a possibility but a reality, he created and included "penitent" groups in his discipleship system (which we'll talk about in the next chapter) as a way to address "those . . . who have made shipwreck of their faith."[11]

---

9 In "Predestination Calmly Considered," Wesley invokes the following scripture passages as primary support for his view regarding "backsliding": Ezekiel 18:24; John 15:1-6; Romans 11:16-22; Colossians 3:3-4; 1 Timothy 1:18-19; Hebrews 6:4-6; 10:26-29; 10:38; and 2 Peter 2:20. See generally Wesley, "Predestination Calmly Considered," ☐☐ 69–78, in Chilcote and Collins, eds., *The Bicentennial Edition of the Works of John Wesley*, 13:301–13 (see chap. 3, n. 17).

10 Wesley, "A Call to Backsliders" (Sermon 86), § 2, ¶ 3 (5), in Outler, ed., *The Bicentennial Edition of the Works of John Wesley*, 3:225 (see chap. 3, n. 12).

11 John Wesley, "Minutes of the First Annual Conference" (Thursday, June 28, 1744), Wesley's answer to Question #2, in *The Bicentennial Edition of the Works of John Wesley*, vol. 10, *The Methodist Societies: The Minutes of Conference*, ed. Henry D. Rack (Nashville: Abingdon Press, 2011), 137.

Of course, all of this raises the inevitable question: "Did Wesley believe that a converted Christian can ever *lose* his or her salvation?" Like many things in Wesleyan theology, the answer is complex, depending on one's interpretation of that sentence. On the one hand, as his quote above makes clear, Wesley *did* believe that one's continuous rejection of God's grace—whether through inattention, carelessness, or conscious intent—results in spiritual death, just as surely as if that individual had never received it in the first place. In "Predestination Calmly Considered," interpreting Ezekiel 18:24, he wrote:

> "When a righteous man turneth away from his righteousness, and committeth iniquity, and dieth in them" (here is temporal death) "for his iniquity that he hath done, he shall die." Here is death eternal.[12]

Later in that same work, he said that our constant spurning of grace can lead to a "total and final loss of . . . faith," and that people who "fall back into . . . pollutions" may "perish everlastingly."[13] Other Wesley writings contain references that affirm that faith can be "lost," and that believers can "fall" from "election" and become "reprobate."[14] Biblical examples include the stories of King Saul, Ananias and Sapphira, and, of course, Judas Iscariot.[15] Each of these began as a person of faith, but because they each consciously rejected God's work and will in their lives, they ended up separated from

---

12 Wesley, "Predestination Calmly Considered," ¶ 69 in Chilcote and Collins, eds., *The Bicentennial Edition of the Works of John Wesley*, 13:301 (see chap. 3, n. 17).

13 Wesley, 13:303, ¶ 70; and 306, ¶ 73.

14 For examples of this language, see John Wesley, "Farther Thoughts upon Christian Perfection," Questions 30–31 (here "loss" refers specifically to the loss not of justification and new birth, but of *Christian Perfection*), in Chilcote and Collins, 13:110; Wesley's commentary on Matthew 18:34; John 6:70; and 1 Corinthians 9:27 in his "Explanatory Notes on the New Testament" in G. Roger Schoenhals, ed., *John Wesley's Commentary on the Bible: A One-Volume Condensation of His Explanatory Notes* (Grand Rapids: Zondervan, 1990), 418, 461, 516; and Wesley's "Letter to Elizabeth Hardy," December 26, 1761, in Campbell, ed., *The Bicentennial Edition of the Works of John Wesley*, 27:279–280. See also Wesley, "Predestination Calmly Considered," ¶¶ 69–78, in Chilcote and Collins, eds., *Works*, 13:301–13.

15 King Saul's rise and rejection as king and his death are described in 1 Samuel 9-10, 15, 28, and 31. The story of Ananias and Sapphira's disobedience is found in Acts 5:11. Judas Iscariot's story of betrayal is found in Matthew 26:14-25, 47-50; and 27:3-10; Mark 14:10-11, 43-46; Luke 22:1-6, 47-48; and John 13:21-27 and 18:1-6.

grace by their own actions. Consequently, if by "losing salvation" one means that humans can nullify and reject (i.e., lose) their justification, new birth, and/or Christian perfection (which we will discuss shortly), then Wesley agreed that this can most certainly occur.

At the same time, while this conscious or unconscious rejection of these certainly can result in one losing "faith" and/or "election," does it constitute losing salvation proper? After all, in his writings Wesley does not use the term "lose," "lost" or "loss" in conjunction with the term "salvation" (as is commonly articulated today). Before rejecting this observation as mere semantics, however, recall that for Wesley, the concept of "salvation" references more than justification, new birth, and/or Christian perfection alone. Instead, these are merely individual *components* of biblical "salvation," which includes everything from prevenient to justifying to sanctifying grace. While, for Wesley, it is possible to "lose" justification, new birth, and/or Christian perfection, it is not accurate to state that one can "lose" prevenient grace (which is part of Wesley's larger concept of "salvation"). Granted, it is merely the invitational dimension, but it is an essential one, nevertheless. Instead, for him, God's offer of love (the prevenient dimension of salvation) is always available even after we backslide;[16] then even "backslidden," or "fallen" Christians have the *possibility* of once again receiving God's grace through repentance and reaffirmation of their faith. As noted earlier, this was precisely the reason behind Wesley's creation of Methodist "penitent" groups. And while Wesley would certainly agree that one can reject prevenient grace to the point where it is effectively voided and ineffective in and for one's life, does that mean that its possibility and promise are "lost," in the sense that they can never again be recovered? Remember, too, that for Wesley "salvation" does not consist of a static state to be achieved or possessed, but a network of *relationships* between us, God, others, and the created order. If so, then is it conceivable that one can "lose" something (e.g., a relationship) that one never possessed in the first place? So, if what I've just described is what is meant by one "losing salvation," then attributing this exact phrase to Wesley becomes more problematic.

Perhaps the closest that Wesley came to addressing this subject in the

---

16 Consider, for example, Jesus's parable of the prodigal son, shared in Luke 15:11-24.

terms popularly articulated today is in his responses to Questions 11–14 of a conversation dated August 1, 1745, between himself and several of his fellow Methodist preachers in Bristol, England:

> Q. 11. Is a believer constrained to obey God? A. At first he is. The love of Christ constraineth him. After this, he may obey, or he may not; no constraint being laid upon him. Q. 12. Can faith be lost, but through disobedience? A. It cannot. A believer first inwardly disobeys, inclines to sin with his heart: Then his intercourse with God is cut off; that is, his faith is lost: And after this, he may fall into outward sin, being now weak, and like another man. Q. 13. How can such an one recover faith? A. By "repenting, and doing the first works." Rev. ii.5) Q. 14. Whence is it that so great a majority of those who believe fall more or less into doubt or fear? A. Chiefly from their own ignorance and unfaithfulness: Often from their not watching unto prayer: Perhaps sometimes from some defect, or want of the power of God in the preaching they hear.[17]

Obviously again, one can certainly "lose faith"—meaning that one's active relationship with God is voided and nullified through inattention or rejection. However, I would argue that the contemporary tendency to combine the word "lose" with the word "salvation" may not be the most accurate way to describe this within a Wesleyan framework. The bottom line is that answering the original question about whether or not Wesley believed that a converted Christian can actually "lose salvation" in large part depends on how one interprets his definition of both "loss" and "salvation."

The Goal of the Christian Life: Perfect Love

Earlier in this chapter, I cited Hebrews 6:1, where we find these words of challenge from the apostle Paul: "Therefore let us go on toward perfection . . ." (NRSV). This phrase, of course, begs the question: Can one in this life ever reach the "perfection" spoken of here? Can anyone on earth ever be *totally renewed* in the imago Dei? Thinking of our podium illustration of

---

17 Wesley, "Minutes of Some Late Conversations Between the Rev. Mr. Wesley and Others," Conversation II, August 2, 1745, Questions 11–14 in Jackson, ed., *The Works of John Wesley*, 8:283 (see chap. 1, n. 2).

chapter 3, can one in this life ever be reunited with the podium? Thinking of the bridge illustration of chapter 4, can one here on earth ever reach the other side of the chasm in spiritual completeness?

As strange as it may seem, Wesley would answer these kinds of questions with a firm (yet qualified) "YES!" He felt that there were different names Christians used to describe this: *holiness; entire sanctification; perfect love; full salvation; second rest*. The phrase, however, that he believed was the most scriptural was **Christian perfection,** and for he and his early Methodists, it was a doctrine of primary importance. "This doctrine," he once wrote, "is the grand depositum which God has lodged with the people called Methodists; and for the sake of propagating this chiefly He appeared to have raised us up."[18]

> **Christian perfection:** a state of maturity in the latter part of sanctification whereby a Christian is able to love others as God loves them. For Wesley, this was the goal of the Christian life, with several synonyms being *holiness, entire sanctification, perfect love, full salvation,* and *second rest.* Identified by Jesus in Matthew 5:48 and by Paul in Hebrews 6:1 and 2 Corinthians 13:9.

Given this, it's unfortunate that the very reason why Wesley believed God "raised up" the people called Methodists in the first place is rarely preached or spoken of from today's pulpits, due to how it is (and was in Wesley's time) misunderstood. Yet, much of the misunderstanding is (and was) caused by a misinterpretation of the word "perfect." Our English word is derived from the Latin term *perfectus*, which refers to absolute purity and flawlessness in every way—a finished, complete work; absolute conformity to the will of God. Wesley called this "absolute perfection,"[19] and agreed that it was not possible in this life. However, this definition is not what is meant when the word "perfect" is used in English translations of the Bible. For instance, in Matthew 5:48 when Jesus says, "Be perfect, as your heavenly

---

18 John Wesley, "Letter to Robert Carr Brackenbury" (September 15, 1790) in Telford, ed., *The Letters of the Rev. John Wesley*, 8:238 (see chap. 4, n. 11).

19 He wrote that there is "[no] absolute perfection on earth." John Wesley, "Christian Perfection" (Sermon 40), §1, ¶ 9, in Outler, ed., *The Bicentennial Edition of the Works of John Wesley*, 2:104 (see chap. 3, n. 1).

Father is perfect" (ASV), the term used is not the Latin word *perfectus* but the Greek word *teleios*.[20] *Teleios* refers not to *absolute* perfection, which cannot be improved upon, but to a maturity that still allows for further growth. It is completeness in terms of a *goal* (Greek *telos*)—in this case, the goal of *love*. To try and clear up some of the confusion over this important concept, in 1741 Wesley wrote a sermon titled "Christian Perfection."

Christian Perfection[21]
by John Wesley

"Not as though I had already attained, either were already perfect." Phil. 3:12.

1. There is scarce any expression in Holy Writ which has given more offence than this. The word perfect is what many cannot bear. The very sound of it is an abomination to them. And whosoever preaches perfection (as the phrase is,) that is, asserts that it is attainable in this life, runs great hazard of being accounted by them worse than a heathen man or a publican.

2. And hence some have advised, wholly to lay aside the use of those expressions, "because they have given so great offence." But are they not found in the oracles of God. If so, by what authority can any Messenger of God lay them aside, even though all men should be offended. We have not so learned Christ; neither may we thus give place to the devil. Whatsoever God hath Spoken that will we speak, whether men will hear or whether they will forbear; knowing that then alone can any Minister of Christ be "pure from the blood of all men," when he hath "not shunned to declare unto them all the counsel of God" [Acts 20:26, 27].

3. We may not, therefore, lay these expressions aside, seeing they are the words of God, and not of man. But we may and ought to explain the meaning of them, that those who are sincere of heart may not err to the right hand or to the left, from the mark

---

20 Olive Tree Bible Software. "Enhanced Strong's Dictionary," Strong's Number g5046, Version 7.5.5, Build 1562 (July 2, 2019).

21 Wesley, "Christian Perfection," in Outler, ed., *The Bicentennial Edition of the Works of John Wesley*, 2:97–124.

of the prize of their high calling. And this is the more needful to be done because in the verse already repeated the Apostle speaks of himself as not perfect: "Not," saith he, "as though I were already perfect." And yet immediately after, in the fifteenth verse, he speaks of himself, yea and many others, as perfect. "Let us," saith he, "as many as be perfect, be thus minded" [Phil. 3:15].

4. In order, therefore, to remove the difficulty arising from this seeming contradiction, as well as to give light to them who are pressing forward to the mark, and that those who are lame be not turned out of the way, I shall endeavor to show,

> First, in what sense Christians are not; and,
> Secondly, in what sense they are, perfect.

I.

1. In the first place I shall endeavor to show in what sense Christians are not perfect. And both from experience and Scripture it appears, First, that they are not perfect in knowledge: they are not so perfect in this life as to be free from ignorance. They know, it may be, in common with other men, many things relating to the present world; and they know, with regard to the world to come, the general truths which God hath revealed. They know, likewise, (what the natural man receiveth not, for these things are spiritually discerned,) "what manner of love" it is wherewith "the Father" hath loved them, "that they should be called the sons of God." [1 John 3:1] They know the mighty working of his Spirit in their hearts; [Eph. 3:16] and the wisdom of his providence, directing all their paths [Prov. 3:6], and causing all things to work together for their good [Rom. 8:28]. Yea, they know in every circumstance of life what the Lord requireth of them, and how to keep a conscience void of offence both toward God and toward man [Acts 24:16].

2. But innumerable are the things which they know not. Touching the Almighty himself, they cannot search him out to perfection. "Lo, these are but a part of his ways; but the thunder of his power who can understand?" [Job 26:14] They cannot understand, I will not say, how "there are Three that bear record in heaven, the Father, the Son, and the Holy Spirit, and these three are one;" [1 John 5:7] or how the eternal Son of God "took upon himself the form of a servant;" [Phil. 2:7] — but not any

one attribute, not any one circumstance of the divine nature. [2 Pet. 1:4] Neither is it for them to know the times and seasons [Acts 1:7] when God will work his great works upon the earth; no, not even those which he hath in part revealed by his servants and Prophets since the world began [see Amos 3:7]. Much less do they know when God, having "accomplished the number of his elect, will hasten his kingdom;" when "the heavens shall pass away with a great noise, and the elements shall melt with fervent heat" [2 Pet. 3:10].

3. They know not the reasons even of many of his present dispensations with the sons of men; but are constrained to rest here,—Though "clouds and darkness are round about him, righteousness and judgment are the habitation of his seat." [Ps. 97:2] Yea, often with regard to his dealings with themselves, doth their Lord say unto them, "What I do, thou knowest not now; but thou shalt know hereafter." [John 13:7] And how little do they know of what is ever before them, of even the visible works of his hands!—How "he spreadeth the north over the empty place, and hangeth the earth upon nothing?" [Job 26:7] How he unites all the parts of this vast machine by a secret chain which cannot be broken? So great is the ignorance, so very little the knowledge, of even the best of men!

4. No one, then, is so perfect in this life, as to be free from ignorance. Nor, Secondly, from mistake; which indeed is almost an unavoidable consequence of it; seeing those who "know but in part" [1 Cor. 13:12] are ever liable to err, touching the things which they know not. It is true, the children of God do not mistake as to the things essential to salvation: They do not "put darkness for light, or light for darkness;" [Isa. 5:20] neither "seek death in the error of their life." [Wisdom 1:12] For they are "taught of God," and the way which he teaches them, the way of holiness, is so plain, that "the wayfaring man, though a fool, need not err therein." [Isa. 35:8] But in things unessential to salvation they do err, and that frequently. The best and wisest of men are frequently mistaken even with regard to facts; believing those things not to have been which really were, or those to have been done which were not. Or, suppose they are not mistaken as to the fact itself, they may be with regard to its circumstances; believing them, or many of them, to have been quite different from what in truth,

they were. And hence cannot but arise many farther mistakes. Hence they may believe either past or present actions which were or are evil, to be good; and such as were or are good, to be evil. Hence also they may judge not according to truth with regard to the characters of men; and that, not only by supposing good men to be better, or wicked men to be worse, than they are, but by believing them to have been or to be good men who were or are very wicked; or perhaps those to have been or to be wicked men, who were or are holy and unreprovable.

5. Nay, with regard to the Holy Scriptures themselves, as careful as they are to avoid it, the best of men are liable to mistake, and do mistake day by day; especially with respect to those parts thereof which less immediately relate to practice. Hence even the children of God are not agreed as to the interpretation of many places in holy writ: Nor is their difference of opinion any proof that they are not the children of God on either side; but it is a proof that we are no more to expect any living man to be infallible than to be omniscient.

6. If it be objected to what has been observed under this and the preceding head, that St. John, speaking to his brethren in the faith says, "Ye have an unction from the Holy One, and ye know all things:" (1 John 2:20) The answer is plain: "Ye know all things that are needful for your souls' health." [cf. 3 John 2] That the Apostle never designed to extend this farther, that he could not speak it in an absolute sense, is clear, First from hence;—that otherwise he would describe the disciple as "above his Master;" seeing Christ himself, as man, knew not all things: "Of that hour," saith he, "knoweth no man; no, not the Son, but the Father only." [Mark 13:32] It is clear, Secondly, from the Apostle's own words that follow: "These things have I written unto you concerning them that deceive you;" [1 John 2:26; cf. 1 John 3:7] as well as from his frequently repeated caution, "Let no man deceive you;" [1 John 3:7; see Mark 13:5; Eph. 5:6; 2 Thess. 2:3] which had been altogether needless, had not those very persons who had that unction from the Holy One [1 John 2:20] been liable, not to ignorance only, but to mistake also.

7. Even Christians, therefore, are not so perfect as to be free either from ignorance or error: We may, Thirdly, add, nor from infirmities.—Only let us take care to understand this word aright:

Only let us not give that soft title to known sins, as the manner of some is. So, one man tells us, "Every man has his infirmity, and mine is drunkenness;" Another has the infirmity of uncleanness; another of taking God's holy name in vain; and yet another has the infirmity of calling his brother, "Thou fool," [Matt. 5:22] or returning "railing for railing." [1 Pet. 3:9] It is plain that all you who thus speak, if ye repent not, shall, with your infirmities, go quick into hell! But I mean hereby, not only those which are properly termed bodily infirmities, but all those inward or outward imperfections which are not of a moral nature. Such are the weakness or slowness of understanding, dullness or confusedness of apprehension, incoherency of thought, irregular quickness or heaviness of imagination. Such (to mention no more of this kind) is the want of a ready or of a retentive memory. Such in another kind, are those which are commonly, in some measure, consequent upon these; namely, slowness of speech, impropriety of language, ungracefulness of pronunciation; to which one might add a thousand nameless defects, either in conversation or behaviour. These are the infirmities which are found in the best of men, in a larger or smaller proportion. And from these none can hope to be perfectly freed till the spirit returns to God that gave it. [Eccles. 12:7]

8. Nor can we expect, till then, to be wholly free from temptation. Such perfection belongeth not to this life. It is true, there are those who, being given up to work all uncleanness with greediness [Eph. 4:19], scarce perceive the temptations which they resist not, and so seem to be without temptation. There are also many whom the wise enemy of souls, seeing to be fast asleep in the dead form of godliness, will not tempt to gross sin, lest they should awake before they drop into everlasting burnings. I know there are also children of God who, being now justified freely [Rom. 5:1], having found redemption in the blood of Christ [Eph. 1:7], for the present feel no temptation. God hath said to their enemies, "Touch not mine anointed, and do my children no harm." [See 1 Chron. 16:22.] And for this season, it may be for weeks or months, he causeth them to "ride on high places;" [Deut. 32:13] he beareth them as on eagles' wings, [Exod. 19:4] above all the fiery darts of the wicked one [Eph. 6:16]. But this state will not last always; as we may learn from that single

consideration,—that the Son of God himself, in the days of his flesh, was tempted even to the end of his life [Heb. 2:18; 4:15; 6:7]. Therefore, so let his servant expect to be; for "it is enough that he be as his Master." [Luke 6:40]

9. Christian perfection, therefore, does not imply (as some men seem to have imagined) an exemption either from ignorance or mistake, or infirmities or temptations. Indeed, it is only another term for holiness. They are two names for the same thing. Thus every one that is perfect is holy, and every one that is holy is, in the Scripture sense, perfect. Yet we may, lastly, observe, that neither in this respect is there any absolute perfection on earth. There is no perfection of degrees, as it is termed; none which does not admit of a continual increase. So that how much soever any man hath attained, or in how high a degree soever he is perfect, he hath still need to "grow in grace," [2 Pet. 3:18] and daily to advance in the knowledge and love of God his Saviour [see Phil. 1:9].

II.

1. In what sense, then, are Christians perfect? This is what I shall endeavor, in the Second place, to show. But it should be premised, that there are several stages in Christian life, as in natural; some of the children of God being but new-born babes; others having attained to more maturity. And accordingly St. John, in his first Epistle, (1 John 2:12, &c.,) applies himself severally to those he terms little children, those he styles young men, and those whom he entitles fathers. "I write unto you, little children," saith the Apostle, "because your sins are forgiven you:" Because thus far you have attained,—being "justified freely," you "have peace with God, through Jesus Christ." [Rom. 5:1] "I write unto you, young men, because ye have overcome the wicked one;" or (as he afterwards addeth,) "because ye are strong, and the word of God abideth in you" [1 John 2:13, 14]. Ye have quenched the fiery darts of the wicked one, [Eph. 6:16] the doubts and fears wherewith he disturbed your first peace; and the witness of God, that your sins are forgiven, now abideth in your heart. "I write unto you, fathers, because ye have known him that is from the beginning" [1 John 2:13] Ye have known both the Father and the Son and the Spirit of Christ, in your inmost soul. Ye are "perfect men, being grown up to the measure of the stature of the fullness of Christ." [Eph. 4:13]

2. It is of these chiefly I speak in the latter part of this discourse: For these only are properly Christians. But even babes in Christ are in such a sense perfect, or born of God, (an expression taken also in divers senses,) as, First, not to commit sin. If any doubt of this privilege of the sons of God, the question is not to be decided by abstract reasonings, which may be drawn out into an endless length, and leave the point just as it was before. Neither is it to be determined by the experience of this or that particular person. Many may suppose they do not commit sin, when they do; but this proves nothing either way. To the law and to the testimony we appeal. "Let God be true, and every man a liar." [Rom. 3:4]. By his Word will we abide, and that alone. Hereby we ought to be judged.

3. Now the Word of God plainly declares, that even those who are justified, who are born again in the lowest sense, "do not continue in sin;" that they cannot "live any longer therein;" (Rom. 6:1, 2;) that they are "planted together in the likeness of the death" of Christ; (Rom. 6:5;) that their "old man is crucified with him," the body of sin being destroyed, so that henceforth they do not serve sin; that being dead with Christ, they are free from sin; (Rom. 6:6, 7;) that they are "dead unto sin, and alive unto God;" (Rom. 6:11;) that "sin hath no more dominion over them," who are "not under the law, but under grace;" but that these, "being free from sin, are become the servants of righteousness." (Rom. 6:14, 18)

4. The very least which can be implied in these words, is, that the persons spoken of therein, namely, all real Christians, or believers in Christ, are made free from outward sin. And the same freedom, which St. Paul here expresses in such variety of phrases, St. Peter expresses in that one: (1 Pet. 4:1, 2) "He that hath suffered in the flesh hath ceased from sin,—that he no longer should live to the desires of men, but to the will of God." For this ceasing from sin, if it be interpreted in the lowest sense, as regarding only the outward behaviour, must denote the ceasing from the outward act, from any outward transgression of the law.

5. But most express are the well-known words of St. John, in the third chapter of his First Epistle, verse 8, &c.: "He that committeth sin is of the devil; for the devil sinneth from the beginning. For this purpose the Son of God was manifested, that he might destroy the works of the devil. Whosoever is born of God doth

not commit sin; for his seed remaineth in him: And he cannot sin because he is born of God." [1 John 3:8, 9] And those in the fifth: (1 John 5:18) "We know that whosoever is born of God sinneth not; but he that is begotten of God keepeth himself, and that wicked one toucheth him not."

6. Indeed it is said this means only, He sinneth not wilfully; or he doth not commit sin habitually; or, not as other men do; or, not as he did before. But by whom is this said? By St. John? No. There is no such word in the text; nor in the whole chapter; nor in all his Epistle; nor in any part of his writings whatsoever. Why then, the best way to answer a bold assertion is simply to deny it. And if any man can prove it from the Word of God, let him bring forth his strong reasons.

7. And a sort of reason there is, which has been frequently brought to support these strange assertions, drawn from the examples recorded in the Word of God: "What!" say they, "did not Abraham himself commit sin,—prevaricating, and denying his wife? Did not Moses commit sin, when he provoked God at the waters of strife? Nay, to produce one for all, did not even David, 'the man after God's own heart,' commit sin, in the matter of Uriah the Hittite; even murder and adultery?" It is most sure he did. All this is true. But what is it you would infer from hence? It may be granted, First, that David, in the general course of his life, was one of the holiest men among the Jews; and, Secondly, that the holiest men among the Jews did sometimes commit sin. But if you would hence infer, that all Christians do and must commit sin as long as they live; this consequence we utterly deny: It will never follow from those premises.

8. Those who argue thus, seem never to have considered that declaration of our Lord: (Matt. 11:11) "Verily I say unto you, Among them that are born of women there hath not risen a greater than John the Baptist: Notwithstanding he that is least in the kingdom of heaven is greater than he." I fear, indeed, there are some who have imagined "the kingdom of heaven," here, to mean the kingdom of glory; as if the Son of God had just discovered to us, that the least glorified saint in heaven is greater than any man upon earth! To mention this is sufficiently to refute it. There can, therefore, no doubt be made, but "the kingdom of heaven," here, (as in the following verse, where it is said to be taken by force [Matt. 11:12])

CHAPTER 5

or, "the kingdom of God," as St. Luke expresses it,—is that kingdom of God on earth whereunto all true believers in Christ, all real Christians, belong. In these words, then, our Lord declares two things: First, that before his coming in the flesh, among all the children of men there had not been one greater than John the Baptist; whence it evidently follows, that neither Abraham, David, nor any Jew was greater than John. Our Lord, Secondly, declares that he which is least in the kingdom of God (in that kingdom which he came to set up on earth, and which the violent now began to take by force) is greater than he:—Not a greater Prophet as some have interpreted the word; for this is palpably false in fact; but greater in the grace of God, and the knowledge of our Lord Jesus Christ. Therefore, we cannot measure the privileges of real Christians by those formerly given to the Jews. Their "ministration," (or dispensation,) we allow "was glorious;" but ours "exceeds in glory." [2 Cor. 3:7-9] So that whosoever would bring down the Christian dispensation to the Jewish standard, whosoever gleans up the examples of weakness, recorded in the Law and the Prophets, and thence infers that they who have "put on Christ" [Gal. 3:27] are endued with no greater strength, doth greatly err, neither "knowing the Scriptures, nor the power of God." [Matt. 22:29]

9. "But are there not assertions in Scripture which prove the same thing, if it cannot be inferred from those examples? Does not the Scripture say expressly, 'Even a just man sinneth seven times a day?'" I answer, No. The Scripture says no such thing. There is no such text in all the Bible. That which seems to be intended is the sixteenth verse of the twenty-fourth chapter of the Proverbs the words of which are these: "A just man falleth seven times, and riseth up again." [Prov. 24:16] But this is quite another thing. For, First, the words "a day" are not in the text. So that if a just man falls seven times in his life, it is as much as is affirmed here. Secondly, here is no mention of falling into sin at all; what is here mentioned is falling into temporal affliction. This plainly appears from the verse before, the words of which are these: "Lay not wait, O wicked man, against the dwelling of the righteous; spoil not his resting place." [Prov. 24:15] It follows, "For a just man falleth seven times, and riseth up again; but the wicked shall fall into mischief." As if he had said, "God will

deliver him out of his trouble; but when thou fallest, there shall be none to deliver thee."

10. "But, however, in other places," continue the objectors, "Solomon does assert plainly, 'There is no man that sinneth not;' (1 Kings 8:46; 2 Chron. 6:36;) yea, 'There is not a just man upon earth that doeth good, and sinneth not.' (Eccles. 7:20.)" I answer, Without doubt, thus it was in the days of Solomon. Yea, thus it was from Adam to Moses, from Moses to Solomon, and from Solomon to Christ. There was then no man that sinned not. Even from the day that sin entered into the world, there was not a just man upon earth that did good and sinned not, until the Son of God was manifested to take away our sins. It is unquestionably true, that "the heir, as long as he is a child, differeth nothing from a servant." [Gal. 4:1] And that even so they (all the holy men of old, who were under the Jewish dispensation) were, during that infant state of the Church, "in bondage under the elements of the world." [Gal. 4:3] "But when the fulness of the time was come, God sent forth his Son, made under the law, to redeem them that were under the law, that they might receive the adoption of sons;" [Gal. 4:4]—that they might receive that "grace which is now made manifest by the appearing of our Saviour, Jesus Christ, who hath abolished death, and brought life and immortality to light through the gospel." [2 Tim. 1:10] Now, therefore, they "are no more servants, but sons." [See Gal. 4:7] So that, whatsoever was the case of those under the law, we may safely affirm with St. John, that, since the gospel was given, "he that is born of God sinneth not." [1 John 5:18]

11. It is of great importance to observe, and that more carefully than is commonly done, the wide difference there is between the Jewish and the Christian dispensation; and that ground of it which the same Apostle assigns in the seventh chapter of his Gospel. (John 7:38, &c) After he had there related, those words of our blessed Lord, "He that believeth on me, as the Scripture hath said, out of his belly shall flow rivers of living water," he immediately subjoins, "This spake he of the Spirit," *ou emellon lambanein oi pisteuontes eis auton,* — which they who should believe on him were afterwards to receive. For the Holy Ghost was not yet given, because that Jesus was not yet glorified." [John 7:39] Now, the Apostle cannot mean here, (as some have

taught,) that the miracle-working power of the Holy Ghost was not yet given. For this was given; our Lord had given it to all the Apostles, when he first sent them forth to preach the gospel. He then gave them power over unclean spirits to cast them out; power to heal the sick; yea, to raise the dead. [Mark 10:8] But the Holy Ghost was not yet given in his sanctifying graces, as he was after Jesus was glorified. It was then when "he ascended up on high, and led captivity captive," that he "received" those "gifts for men, yea, even for the rebellious, that the Lord God might dwell among them." [Ps. 68:18; cf. Eph. 4:8] And when the day of Pentecost was fully come, [Acts 2:1] then first it was, that they who "waited for the promise of the Father" [Acts 1:4] were made more than conquerors [Rom. 8:37] over sin by the Holy Ghost given unto them.

12. That this great salvation from sin was not given till Jesus was glorified, St. Peter also plainly testifies; where, speaking of his brethren in the flesh, as now "receiving the end of their faith, the salvation of their souls," he adds, (1 Peter 1:9, 10, &c.,) "Of which salvation the Prophets have inquired and searched diligently, who prophesied of the grace" that is, the gracious dispensation, "that should come unto you: Searching what, or what manner of time the Spirit of Christ which was in them did signify, when it testified beforehand the sufferings of Christ. and the glory," the glorious salvation, "that should follow. Unto whom it was revealed, that not unto themselves, but unto us they did minister the things which are now reported unto you by them that have preached the gospel unto you with the Holy Ghost sent down from heaven;" [1 Pet. 1:12] viz., at the day of Pentecost, and so unto all generations, into the hearts of all true believers. On this ground, even "the grace which was brought unto them by the revelation of Jesus Christ," [1 Pet. 1:13] the Apostle might well build that strong exhortation, "Wherefore girding up the loins of your mind,—as he which hath called you is holy, so be ye holy in all manner of conversation." [1 Pet. 1:13]

13. Those who have duly considered these things must allow, that the privileges of Christians are in no wise to be measured by what the Old Testament records concerning those who were under the Jewish dispensation; seeing the fullness of time is now come; the Holy Ghost is now given; the great salvation of God is

brought unto men, by the revelation of Jesus Christ. The kingdom of heaven is now set up on earth; concerning which the Spirit of God declared of old, (so far is David from being the pattern or standard of Christian perfection,) "He that is feeble among them at that day, shall be as David; and the house of David shall be as God, as the angel of the Lord before them." (Zech. 12:8.)

14. If, therefore, you would prove that the Apostle's words, "He that is born of God sinneth not," [1 John 5:18] are not to be understood according to their plain, natural, obvious meaning, it is from the New Testament you are to bring your proofs, else you will fight as one that beateth the air. [1 Cor. 9:26] And the first of these which is usually brought is taken from the examples recorded in the New Testament. "The Apostles themselves," it is said, "committed sin; nay, the greatest of them, Peter and Paul: St. Paul, by his sharp contention with Barnabas; [Acts 15:39] and St. Peter, by his dissimulation at Antioch." [Gal. 2:11] Well: Suppose both Peter and Paul did then commit sin; what is it you would infer from hence? That all the other Apostles committed sin sometimes? There is no shadow of proof in this. Or would you thence infer, that all the other Christians of the apostolic age committed sin? Worse and worse: This is such an inference as, one would imagine, a man in his senses could never have thought of. Or will you argue thus: "If two of the Apostles did once commit sin, then all other Christians, in all ages, do and will commit sin as long as they live?" Alas, my brother! a child of common understanding would be ashamed of such reasoning as this. Least of all can you with any colour of argument infer, that any man must commit sin at all. No: God forbid we should thus speak! No necessity of sinning was laid upon them. The grace of God was surely sufficient for them. And it is sufficient for us at this day. With the temptation which fell on them, there was a way to escape; as there is to every soul of man in every temptation. So that whosoever is tempted to any sin, need not yield; for no man is tempted above that he is able to bear. [1 Cor. 10:13]

15. "But St. Paul besought the Lord thrice, and yet he could not escape from his temptation." Let us consider his own words literally translated: "There was given to me a thorn to the flesh, an angel" (or messenger) "of Satan, to buffet me. Touching this, I besought the Lord thrice, that it" (or he) "might depart from

me. And he said unto me, My grace is sufficient for thee: For my strength is made perfect in weakness. Most gladly, therefore, will I rather glory in" these "my weaknesses, that the strength of Christ may rest upon me. Therefore I take pleasure in weaknesses;—for when I am weak, then am I strong." [2 Cor. 12:7-10]

16. As this scripture is one of the strong-holds of the patrons of sin, it may be proper to weigh it thoroughly. Let it be observed then, First, it does by no means appear that this thorn, whatsoever it was, occasioned St. Paul to commit sin; much less laid him under any necessity of doing so. Therefore, from hence it can never be proved that any Christian must commit sin. Secondly, the ancient Fathers inform us, it was bodily pain: "a violent headache, saith Tertullian; (De Pudic.) to which both Chrysostom and St. Jerome agree. St. Cyprian [De Mortalitate] expresses it, a little more generally, in those terms: "Many and grievous torments of the flesh and of the body." [*Carnis et corporis multa ac gravia tormenta.*] Thirdly, to this exactly agree the Apostle's own words, "A thorn to the flesh to smite, beat, or buffet me." "My strength is made perfect in weakness:"—Which same word occurs no less than four times in these two verses only. But, Fourthly, whatsoever it was, it could not be either inward or outward sin. It could no more be inward stirrings, than outward expressions, of pride, anger, or lust. This is manifest, beyond all possible exception from the words that immediately follow: "Most gladly will I glory in" these "my weaknesses, that the strength of Christ may rest upon me." [2 Cor. 12:9] What! Did he glory in pride, in anger, in lust? Was it through these weaknesses, that the strength of Christ rested upon him? He goes on: "Therefore I take pleasure in weaknesses; for when I am weak, then am I strong;" [2 Cor. 12:10] that is, when I am weak in body, then am I strong in spirit. But will any man dare to say, "When I am weak by pride or lust, then am I strong in spirit?" I call you all to record this day, who find the strength of Christ resting upon you, can you glory in anger, or pride, or lust? Can you take pleasure in these infirmities? Do these weaknesses make you strong? Would you not leap into hell, were it possible, to escape them? Even by yourselves, then, judge, whether the Apostle could glory and take pleasure in them! Let it be, Lastly, observed, that this thorn was given to St. Paul above fourteen

years before he wrote this Epistle; [2 Cor. 12:2] which itself was wrote several years before he finished his course. [See Acts 20:24; 2 Tim. 4:7.] So that he had after this, a long course to run, many battles to fight, many victories to gain, and great increase to receive in all the gifts of God, and the knowledge of Jesus Christ. Therefore from any spiritual weakness (if such it had been) which he at that time felt, we could by no means infer that he was never made strong; that Paul the aged, the father in Christ, still laboured under the same weaknesses; that he was in no higher state till the day of his death. From all which it appears that this instance of St. Paul is quite foreign to the question, and does in no wise clash with the assertion of St. John, "He that is born of God sinneth not." [1 John 5:18]

17. "But does not St. James directly contradict this? His words are, 'In many things we offend all,' (Jas. 3:2:) And is not offending the same as committing sin?" In this place, I allow it is: I allow the persons here spoken of did commit sin; yea, that they all committed many sins. But who are the persons here spoken of? Why, those many masters or teachers whom God had not sent; (probably the same vain men who taught that faith without works [Jas. 2:20], which is so sharply reproved in the preceding chapter;) not the Apostle himself, nor any real Christian. That in the word we (used by a figure of speech common in all other, as well as the inspired, writings) the Apostle could not possibly include himself or any other true believer, appears evidently, First, from the same word in the ninth verse: — "Therewith," saith he, "bless we God and therewith curse we men. Out of the same mouth proceedeth blessing and cursing." [Jas. 3:9] True; but not out of the mouth of the Apostle, nor of anyone who is in Christ a new creature. [2 Cor. 5:17] Secondly, from the verse immediately preceding the text, and manifestly connected with it: "My brethren, be not many masters," (or teachers,) "knowing that we shall receive the greater condemnation." "For in many things we offend all." [Jas. 3:1] We! Who Not the Apostles, not true believers; but they who know they should receive the greater condemnation, because of those many offences. But this could not be spoke of the Apostle himself, or of any who trod in his steps, seeing "there is no condemnation to them who walk not after the flesh, but after the Spirit." [Rom. 8:2] Nay, Thirdly, the

CHAPTER 5

very verse itself proves, that "we offend all," cannot be spoken either of all men, or of all Christians: For in it there immediately follows the mention of a man who offends not, as the we first mentioned did; from whom, therefore, he is professedly contradistinguished, and pronounced a perfect man.

18. So clearly does St. James explain himself, and fix the meaning of his own words. Yet, lest any one should still remain in doubt, St. John, writing many years after St. James, puts the matter entirely out of dispute, by the express declarations above recited. But here a fresh difficulty may arise: How shall we reconcile St. John with himself? In one place he declares, "Whosoever is born of God doth not commit sin;" [1 John 3:9] and again,—"We know that he which is born of God sinneth not." [1 John 5:18] And yet in another he saith, "If we say that we have no sin, we deceive ourselves, and the truth is not in us;" [1 John 1:8] and again,—"If we say that we have not sinned, we make him a liar, and his word is not in us." [1 John 1:10]

19. As great a difficulty as this may at first appear, it vanishes away, if we observe, First, that the tenth verse fixes the sense of the eighth: "If we say we have no sin," in the former, being explained by, "If we say we have not sinned," in the latter verse. [1 John 1:10, 8] Secondly, that the point under present consideration is not whether we have or have not sinned heretofore; and neither of these verses asserts that we do sin, or commit sin now. Thirdly, that the ninth verse explains both the eighth and tenth. "If we confess our sins, he is faithful and just to forgive us our sins, and to cleanse us from all unrighteousness:" As if he had said, "I have before affirmed, 'The blood of Jesus Christ cleanseth us from all sin; but let no man say, I need it not; I have no sin to be cleansed from. If we say that we have no sin, that we have not sinned, we deceive ourselves, and make God a liar: But if we confess our sins, he is faithful and just,' not only 'to forgive our sins,' but also 'to cleanse us from all unrighteousness:' [1 John 1:8-10] that we may 'go and sin no more.'" [John 8:11]

20. St. John, therefore, is well consistent with himself, as well as with the other holy writers; as will yet more evidently appear if we place all his assertions touching this matter in one view: He declares, First, the blood of Jesus Christ cleanseth us from all sin. Secondly, no man can say, I have not sinned, I have no sin to be

cleansed from. Thirdly, but God is ready both to forgive our past sins and to save us from them for the time to come. [1 John 1:7-10] Fourthly, "These things I write unto you," saith the Apostle, "that ye may not sin. But if any man" should "sin," or have sinned, (as the word might be rendered,) he need not continue in sin; seeing "we have an Advocate with the Father, Jesus Christ the righteous." [1 John 2:1-2] Thus far all is clear. But lest any doubt should remain in a point of so vast importance, the Apostle resumes this subject in the third chapter, and largely explains his own meaning. "Little children," saith he, "let no man deceive you:" (As though I had given any encouragement to those that continue in sin:) "He that doeth righteousness is righteous, even as He is righteous. He that committeth sin is of the devil; for the devil sinneth from the beginning. For this purpose the Son of God was manifested, that he might destroy the works of the devil. Whosoever is born of God doth not commit sin: For his seed remaineth in him; and he cannot sin, because he is born of God. In this the children of God are manifest, and the children of the devil." (1 John 3:7-10) Here the point, which till then might possibly have admitted of some doubt in weak minds, is purposely settled by the last of the inspired writers, and decided in the clearest manner. In conformity, therefore, both to the doctrine of St. John, and to the whole tenor of the New Testament, we fix this conclusion—A Christian is so far perfect, as not to commit sin.

21. This is the glorious privilege of every Christian; yea, though he be but a babe in Christ. But it is only of those who are strong in the Lord, and "have overcome the wicked one," or rather of those who "have known him that is from the beginning," [1 John 2:13, 14] that it can be affirmed they are in such a sense perfect, as, Secondly, to be freed from evil thoughts and evil tempers. First, from evil or sinful thoughts. But here let it be observed, that thoughts concerning evil are not always evil thoughts; that a thought concerning sin, and a sinful thought, are widely different. A man, for instance, may think of a murder which another has committed; and yet this is no evil or sinful thought. So our blessed Lord himself doubtless thought of, or understood the thing spoken by the devil, when he said, "All these things will I give thee, if thou wilt fall down and worship me." [Matt. 4:9] Yet had he no evil or sinful thought; nor indeed

was capable of having any. And even hence it follows, that neither have real Christians: for "every one that is perfect is as his Master." (Luke 6:40) Therefore, if He was free from evil or sinful thoughts, so are they likewise.

22. And, indeed, whence should evil thoughts proceed, in the servant who is as his Master "Out of the heart of man" (if at all) "proceed evil thoughts." (Mark 7:21) If, therefore, his heart be no longer evil, then evil thoughts can no longer proceed out of it. If the tree were corrupt, so would be the fruit: But the tree is good; The fruit, therefore is good also; (Matt. 22:33) our Lord himself bearing witness, "Every good tree bringeth forth good fruit. A good tree cannot bring forth evil fruit," as "a corrupt tree cannot bring forth good fruit." (Matt 7:17, 18)

23. The same happy privilege of real Christians, St. Paul asserts from his own experience. "The weapons of our warfare," saith he, "are not carnal, but mighty through God to the pulling down of strongholds; casting down imaginations" (or reasonings rather, for so the word *logismous* signifies; all the reasonings of pride and unbelief against the declarations, promises, or gifts of God) "and every high thing that exalteth itself against the knowledge of God, and bringing into captivity every thought to the obedience of Christ." (2 Cor. 10:4, &c.)

24. And as Christians indeed are freed from evil thoughts, so are they, Secondly, from evil tempers. This is evident from the above-mentioned declaration of our Lord himself: "The disciple is not above his Master; but every one that is perfect shall be as his Master." [Luke 6:40] He had been delivering, just before, some of the sublimest doctrines of Christianity, and some of the most grievous to flesh and blood. "I say unto you, love your enemies, do good to them which hate you;—and unto him that smiteth thee on the one cheek, offer also the other." [Luke 6:29] Now these he well knew the world would not receive; and, therefore, immediately adds, "Can the blind lead the blind? Will they not both fall into the ditch?" [Luke 6:39] As if he had said, "Do not confer with flesh and blood touching these things,—with men void of spiritual discernment, the eyes of whose understanding God hath not opened,—lest they and you perish together." In the next verse he removes the two grand objections with which these wise fools meet us at every

turn: "These things are too grievous to be borne," or, "They are too high to be attained," [Matt. 23:4] saying, "'The disciple is not above his Master;' therefore, if I have suffered, be content to tread in my steps. And doubt ye not then, but I will fulfill my word: 'For every one that is perfect shall be as his Master.'" [Luke 6:40] But his Master was free from all sinful tempers. So, therefore, is his disciple, even every real Christian.

25. Every one of these can say, with St. Paul, "I am crucified with Christ: Nevertheless I live; yet not I, but Christ liveth in me:" [Gal 2:20]—Words that manifestly describe a deliverance from inward as well as from outward sin. This is expressed both negatively, I live not; (my evil nature, the body of sin, is destroyed;) and positively, Christ liveth in me; and, therefore, all that is holy, and just, and good. Indeed, both these, Christ liveth in me, and I live not, are inseparably connected; for "what communion hath light with darkness, or Christ with Belial" [2 Cor. 6:15]

26. He, therefore, who liveth in true believers, hath "purified their hearts by faith;" [Acts 15:9] insomuch that every one that hath Christ in him the hope of glory, [Col. 1:27] "purifieth himself, even as he is pure" (1 John 3:3.) He is purified from pride; for Christ was lowly of heart. [Matt. 11:29] He is pure from self-will or desire; for Christ desired only to do the will of his Father, and to finish his work. [John 4:34; 5:30] And he is pure from anger, in the common sense of the word; for Christ was meek and gentle, patient and long-suffering. I say, in the common sense of the word; for all anger is not evil. We read of our Lord himself, (Mark 3:5,) that he once "looked round with anger." But with what kind of anger? The next word shows, *sullupoumenos*, being, at the same time "grieved for the hardness of their hearts." [Mark 3:6] So then he was angry at the sin, and in the same moment grieved for the sinners; angry or displeased at the offence, but sorry for the offenders. With anger, yea, hatred, he looked upon the thing; with grief and love upon the persons. Go, thou that art perfect, and do likewise. Be thus angry, and thou sinnest not; [see Eph. 4:26] feeling a displacency at every offence against God, but only love and tender compassion to the offender.

27. Thus doth Jesus "save his people from their sins:" [Matt. 1:21] And not only from outward sins, but also from the sins of their hearts; from evil thoughts and from evil tempers.—"True,"

say some, "we shall thus be saved from our sins; but not till death; not in this world." But how are we to reconcile this with the express words of St. John? "Herein is our love made perfect, that we may have boldness in the day of judgment. Because as he is, so are we in this world." The Apostle here, beyond all contradiction, speaks of himself and other living Christians, of whom (as though he had foreseen this very evasion, and set himself to overturn it from the foundation) he flatly affirms, that not only at or after death but in this world they are as their Master. (1 John 4:17.)

28. Exactly agreeable to this are his words in the first chapter of this Epistle, (1 John 1:5, &c.,) "God is light, and in him is no darkness at all. If we walk in the light,—we have fellowship one with another, and the blood of Jesus Christ his Son cleanseth us from all sin." And again, "If we confess our sins, he is faithful and just to forgive us our sins, and to cleanse us from all unrighteousness." [1 John 1:9] Now it is evident, the Apostle here also speaks of a deliverance wrought in this world. For he saith not, the blood of Christ will cleanse at the hour of death, or in the day of judgment, but, it "cleanseth," at the time present, "us," living Christians, "from all sin." And it is equally evident, that if any sin remain, we are not cleansed from all sin: If any unrighteousness remain in the soul, it is not cleansed from all unrighteousness. Neither let any sinner against his own soul say, that this relates to justification only, or the cleansing us from the guilt of sin. First, because this is confounding together what the Apostle clearly distinguishes, who mentions first, to forgive us our sins, and then to cleanse us from all unrighteousness. "Secondly, because this is asserting justification by works, in the strongest sense possible; it is making all inward as well as outward holiness necessarily previous to justification. For if the cleansing here spoken of is no other than the cleansing us from the guilt of sin, then we are not cleansed from guilt; that is, are not justified, unless on condition of "walking in the light, as he is in the light." [1 John 1:7] It remains, then, that Christians are saved in this world from all sin, from all unrighteousness; that they are now in such a sense perfect, as not to commit sin, and to be freed from evil thoughts and evil tempers."

29. Thus hath the Lord fulfilled the things he spake by his holy prophets, which have been since the world began;—by

Moses in particular, saying, (Deut. 30:6) I "will circumcise thine heart, and the heart of thy seed, to love the Lord thy God with all thy heart, and with all thy soul;" by David, crying out, "Create in me a clean heart, and renew a right spirit within me;" [Ps. 51:10]—and most remarkably by Ezekiel, in those words: "Then will I sprinkle clean water upon you, and ye shall be clean; From all your filthiness, and from all your idols, will I cleanse you. A new heart also will I give you, and a new spirit will I put within you;—and cause you to walk in my statutes, and ye shall keep my judgments, and do them.—Ye shall be my people, and I will be your God. I will also save you from all your uncleannesses.—Thus saith the Lord your God, In the day that I shall have cleansed you from all your iniquities,—the Heathen shall know that I the Lord build the ruined places;—I the Lord have spoken it, and I will do it." (Ezek. 36:25, &c.)

30. "Having therefore these promises, dearly beloved," both in the Law and in the Prophets, and having the prophetic word confirmed unto us in the Gospel, by our blessed Lord and his Apostles; "let us cleanse ourselves from all filthiness of flesh and spirit, perfecting holiness in the fear of God." [2 Cor. 7:1] "Let us fear, lest" so many "promises being made us of entering into his rest," which he that hath entered into, has ceased from his own works, "any of us should come short of it." [Heb. 4:1] "This one thing let us do, forgetting those things which are behind, and reaching forth unto those things which are before, let us press toward the mark, for the prize of the high calling of God in Christ Jesus;" [Phil. 3:13, 14] crying unto him day and night, till we also are "delivered from the bondage of corruption, into the glorious liberty of the sons of God!" [Rom. 8:21]

* * *

{**NOTE:** the lyrics to Charles Wesley's hymn "The Promise of Sanctification" appeared here in Wesley's original text. In the interest of space, they have been omitted in this printing.}

One of the greatest assets of this sermon is Wesley's explanations both as to what Christian perfection is NOT and what it IS in order to help readers better understand its fundamental nature and character. Without repeating

CHAPTER 5

these verbatim, allow me to summarize the main arguments in more contemporary language.

First, for Wesley, Christian perfection is ***not* spiritual infallibility.** Paragraphs 1–6 of section 1 indicate that even "perfected" Christians are subject to making mistakes of knowledge, wisdom, judgment, application, and performance. Wesley often refers to these kinds of things as "involuntary transgressions," and distinguishes them from intentional "sin"—both can cause hurt and harm to others; but unlike the former, the latter requires some degree of intentionality. Consequently, Christian perfection does not create any kind of "superior Christianity" that makes us "better than" other Christians or eliminates our own need for God's forgiveness and grace. To the contrary: a "Perfected" Christian will be filled with such humility that they are extremely cautious about any self-testimony regarding it.

Second, Christian perfection is ***not* immunity from the brokenness of life on earth.** Paragraphs 7-8 of Section 1 remind readers that all Christians, even "perfected" ones, are subject to the "infirmities" of our fallen world, including the laws of nature, what we today identify as germs and disease, and temptation. In fact, 1 Peter 5:8 indicates that the closer we are to God, the more strenuously the forces of evil fight to bring us down. So, far from being *free* from temptation, "perfected" Christians may, in fact, be more of a target!

Finally, for Wesley, Christian perfection is also ***not* a static, unchanging state.** Unlike traditional definitions of a "state," one who has achieved "perfection in love" can still grow and improve in their practice of love. In paragraph 9 of section 1, Wesley writes that

> there is no perfection of degrees, as it is termed; none which does not admit of a continual increase. So that how much soever any man hath attained, or in how high a degree soever he is perfect, he hath still need to "grow in grace," and daily to advance in the knowledge and love of God his Saviour.[22]

In other words, no one can ever say that he or she has "arrived," as even this "state" or mode of being allows for growth in perfection.

How is this possible, you might ask? How can "perfection" be improved upon? Let me share two examples to illustrate how this apparent

---

22 Wesley, § 1, ¶ 9, in Outler, 2:104.

inconsistency in logic is possible. First, when my wife, Trish, and I were married, I loved her 100 percent, with all my heart and soul—in other words, with a "perfect" love. Thirty years later (as of the writing of this book), I still love her 100 percent, with all my heart and soul—again, with a "perfect" love. However, today's 100 percent love is stronger, more mature, and more complete than the 100 percent love of thirty years ago—my "perfect" love has (I like to think) grown and improved over the years. While it may not make logical sense to say that 100 percent can be improved upon, it nevertheless is a reality of life that *this* kind of perfection *can* be improved upon. This is why I believe one of the best ways to describe the work of biblical *teleios* is to talk about it in terms of *maturity*—in fact, for a clearer meaning of this concept, try substituting the word "mature" or "maturity" in biblical texts where the English word "perfect" or one of its conjugations is found.[23]

A second example is to think once more of Wesley's "House of Religion" analogy (fig. 5.3). Upon achieving Christian perfection, one might assume that all the rooms in one's spiritual house are filled with God's love. For that moment, you would be correct. However, the "house" of our spiritual lives is never static; it is constantly changing: rooms occasionally disappear (for example, when we lose a loved one, change jobs, or move to a new home); and new rooms are occasionally added (for example, upon the birth of a child, getting married, making a new friend, or joining a new church). If one merely rests one's laurels on the completeness of one's house of faith when one first reached Christian perfection, then over time that completeness ceases to be truly complete, because the room configuration of one's house of salvation is now different. The result is a spiritual "state" that is constantly changing, requiring daily surrender to God in order to continue to be "perfected in love."

In addition to these three ways of talking about what Christian perfection is not, let me also briefly summarize from Wesley's sermon four things that it *is*. First, it can be characterized as **freedom from the root of sin**, begun during sanctification. Section 2, paragraphs 2–21, remind us of Wesley's extraordinary claim that a converted Christian *need not* voluntarily sin. But he also reminds us there that the key to this ability is to "abide in Christ" so closely that "whosoever is tempted to any sin, *need not yield*."[24] So, though

---

23 For example: Matthew 5:48; 2 Corinthians 13:9; Hebrews 6:1; 1 John 2:5; 4:12.
24 Wesley, § 2, ¶ 14, in Outler, 2:112 (emphasis added).

one who has been "perfected in love" still experiences temptation, the power to overcome it can be readily called upon because they are walking closely with God daily.

Christian perfection can also be understood as one possessing a **full, wholehearted love for God and neighbor.** Wesley wrote that "perfect love . . . is love excluding sin; love filling the heart, taking up the whole capacity of the soul."[25] In like manner, 1 John 4:18 says "There is no fear in love, but perfect love casts out fear" (NRSV). Consider that there are at least two ways to get air out of a container: (1) vacuum the air out; or (2) simply *fill* the container with something else (such as a water). In the latter method, the insertion of water excludes the air from the space entirely. So it is with God's perfect love in our lives—its presence excludes or "casts out" sin, fear, and any other manifestation of evil, to the point where our first inclination in all situations involves a wholehearted love toward others arising from our love for God.

Third, Christian perfection means that we possess **purity of Godly *intention*.** In Matthew 22:37-38, Jesus commands us to love the Lord our God with all our hearts, with all our souls, and with all our minds. For Wesley, this single-minded love for God is the essence of Christian perfection. "This it is to be a perfect man," he once wrote, "to be 'sanctified throughout;' even 'to have a heart so all-flaming with the love of God,' . . . as continually to offer up every thought, word, and work, as a spiritual sacrifice, acceptable to God through Christ."[26]

In sum, for Wesley, Christian perfection simply means to look at how God is perfect and then to imitate God in that way. Since God is perfect in *love*, then to be "perfect" means that we are **to love others as God loves us**—unconditionally, completely, patiently, without pretense or prejudice. In his "Brief Thoughts on Christian Perfection" (1767), he wrote, "By perfection I mean the humble, gentle, patient love of God, and our neighbour, ruling our tempers, words, and actions."[27]

---

[25] Wesley, "The Scripture Way of Salvation," § 1, ¶ 9, in Outler, ed., *Works* 2:160.

[26] Wesley, "A Plain Account of Christian Perfection," ¶ 15 (6), in Chilcote and Collins, eds., *The Bicentennial Edition of the Works of John Wesley*, 13:155.

[27] John Wesley, "Brief Thoughts on Christian Perfection" (1767), ¶ 1, in Chilcote and Collins, 13:199.

While there is no record to indicate whether or not Wesley ever believed that he himself had achieved Christian perfection, throughout his ministry he did report knowing people—though rare—who he believed *had* achieved it.[28] Still, he felt strongly enough about it that it became one of the primary emphases of early Methodist doctrine, and he also believed that its achievement should be the goal of every Christian.

If this is so, then what are some of the ways that God's grace is manifested to enable us to reach this goal? Specifically, what are some of the tools or vehicles by which God's prevenient, justifying, sanctifying and perfecting grace are conveyed to humans? This will be the topic of our next chapter.

Discussion Questions

1. In what ways have you grown in your faith (i.e., experienced sanctification) since you became a Christian?

2. Identify some of the "acts of piety" and "acts of mercy" that are active in your own spiritual life. How does your use of these help you feel closer to God? Which one(s) might you want to include in the future as ways to grow in your relationship with God?

3. Which fruit of the Spirit are ones that you most need to work on developing in your life of faith?

4. Identify and name two or three ways you realize that you are not yet "complete" as a Christian—things that may need the work of "repentance of believers" in your life.

5. Based on Wesley's definition and understanding of the nature and practice of Christian perfection, do you know people who may have achieved this maturity, even if they never claimed it for themselves? Briefly describe their character and some of the qualities of faith that make you think they have achieved Christian perfection.

---

28 Even still, in Wesley's day, Thomas Maxfield and George Bell led a group of Methodists who claimed a "perfection of angels"—perfection that could not be improved upon—for themselves. Their teachings and practices caused much confusion and division in part of early British Methodism, resulting in Wesley finally banning them from the Methodist movement.

Part Three

The Means of *Grace* and *the Sacraments*

CHAPTER 6

THE MEANS OF GRACE

To this point, we have walked through the three major stages, or "movements," of Wesley's vision of the Christian life: prevenient grace; justifying grace; and sanctifying grace. So far, however, we have only described these conceptually. What do they look like practically? Put another way: how, in what specific forms, do these manifestations of God's grace come to us? What do they look like in everyday life?

To answer that, think about either a relationship that you *wish* to have or one you already have that you wish to *grow* in. I cannot have or grow in that relationship simply by wanting, wishing, or willing it to be. Instead, I have to intentionally find ways to get to know, connect, and interact with a person, whether that be by talking with him or her directly; communicating via email, text, social media, or letter; or—better still—by simply spending time with and being present with that person. In the same way, I cannot expect to experience or grow in a relationship with God merely by thinking about it hard enough, or by simply wanting or willing it to be so. Instead, I have to find ways to intentionally reach out to and connect with God through some type, method, or means of interaction. The point is: *relationships are neither created nor developed by themselves in a vacuum, but instead require a means of conveyance between two people* in order for the relationship to be established and grown.

In terms of our relationship with God as humans, Wesley called these things **means of grace**—specific tools, preveniently established and given to us *by* God, that we can use to reach out and connect and interact *with* God. Listen to his definition: "By 'means of grace' I understand outward signs, words, or actions, ordained of God, and appointed for this end, to be the ordinary channels whereby he might convey to men, preventing, justifying, or sanctifying grace."[1]

> **Means of grace:** Specific outward actions, practices, and experiences by and through which the grace

---

1 John Wesley's "The Means of Grace" (Sermon 16), § 2, ¶ 1, in Outler, ed., *The Bicentennial Edition of the Works of John Wesley*, 1:381 (see chap. 3, n. 16).

> of God can be experienced in everyday life, and through which we can build and grow a relationship with God. These consist of at least two major categories: instituted means, and prudential means.

These "outward signs, words, or actions," then, are both the practical ways that we actually *experience* God and God's grace in everyday life but are also ways by which we can *grow* in that relationship.[2] Consequently, through these, we experience God's prevenient, justifying, and sanctifying grace. In general, Wesley understood there to be at least two broad categories, or types, of means of grace from God.[3]

The Instituted Means of Grace

The first category was most commonly called the **"instituted" means of grace**, because it consisted of means that were initiated or commanded (i.e., "instituted") by Christ himself, either through his words or his *actions*. These were often called by other names: "ordinances of God"; "ordinances of Christ"; or even at times as another way to refer to "acts of piety" (discussed in the previous chapter). Wesley identified at least five of these in the New Testament and believed that each of them was instituted by Christ himself for *all* Christians in *all* times and contexts—there is no Christian anywhere at *any time* in history that did not need to use and practice these five means of grace in their walk with God.[4]

> **Instituted means of grace**: Means of grace that are initiated or commanded by Christ's explicit words or

---

2 Note from Wesley's definition that he did *not* understand there to be three *separate, distinct* graces from God, but merely three forms of *one* grace. Nevertheless, at various stages and points within one's Christian life, that *one* grace can be manifested in various ways—sometimes all three at one time. In other words, just because one is experiencing the sanctifying grace stage of one's Christian faith does not mean that prevenient or justifying grace is inoperative. Instead, they often work concurrently within one's life.

3 In addition to the two major categories that we will discuss here—the instituted and prudential means of grace—a third category (the "general" means of grace) has also been identified as being used by Wesley but will not be discussed here due to space limitations.

4 See generally Wesley, "Minutes of Several Conversations Between the Rev. Mr. Wesley and Others" (1744–1789), Question 48, Answer 1, in Jackson, ed., *The Works of John Wesley*, 8:322–23 (see chap. 1, n. 2).

implicitly through his action and are therefore meant to be used by all Christians in all times and contexts. Also called "ordinances of God/Christ" and acts of piety. The "chief" of these are prayer, "searching the Scriptures," and the Lord's Supper, along with fasting and "Christian conferencing."

Wesley described the first three ("chief") of these in his 1739 sermon "The Means of Grace," along with a general overview of the nature and purpose of the means themselves, and a few cautions about their use and practice.

The Means of Grace[5]
by John Wesley

"Ye are gone away from mine ordinances and have not kept them." Mal. 3:7.

I.

1. But are there any ordinances now, since life and immortality were brought to light by the gospel? Are there, under the Christian dispensation, any means ordained of God, as the usual channels of his grace? This question could never have been proposed in the apostolical church, unless by one who openly avowed himself to be a Heathen; the whole body of Christians being agreed, that Christ had ordained certain outward means, for conveying his grace into the souls of men. Their constant practice set this beyond all dispute; for so long as "all that believed were together, and had all things common," (Acts 2:44) "they continued steadfastly in the teaching of the Apostles, and in the breaking of bread, and in prayers." (Acts 2:42)

2. But in process of time, when "the love of many waxed cold," some began to mistake the means for the end, and to place religion rather in doing those outward works, than in a heart renewed after the image of God. They forgot that "the end of" every "commandment is love, out of a pure heart," with "faith unfeigned;" the loving the Lord their God with all their

---

5 Wesley, "The Means of Grace," in Outler, ed., *The Bicentennial Edition of the Works of John Wesley*, 1:378–97.

heart, and their neighbour as themselves; and the being purified from pride, anger, and evil desire, by a "faith of the operation of God." Others seemed to imagine, that though religion did not principally consist in these outward means, yet there was something in them wherewith God was well pleased: something that would still make them acceptable in his sight, though they were not exact in the weightier matters of the law, in justice, mercy, and the love of God.

3. It is evident, in those who abused them thus, they did not conduce to the end for which they were ordained: Rather, the things which should have been for their health, were to them an occasion of falling. They were so far from receiving any blessing therein, that they only drew down a curse upon their head; so far from growing more heavenly in heart and life, that they were two-fold more the children of hell than before. Others, clearly perceiving that these means did not convey the grace of God to those children of the devil, began, from this particular case, to draw a general conclusion,—that they were not means of conveying the grace of God.

4. Yet the number of those who abused the ordinances of God, was far greater than of those who despised them, till certain men arose, not only of great understanding, (sometimes joined with considerable learning,) but who likewise appeared to be men of love, experimentally acquainted with true, inward religion. Some of these were burning and shining lights, persons famous in their generations, and such as had well deserved of the church of Christ, for standing in the gap against the overflowings of ungodliness.

It cannot be supposed, that these holy and venerable men intended any more, at first, than to show that outward religion is nothing worth, without the religion of the heart; that "God is a Spirit, and they who worship him must worship him in spirit and in truth;" that, therefore, external worship is lost labour, without a heart devoted to God; that the outward ordinances of God then profit much, when they advance inward holiness, but, when they advance it not, are unprofitable and void, are lighter than vanity; yea, that when they are used, as it were in the place of this, they are an utter abomination to the Lord.

THE MEANS OF GRACE

5. Yet is it not strange, if some of these, being strongly convinced of that horrid profanation of the ordinances of God, which had spread itself over the whole church, and well nigh driven true religion out of the world,—in their fervent zeal for the glory of God, and the recovery of souls from that fatal delusion,—spake as if outward religion were absolutely nothing, as if it had no place in the religion of Christ. It is not surprising at all, if they should not always have expressed themselves with sufficient caution; so that unwary hearers might believe they condemned all outward means, as altogether unprofitable, and as not designed of God to be the ordinary channels of conveying his grace into the souls of men.

Nay, it is not impossible, some of these holy men did, at length, themselves fall into this opinion; in particular those who, not by choice, but by the providence of God, were cut off from all these ordinances; perhaps wandering up and down, having no certain abiding-place, or dwelling in dens and caves of the earth. These, experiencing the grace of God in themselves, though they were deprived of all outward means, might infer that the same grace would be given to them who of set purpose abstained from them.

6. And experience shows how easily this notion spreads, and insinuates itself into the minds of men; especially of those who are thoroughly awakened out of the sleep of death, and begin to feel the weight of their sins a burden too heavy to be borne. These are usually impatient of their present state; and, trying every way to escape from it, they are always ready to catch at any new thing, any new proposal of ease or happiness. They have probably tried most outward means, and found no ease in them; it may be, more and more of remorse, and fear, and sorrow, and condemnation. It is easy, therefore, to persuade these, that it is better for them to abstain from all those means. They are already weary of striving (as it seems) in vain, of labouring in the fire; and are therefore glad of any pretence to cast aside that wherein their soul has no pleasure, to give over the painful strife, and sink down into an indolent inactivity.

II.

1. In the following discourse, I propose to examine at large, whether there are any means of grace. By "means of grace" I

understand outward signs, words, or actions, ordained of God, and appointed for this end, to be the ordinary channels whereby he might convey to men, preventing, justifying, or sanctifying grace.

I use this expression, means of grace, because I know none better; and because it has been generally used in the Christian church for many ages;—in particular by our own Church, which directs us to bless God both for the means of grace, and hope of glory; and teaches us, that a sacrament is "an outward sign of inward grace, and a means whereby we receive the same."

The chief of these means are prayer, whether in secret or with the great congregation; searching the Scriptures; (which implies reading, hearing, and meditating thereon;) and receiving the Lord's Supper, eating bread and drinking wine in remembrance of Him: And these we believe to be ordained of God, as the ordinary channels of conveying his grace to the souls of men.

2. But we allow, that the whole value of the means depends on their actual subservience to the end of religion; that, consequently, all these means, when separate from the end, are less than nothing and vanity; that if they do not actually conduce to the knowledge and love of God, they are not acceptable in his sight; yea, rather, they are an abomination before him, a stink in his nostrils; he is weary to bear them. Above all, if they are used as a kind of commutation for the religion they were designed to subserve, it is not easy to find words for the enormous folly and wickedness of thus turning God's arms against himself; of keeping Christianity out of the heart by those very means which were ordained for the bringing it in.

3. We allow, likewise, that all outward means whatever, if separate from the Spirit of God, cannot profit at all, cannot conduce, in any degree, either to the knowledge or love of God. Without controversy, the help that is done upon earth, He doeth it himself. It is He alone who, by his own almighty power, worketh in us what is pleasing in his sight; and all outward things, unless He work in them and by them, are mere weak and beggarly elements. Whosoever, therefore, imagines there is any intrinsic power in any means whatsoever, does greatly err, not knowing the Scriptures, neither the power of God. We know that there is no inherent power in the words that are spoken in prayer, in the

letter of Scripture read, the sound thereof heard, or the bread and wine received in the Lord's Supper; but that it is God alone who is the Giver of every good gift, the Author of all grace; that the whole power is of him, whereby, through any of these, there is any blessing conveyed to our soul. We know, likewise, that he is able to give the same grace, though there were no means on the face of the earth. In this sense, we may affirm, that, with regard to God, there is no such thing as means; seeing he is equally able to work whatsoever pleaseth him, by any, or by none at all.

4. We allow farther, that the use of all means whatever will never atone for one sin; that it is the blood of Christ alone, whereby any sinner can be reconciled to God; there being no other propitiation for our sins, no other fountain for sin and uncleanness. Every believer in Christ is deeply convinced that there is no merit but in Him; that there is no merit in any of his own works; not in uttering the prayer, or searching the Scripture, or hearing the word of God, or eating of that bread and drinking of that cup. So that if no more be intended by the expression some have used, "Christ is the only means of grace," than this,—that He is the only meritorious cause of it, it cannot be gainsayed by any who know the grace of God.

5. Yet once more: We allow, though it is a melancholy truth, that a large proportion of those who are called Christians, do to this day abuse the means of grace to the destruction of their souls. This is doubtless the case with all those who rest content in the form of godliness, without the power. Either they fondly presume they are Christians already, because they do thus and thus,—although Christ was never yet revealed in their hearts, nor the love of God shed abroad therein:—Or else they suppose they shall infallibly be so barely because they use these means; idly dreaming, (though perhaps hardly conscious thereof,) either that there is some kind of power therein, whereby, sooner or later, (they know not when,) they shall certainly be made holy; or that there is a sort of merit in using them, which will surely move God to give them holiness, or accept them without it.

6. So little do they understand that great foundation of the whole Christian building, "By grace are ye saved:" Ye are saved from your sins, from the guilt and power thereof, ye are restored to the favour and image of God, not for any works, merits, or

deservings of yours, but by the free grace, the mere mercy of God, through the merits of his well-beloved Son: Ye are thus saved, not by any power, wisdom, or strength, which is in you, or in any other creature; but merely through the grace or power of the Holy Ghost, which worketh all in all.

7. But the main question remains: "We know this salvation is the gift and the work of God; but how (may one say who is convinced he hath it not) may I attain thereto?" If you say, "Believe, and thou shalt be saved!" he answers, "True; but how shall I believe?" You reply, "Wait upon God." "Well; but how am I to wait? In the means of grace, or out of them? Am I to wait for the grace of God which bringeth salvation, by using these means, or by laying them aside?"

8. It cannot possibly be conceived, that the word of God should give no direction in so important a point; or, that the Son of God, who came down from heaven for us men and for our salvation, should have left us undetermined with regard to a question wherein our salvation is so nearly concerned. And, in fact, he hath not left us undetermined; he hath shown us the way wherein we should go. We have only to consult the oracles of God; to inquire what is written there; and, if we simply abide by their decision, there can no possible doubt remain.

III.

1. According to this, according to the decision of holy writ all who desire the grace of God are to wait for it in the means which he hath ordained; in using, not in laying them aside.

And, First, all who desire the grace of God are to wait for it in the way of prayer. This is the express direction of our Lord himself. In his Sermon upon the Mount, after explaining at large wherein religion consists, and describing the main branches of it, he adds, "Ask, and it shall be given you; seek, and ye shall find; knock, and it shall be opened unto you: For everyone that asketh receiveth; and he that seeketh findeth; and to him that knocketh it shall be opened." (Matt. 7:7, 8) Here we are in the plainest manner directed to ask, in order to, or as a means of, receiving; to seek, in order to find, the grace of God, the pearl of great price; and to knock, to continue asking and seeking, if we would enter into his kingdom.

2. That no doubt might remain, our Lord labours this point in a more peculiar manner. He appeals to every man's own heart: "What man is there of you, who, if his son ask bread, will give him a stone? Or, if he ask a fish, will he give him a serpent? If ye then, being evil, know how to give good gifts unto your children, how much more shall your Father which is in heaven," the Father of angels and men, the Father of the spirits of all flesh, "give good things to them that ask him" (Matt. 7:9-11.) Or, as he expresses himself on another occasion, including all good things in one, "How much more shall your heavenly Father give the Holy Spirit to them that ask him" (Luke 11:13.) It should be particularly observed here, that the persons directed to ask had not then received the Holy Spirit: Nevertheless our Lord directs them to use this means, and promises that it should be effectual; that upon asking they should receive the Holy Spirit, from him whose mercy is over all his works.

3. The absolute necessity of using this means, if we would receive any gift from God, yet farther appears from that remarkable passage which immediately precedes these words: "And he said unto them," whom he had just been teaching how to pray, "Which of you shall have a friend, and shall go unto him at midnight, and shall say unto him, Friend, lend me three loaves: And he from within shall answer, Trouble me not; I cannot rise and give thee. I say unto you, though he will not rise and give him, because he is his friend, yet because of his importunity, he will rise, and give him as many as he needeth. And I say unto you, Ask, and it shall be given you." (Luke 11:5, 7-9) "Though he will not give him, because he is his friend, yet because of his importunity he will rise and give him as many as he needeth." How could our blessed Lord more plainly declare, that we may receive of God, by this means, by importunately asking, what otherwise we should not receive at all.

4. "He spake also another parable, to this end, that men ought always to pray, and not to faint," till through this means they should receive of God whatsoever petition they asked of him: "There was in a city a judge which feared not God, neither regarded man. And there was a widow in that city, and she came unto him, saying, Avenge me of my adversary. And he would not for a while; but afterward he said within himself, Though I

fear not God, nor regard man, yet because this widow troubleth me, I will avenge her, lest, by her continual coming, she weary me." (Luke 18:1-5) The application of this our Lord himself hath made: "Hear what the unjust judge saith!" Because she continues to ask, because she will take no denial, therefore I will avenge her. "And shall not God avenge his own elect, which cry day and night unto him I tell you he will avenge them speedily," if they pray and faint not.

5. A direction, equally full and express, to wait for the blessings of God in private prayer, together with a positive promise, that, by this means, we shall obtain the request of our lips, he hath given us in those well-known words: "Enter into thy closet, and, when thou hast shut thy door, pray to thy Father which is in secret; and thy Father, which seeth in secret, shall reward thee openly." (Matt. 6:6)

6. If it be possible for any direction to be more clear, it is that which God hath given us by the Apostle, with regard to prayer of every kind, public or private, and the blessing annexed thereto: "If any of you lack wisdom, let him ask of God, that giveth to all men liberally," (if they ask; otherwise "ye have not, because ye ask not," (James 4:2) "and upbraideth not; and it shall be given him." (James 1:5)

If it be objected, "But this is no direction to unbelievers; to them who know not the pardoning grace of God: For the Apostle adds, 'But let him ask in faith;' otherwise, 'let him not think that he shall receive any thing of the Lord:'" I answer, The meaning of the word faith, in this place, is fixed by the Apostle himself, as if it were on purpose to obviate this objection, in the following: "Let him ask in faith, nothing wavering," nothing doubting, *mhden diakrinomenos*. Not doubting but God heareth his prayer, and will fulfil the desire of his heart.

The gross, blasphemous absurdity of supposing faith, in this place, to be taken in the full Christian meaning, appears hence: It is supposing the Holy Ghost to direct a man who knows he has not faith, (which is here termed wisdom,) to ask it of God, with a positive promise that "it shall be given him;" and then immediately to subjoin, that it shall not be given him, unless he have it before he asks for it! But who can bear such a supposition? From this scripture, therefore, as well as those cited above, we must infer, that all who desire the grace of God are to wait for it in the way of prayer.

7. Secondly. All who desire the grace of God are to wait for it in searching the Scriptures.

Our Lord's direction, with regard to the use of this means, is likewise plain and clear. "Search the Scriptures," saith he to the unbelieving Jews, "for they testify of me." (John 5:39) And for this very end did he direct them to search the Scriptures, that they might believe in him.

The objection, that "this is not a command, but only an assertion, that they did search the Scriptures," is shamelessly false. I desire those who urge it, to let us know how a command can be more clearly expressed, than in those terms, *Ereunate tas grajas*. It is as peremptory as so many words can make it.

And what a blessing from God attends the use of this means, appears from what is recorded concerning the Bereans; who, after hearing St. Paul, "searched the Scriptures daily, whether those things were so. Therefore many of them believed;"—found the grace of God, in the way which he had ordained. (Acts 17:11, 12)

It is probable, indeed, that in some of those who had "received the word with all readiness of mind," "faith came," as the same Apostle speaks, "by hearing," and was only confirmed by reading the Scriptures: But it was observed above, that under the general term of searching the Scriptures, both hearing, reading, and meditating are contained.

8. And that this is a means whereby God not only gives, but also confirms and increases, true wisdom, we learn from the words of St. Paul to Timothy: "From a child thou hast known the Holy Scriptures, which are able to make thee wise unto salvation through faith which is in Christ Jesus." (2 Tim. 3:15) The same truth (namely, that this is the great means God has ordained for conveying his manifold grace to man) is delivered, in the fullest manner that can be conceived, in the words which immediately follow: "All Scripture is given by inspiration of God;" consequently, all Scripture is infallibly true; "and is profitable for doctrine, for reproof, for correction, for instruction in righteousness;" to the end "that the man of God may be perfect, throughly furnished unto all good works." (2 Tim. 3:16, 17)

9. It should be observed, that this is spoken primarily and directly of the Scriptures which Timothy had known from a child; which must have been those of the Old Testament, for the New was not then wrote. How far then was St. Paul (though he was "not a whit behind the very chief of the Apostles," nor, therefore, I presume, behind any man now upon earth) from making light of the Old Testament! Behold this, lest ye one day "wonder and perish," ye who make so small account of one half of the oracles of God! Yea, and that half of which the Holy Ghost expressly declares, that it is "profitable," as a means ordained of God, for this very thing, "for doctrine, for reproof, for correction, for instruction in righteousness;" to the end, "the man of God may be perfect, throughly furnished unto all good works."

10. Nor is this profitable only for the men of God, for those who walk already in the light of his countenance; but also for those who are yet in darkness, seeking him whom they know not. Thus St. Peter, "We have also a more sure word of prophecy:" Literally, "And we have the prophetic word more sure;" *kai ecomen bebaioteron ton projhtikon logon,* confirmed by our being "eye-witnesses of his Majesty," and "hearing the voice which came from the excellent glory;" unto which—prophetic word; so he styles the Holy Scriptures—"ye do well that ye take heed, as unto a light that shineth in a dark place, until the day dawn, and the Day-star arise in your hearts." (2 Peter 1:19) Let all, therefore, who desire that day to dawn upon their hearts, wait for it in searching the Scriptures.

11. Thirdly. All who desire an increase of the grace of God are to wait for it in partaking of the Lord's Supper: For this also is a direction himself hath given. "The same night in which he was betrayed, he took bread, and brake it, and said, Take, eat; this is my body;" that is, the sacred sign of my body: "This do in remembrance of me." Likewise, "he took the cup, saying, This cup is the new testament," or covenant, "in my blood;" the sacred sign of that covenant; "this do ye in remembrance of me." "For as often as ye eat this bread, and drink this cup, ye do show forth the Lord's death till he come:" (1 Cor. 11:23, &c.) Ye openly exhibit the same, by these visible signs, before God, and angels, and men; ye manifest your solemn remembrance of his death, till he cometh in the clouds of heaven.

Only "let a man" first "examine himself," whether he understand the nature and design of this holy institution, and whether he really desire to be himself made conformable to the death of Christ; and so, nothing doubting, "let him eat of that bread, and drink of that cup." (1 Cor. 11:28)

Here, then, the direction first given by our Lord is expressly repeated by the Apostle: "Let him eat; let him drink;" (*esqietv, pinetv*, both in the imperative mood;) words not implying a bare permission only, but a clear, explicit command; a command to all those either who already are filled with peace and joy in believing, or who can truly say, "The remembrance of our sins is grievous unto us, the burden of them is intolerable."

12. And that this is also an ordinary, stated means of receiving the grace of God, is evident from those words of the Apostle, which occur in the preceding chapter: "The cup of blessing which we bless, is it not the communion," or communication, "of the blood of Christ? The bread which we break, is it not the communion of the body of Christ?" (1 Cor. 10:16) Is not the eating of that bread, and the drinking of that cup, the outward, visible means, whereby God conveys into our souls all that spiritual grace, that righteousness, and peace, and joy in the Holy Ghost, which were purchased by the body of Christ once broken and the blood of Christ once shed for us? Let all, therefore, who truly desire the grace of God, eat of that bread, and drink of that cup.

IV.

1. But as plainly as God hath pointed out the way wherein he will be inquired after, innumerable are the objections which men, wise in their own eyes, have, from time to time, raised against it. It may be needful to consider a few of these; not because they are of weight in themselves, but because they have so often been used, especially of late years, to turn the lame out of the way; yea, to trouble and subvert those who did run well, till Satan appeared as an angel of light.

The first and chief of these is, "You cannot use these means (as you call them) without trusting in them." I pray, where is this written I expect you should show me plain Scripture for your assertion: Otherwise I dare not receive it; because I am not convinced that you are wiser than God.

If it really had been as you assert, it is certain Christ must have known it. And if he had known it, he would surely have warned us; he would have revealed it long ago. Therefore, because he has not, because there is no tittle of this in the whole revelation of Jesus Christ, I am as fully assured your assertion is false, as that this revelation is of God. "However, leave them off for a short time, to see whether you trusted in them or no." So I am to disobey God, in order to know whether I trust in obeying him! And do you avow this advice? Do you deliberately teach to "do evil, that good may come?" O tremble at the sentence of God against such teachers! Their "damnation is just."

"Nay, if you are troubled when you leave them off, it is plain you trusted in them." By no means. If I am troubled when I wilfully disobey God, it is plain his Spirit is still striving with me; but if I am not troubled at wilful sin, it is plain I am given up to a reprobate mind.

But what do you mean by "trusting in them"—looking for the blessing of God therein? Believing, that if I wait in this way, I shall attain what otherwise I should not? So I do. And so I will, God being my helper, even to my life's end. By the grace of God I will thus trust in them, till the day of my death; that is, I will believe, that whatever God hath promised, he is faithful also to perform. And seeing he hath promised to bless me in this way, I trust it shall be according to his word.

2. It has been, Secondly, objected, "This is seeking salvation by works." Do you know the meaning of the expression you use? What is seeking salvation by works? In the writings of St. Paul, it means, either seeking to be saved by observing the ritual works of the Mosaic law; or expecting salvation for the sake of our own works, by the merit of our own righteousness. But how is either of these implied in my waiting in the way God has ordained, and expecting that he will meet me there, because he has promised so to do?

I do expect that he will fulfil his word, that he will meet and bless me in this way. Yet not for the sake of any works which I have done, nor for the merit of my righteousness; but merely through the merits, and sufferings, and love of his Son, in whom he is always well pleased.

3. It has been vehemently objected, Thirdly, "that Christ is the only means of grace." I answer, this is mere playing upon words. Explain your term, and the objection vanishes away. When we say, "Prayer is a means of grace," we understand a channel through which the grace of God is conveyed. When you say, "Christ is the means of grace," you understand the sole price and purchaser of it; or, that "no man cometh unto the Father, but through him." And who denies it? But this is utterly wide of the question.

4. "But does not the Scripture" (it has been objected, Fourthly) "direct us to wait for salvation? Does not David say, 'My soul waiteth upon God, for of him cometh my salvation'? And does not Isaiah teach us the same thing, saying, 'O Lord, we have waited for thee'?" All this cannot be denied. Seeing it is the gift of God, we are undoubtedly to wait on him for salvation. But how shall we wait? If God himself has appointed a way, can you find a better way of waiting for him? But that he hath appointed a way hath been shown at large, and also what that way is. The very words of the Prophet, which you cite, put this out of the question. For the whole sentence runs thus:—"In the way of thy judgments," or ordinances, "O Lord, have we waited for thee." (Isaiah 26:8) And in the very same way did David wait, as his own words abundantly testify: "I have waited for thy saving health, O Lord, and have kept thy law. Teach me, O Lord, the way of thy statutes, and I shall keep it unto the end."

5. "Yea," say some, "but God has appointed another way.—'Stand still, and see the salvation of God.'" Let us examine the Scriptures to which you refer. The first of them, with the context, runs thus:—"And when Pharaoh drew nigh, the children of Israel lifted up their eyes; and they were sore afraid. And they said unto Moses, Because there were no graves in Egypt, hast thou taken us away to die in the wilderness? And Moses said unto the people, Fear ye not; stand still, and see the salvation of the Lord. And the Lord said unto Moses, Speak unto the children of Israel that they go forward. But lift thou up thy rod, and stretch out thine hand over the sea, and divide it. And the children of Israel shall go on dry ground through the midst of the sea." (Exod. 14:10, &c.) This was the salvation of God, which they stood still to see, by marching forward with all their might!

The other passage, wherein this expression occurs stands thus: "There came some that told Jehoshaphat, saying, There cometh a great multitude against thee, from beyond the sea. And Jehoshaphat feared, and set himself to seek the Lord, and proclaimed a fast throughout all Judah. And Judah gathered themselves together to ask help of the Lord: Even out of all the cities they came to seek the Lord. And Jehoshaphat stood in the congregation, in the house of the Lord.—Then upon Jahaziel came the Spirit of the Lord. And he said, Be not dismayed by reason of this great multitude. To-morrow go ye down against them: Ye shall not need to fight in this battle. Set yourselves: Stand ye still, and see the salvation of the Lord. And they rose early in the morning, and went forth. And when they began to sing and to praise, the Lord set ambushments against the children of Moab, Ammon, and mount Seir:—and everyone helped to destroy another." (2 Chron. 20:2, &c.) Such was the salvation which the children of Judah saw. But how does all this prove, that we ought not to wait for the grace of God in the means which he hath ordained?

6. I shall mention but one objection more, which, indeed, does not properly belong to this head: Nevertheless, because it has been so frequently urged, I may not wholly pass it by.

"Does not St. Paul say, 'If ye be dead with Christ, why are ye subject to ordinances'? (Col. 2:20) Therefore a Christian, one that is dead with Christ, need not use the ordinances any more."

So you say, "If I am a Christian, I am not subject to the ordinances of Christ!" Surely, by the absurdity of this, you must see at the first glance, that the ordinances here mentioned cannot be the ordinances of Christ: That they must needs be the Jewish ordinances, to which it is certain a Christian is no longer subject.

And the same undeniably appears from the words immediately following, "Touch not, taste not, handle not;" all evidently referring to the ancient ordinances of the Jewish law.

So that this objection is the weakest of all. And, in spite of all, that great truth must stand unshaken; — that all who desire the grace of God, are to wait for it in the means which he hath ordained.

V.

1. But this being allowed, that all who desire the grace of God are to wait for it in the means he hath ordained; it may still be

inquired, how those means should be used, both as to the order and the manner of using them. With regard to the former, we may observe, there is a kind of order, wherein God himself is generally pleased to use these means in bringing a sinner to salvation. A stupid, senseless wretch is going on in his own way, not having God in all his thoughts, when God comes upon him unawares, perhaps by an awakening sermon or conversation, perhaps by some awful providence, or, it may be, an immediate stroke of his convincing Spirit, without any outward means at all. Having now a desire to flee from the wrath to come, he purposely goes to hear how it may be done. If he finds a preacher who speaks to the heart, he is amazed, and begins searching the Scriptures, whether these things are so. The more he hears and reads, the more convinced he is; and the more he meditates thereon day and night. Perhaps he finds some other book which explains and enforces what he has heard and read in Scripture. And by all these means, the arrows of conviction sink deeper into his soul. He begins also to talk of the things of God, which are ever uppermost in his thoughts; yea, and to talk with God; to pray to him; although, through fear and shame, he scarce knows what to say. But whether he can speak or no, he cannot but pray, were it only in "groans which cannot be uttered." Yet, being in doubt, whether "the high and lofty One that inhabiteth eternity" will regard such a sinner as him, he wants to pray with those who know God, with the faithful, in the great congregation. But here he observes others go up to the table of the Lord. He considers, "Christ has said, 'Do this!' How is it that I do not? I am too great a sinner. I am not fit. I am not worthy." After struggling with these scruples a while, he breaks through. And thus he continues in God's way, in hearing, reading, meditating, praying, and partaking of the Lord's Supper, till God, in the manner that pleases him, speaks to his heart, "Thy faith hath saved thee. Go in peace."

2. By observing this order of God, we may learn what means to recommend to any particular soul. If any of these will reach a stupid, careless sinner, it is probably hearing, or conversation. To such, therefore, we might recommend these, if he has ever any thought about salvation. To one who begins to feel the weight of his sins, not only hearing the Word of God, but reading it too, and perhaps other serious books, may be a means of deeper

conviction. May you not advise him also, to meditate on what he reads, that it may have its full force upon his heart? Yea, and to speak thereof, and not be ashamed, particularly among those who walk in the same path. When trouble and heaviness take hold upon him, should you not then earnestly exhort him to pour out his soul before God; "always to pray and not to faint;" and when he feels the worthlessness of his own prayers, are you not to work together with God, and remind him of going up into the house of the Lord, and praying with all that fear him? But if he does this, the dying word of his Lord will soon be brought to his remembrance; a plain intimation that this is the time when we should second the motions of the blessed Spirit. And thus may we lead him, step by step, through all the means which God has ordained; not according to our own will, but just as the Providence and the Spirit of God go before and open the way.

3. Yet, as we find no command in holy writ for any particular order to be observed herein, so neither do the providence and the Spirit of God adhere to any without variation; but the means into which different men are led, and in which they find the blessing of God, are varied, transposed, and combined together, a thousand different ways. Yet still our wisdom is to follow the leadings of his providence and his Spirit; to be guided herein, (more especially as to the means wherein we ourselves seek the grace of God,) partly by his outward providence, giving us the opportunity of using sometimes one means, sometimes another, partly by our experience, which it is whereby his free Spirit is pleased most to work in our heart. And in the mean time, the sure and general rule for all who groan for the salvation of God is this,—whenever opportunity serves, use all the means which God has ordained; for who knows in which God will meet thee with the grace that bringeth salvation?

4. As to the manner of using them, whereon indeed it wholly depends whether they should convey any grace at all to the user; it behoves us,

First, always to retain a lively sense, that God is above all means. Have a care, therefore, of limiting the Almighty. He doeth whatsoever and whensoever it pleaseth him. He can convey his grace, either in or out of any of the means which he hath appointed. Perhaps he will. "Who hath known the mind of the

Lord or who hath been his counsellor?" Look then every moment for his appearing! Be it at the hour you are employed in his ordinances; or before, or after that hour; or when you are hindered therefrom: He is not hindered. He is always ready, always able, always willing to save. "It is the Lord: Let him do what seemeth him good!"

Secondly. Before you use any means, let it be deeply impressed on your soul;—there is no power in this. It is, in itself, a poor, dead, empty thing: Separate from God, it is a dry leaf, a shadow. Neither is there any merit in my using this; nothing intrinsically pleasing to God; nothing whereby I deserve any favour at his hands, no, not a drop of water to cool my tongue. But, because God bids, therefore I do; because he directs me to wait in this way, therefore here I wait for his free mercy, whereof cometh my salvation.

Settle this in your heart, that the *opus operatum*, the mere work done, profiteth nothing; that there is no power to save, but in the Spirit of God, no merit, but in the blood of Christ; that, consequently, even what God ordains, conveys no grace to the soul, if you trust not in Him alone. On the other hand, he that does truly trust in Him, cannot fall short of the grace of God, even though he were cut off from every outward ordinance, though he were shut up in the centre of the earth.

Thirdly. In using all means, seek God alone. In and through every outward thing, look singly to the power of his Spirit; and the merits of his Son. Beware you do not stick in the work itself; if you do, it is all lost labour. Nothing short of God can satisfy your soul. Therefore, eye him in all, through all, and above all. Remember also, to use all means, as means; as ordained, not for their own sake, but in order to the renewal of your soul in righteousness and true holiness. If, therefore, they actually tend to this, well; but if not, they are dung and dross.

Lastly. After you have used any of these, take care how you value yourself thereon: How you congratulate yourself as having done some great thing. This is turning all into poison. Think, "If God was not there, what does this avail? Have I not been adding sin to sin? How long O Lord! save, or I perish! O lay not this sin to my charge!" If God was there, if his love flowed into your heart, you have forgot, as it were, the outward work. You see,

> you know, you feel, God is all in all. Be abased. Sink down before
> him. Give him all the praise. "Let God in all things be glorified
> through Christ Jesus." Let all your bones cry out, "My song shall
> be always of the loving-kindness of the Lord: With my mouth will
> I ever be telling of thy truth, from one generation to another!"

In the first six paragraphs of section 3, we see how Wesley believed that **prayer** was the primary means of communication and interaction between God and humans. In a 1760 letter, he wrote, "Prayer is certainly the grand means of drawing near to God; and all others are helpful to us only so far as they are mixed with or prepare us for this."[6] Elsewhere, he wrote that "prayer may be said to be the breath of our spiritual life. One who lives cannot possibly cease breathing."[7] Let me invite you to pause from reading for just a moment and take a deep breath in for three seconds . . . then out for three seconds. Now, do it again . . . and once more. How do you feel? Probably very good! Why? Because in physical breathing, we breathe in life-giving, life-sustaining oxygen and breathe out toxic carbon dioxide. The result is a healthier body. In the same way, prayer allows us to metaphorically breathe in the life-giving, life-sustaining presence of God, and breathe out the "toxins" of our spiritual lives through confession and pardon. In his words above, Wesley essentially is saying that just as our physical bodies need breath, so our spiritual bodies need the presence of God through prayer. Consequently, for Wesley, the "neglect of private prayer" is one of the most common causes of what he called "the wilderness state of Christianity"—a sense of spiritual dryness and purposelessness.[8]

A second "chief" instituted means identified in section 3, paragraphs 7–10 in the sermon above is what Wesley called "**searching the Scriptures.**" In today's context, we might be tempted to think of this as Bible study. But it

---

6   John Wesley, "Letter to Jane Catherine March" (March 29, 1760) in Campbell, ed., *The Bicentennial Edition of the Works of John Wesley*, 27:190 (see chap. 1, n. 2).

7   John Wesley, *John Wesley's Explanatory Notes on the New Testament*, commentary on 1 Thessalonians 5:16-17, in *John Wesley's Commentary on the Bible: A One-Volume Condensation of His Explanatory Notes*, ed. G. Roger Schoenhals (Grand Rapids: Zondervan, 1990), 55.

8   Read more about this state and prayer's role in preventing it in section 2, paragraph 4 of Wesley's Sermon 46, "The Wilderness State" in Outler, ed., *The Bicentennial Edition of the Works of John Wesley*, 2:209 (see chap. 3, n. 1).

is, in actuality, much more than this. Through this means, he believed, one should engage in "searching the Scriptures" by

> (i.) Reading: Constantly, some part of everyday; regularly, all the Bible in order; carefully, with the Notes; seriously, with prayer before and after; fruitfully, immediately practicing what you learn there?
>
> (ii.) Meditating: At set times? by any rule?
>
> (iii.) Hearing: Every morning? carefully; with prayer before, at, after; immediately putting in practice? Have you a New Testament always about you?[9]

In other places, he referenced it including the singing of scripture, as well. In short, "searching the Scriptures" involves any way or form by which we interact with Holy Scripture.

In Section 3, paragraphs 11-12 of the sermon above, Wesley references the third Instituted means of grace: **the Lord's Supper (or Holy Communion/ the Eucharist).** Since we will be focusing on this means in chapter 7, I will not expound on it here. Instead, in addition to the three "chief" means listed in this sermon, let me highlight two additional instituted means that Wesley identified in some of his later writings.[10]

The first is spiritual **fasting.** In keeping with the practice both of Jesus[11] and of the early church, Wesley fasted from food every Friday as an aid to spiritual growth and encouraged his Methodists to do the same. Today, fasting is often thought of only in terms of giving up some type or amount of food, such as chocolate, meats, sweets, and so on. While these certainly can be *part of* this practice, for Wesley fasting is not so much about *giving up* something as it is about *taking on* something else—its purpose is to draw us away from earthly things so that we can commit more time and focus to spiritual things.

---

9 Wesley, "Minutes of Several Conversations Between the Rev. Mr. Wesley and Others," Question 48, Answer I (2), in Jackson, ed., *The Works of John Wesley*, 8:323.

10 One may question why *Christian baptism* was not included in Wesley's list of "chief" instituted means of grace. The answer lies in his belief that means of grace are tools by and through which God's grace can flow *continuously* (i.e., repeatedly). However, while Wesley did acknowledge baptism to be a means of God's grace in general (since it does convey grace), nevertheless he does not reference it in his general discussions of means of grace, since in it, God's grace flows only *one, complete time* (i.e., it is not repeatable).

11 Matthew 6:16-18.

CHAPTER 6

When practiced in conjunction with prayer and "scripture searching," fasting can be a great aid in sanctification by enriching and growing one's spiritual life. He did not believe, however, that its practice needs to include acts of extreme asceticism. For example, it can take the form of something as simple as fasting from food after dinner one night until lunchtime the next day.[12] In the spirit of Wesley's understanding, today we might include fasts from things such as watching TV, interacting on social media, attending movies, and so on, so that we might spend more time in prayer or with our families, give to or serve in a worthy mission project at our church, and so on.

The fifth and final instituted means of grace that Wesley found in scripture was something he called **Christian conferencing**—connection and interaction with other Christians. Wesley was convinced that an important reason for the growth and vitality of early Christianity was because it emphasized believers gathering together regularly in small groups for fellowship, nurture, and accountability. In the preface to his 1739 edition of *Hymns and Sacred Poems*, he explained how Christianity is intended to be lived out *in community* (what he called "social" religion):

> Directly opposite to this is the gospel of Christ. Solitary religion is not to be found [in the Bible]. "Holy solitaries" is a phrase no more consistent with the gospel than holy adulterers. The gospel of Christ knows of no religion but social; no holiness but social holiness. Faith working by love, is the length and breadth and depth and height of Christian perfection.[13]

Consequently, he felt that every Christian needs to be part of an intimate group not only where they can share the concerns and difficulties of life and find support through them, but also where they can be lovingly challenged in their faith walk. We find this similarly expressed in Hebrews 10:24-25, "Let us consider how to provoke one another to love and good deeds, not neglecting to meet together . . . but encouraging one another" (NRSV). And while Wesley believed that the exact manner/form of these small groups could be a flexible prudential means of grace, Jesus's own small group of

---

12 For Wesley, liquids were always allowed (and encouraged) during the period of fasting.

13 John Wesley, preface to "Hymns and Sacred Poems" (1739), ¶ 5, in Chilcote and Collins, eds., *The Bicentennial Edition of the Works of John Wesley*, 13:39 (see chap. 3, n. 17).

twelve disciples illustrated the importance of *some* type of "Christian conferencing" for all Christians.

The Prudential Means of Grace

As mentioned earlier in this chapter, Wesley also conceived of a second major category that he called the **prudential means of grace**, because it consisted of means that are *prudent* (shrewdly useful and beneficial) for the development of the spiritual lives of *particular* Christians in *specific* contexts. While they are *not* things specifically commanded or initiated by Christ (they more often are extra-biblical products of church tradition), nevertheless Christ's presence is presumed in and through them because of the positive spiritual fruit that their use produces. In fact, the relational nature and purpose of most of these indicates that they at times can be understood simply as another way of describing Wesley's acts of mercy.[14] Finally, since prudential means of grace are ones that God raises up for particular Christians in specific contexts (as opposed to the instituted means' universal nature), these might from time to time and place to place need to be modified or even eliminated altogether if they no longer seem to bear spiritual fruit.

> **Prudential means of grace**: Means of grace in which Christ's presence is presumed based on observation of their spiritual fruit, and which are therefore useful ("prudent") for specific Christians in particular times and contexts. Due to their relational nature, they are often closely connected to acts of mercy.

Wesley identified several prudential means of grace at work in his time and context, but by far the most important one for his work was the **Methodist society structure** (also outlined briefly in Wesley's sermon "On God's Vineyard" in chapter 2). This was the specific manifestation of "Christian conferencing" in eighteenth-century England and was at the very heart of the early Methodist movement. It began when people began responding to

---

14 While the direct correspondence between prudential means of grace and acts of mercy is not as clear as it is between the instituted means of grace and acts of piety, nevertheless most prudential means help to connect people to one another in significant ways. That is, they are uniquely social in nature.

CHAPTER 6

Wesley's ministry by wanting to know more about what he was preaching. His answer was to form these inquirers into small groups (originally called **societies**) which would meet for prayer, Bible study, testimony, encouragement, and accountability. Soon, however, these societies grew so large that Wesley split them into several smaller groups, all of which were designed to function within the established Church of England to help bring renewal (see fig. 6.1).

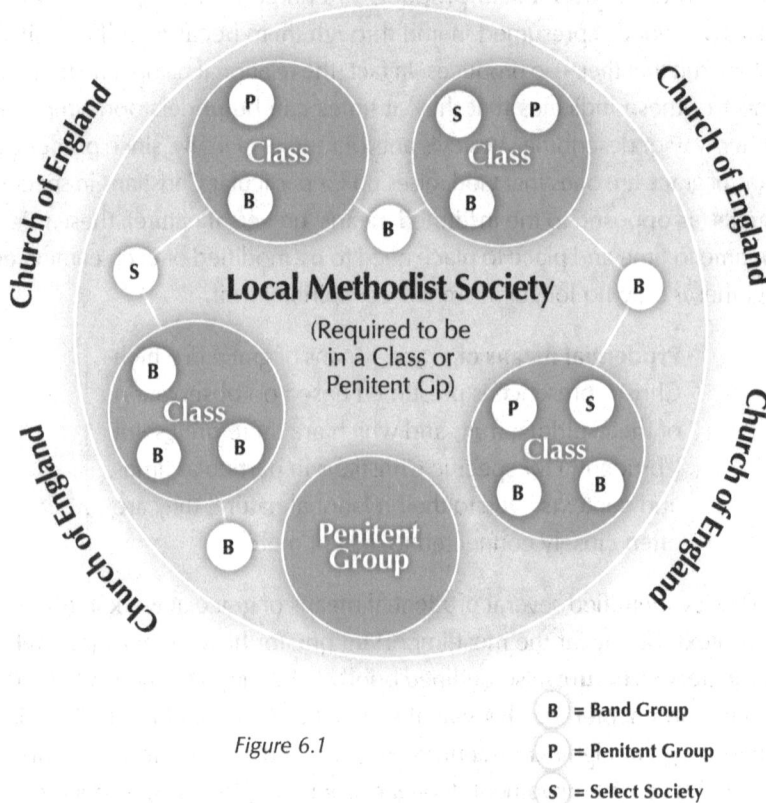

Figure 6.1

B = Band Group
P = Penitent Group
S = Select Society

First, there were the **classes**, which were the very heart of this structure. Wesley explained that "any person desiring to save his soul may be united with the [the Methodists by being] . . . placed in such a class as convenient for him, where he spends about an hour in a week."[15] In other words, to be part of a local Methodist Society, one first had to be part of a Methodist class. Since the only requirement was "a desire to save [one's] soul," one did not have to be already converted to belong or participate—the classes were for spiritual *seekers*. In fact, research from the writings of those impacted by Wesley's ministry indicates that most early Methodists were converted, not during Wesley's *preaching*, but as they participated in a *class*. During the meeting itself, around twelve people reported on their spiritual progress, shared their needs and challenges, and received support and prayer from the others in the group.[16] Members were held accountable to their practice of the Methodist discipline and "General Rules" (described below), and each class was led by a man or woman appointed by either Wesley or their society pastor, whose job it was "to see each person in his class once a week at least, in order to receive what they are willing to give towards the relief of the poor; to inquire how their souls prosper; to advise, reprove, comfort, or exhort, as occasion may require."[17]

For those who demonstrated clear fruits of conversion and a desire for further spiritual growth, Wesley also established **bands**. These met *in addition to* the participant's class and consisted of about five to eight people (instead of the twelve or so in a class). Roughly 20 percent of early Methodists participated in a band. These were divided by age, sex, and marital status, because each experienced faith in a different way. In addition, as opposed to the mandatory nature of the classes and the fact that their leaders were appointed, bands were always voluntary, and band groups chose their own leader from among themselves. Since the bands were only for those who had demonstrated clear fruit of conversion, the depth of discussion was more intimate than that found in the classes. For example, members could ask each other questions such as: "What known sins have you committed since our last meeting? What temptations have you met with? How were you delivered?

---

15 Wesley, "On God's Vineyard," § 3, ¶ 1, in Outler, ed., *The Bicentennial Edition of the Works of John Wesley*, 3:511–12 (see chap. 3, n. 12).

16 Note: Classes were *not* primarily for instruction, as we might think of Sunday school classes today.

17 John Wesley, "The Nature, Design and General Rules of the United Societies" (1743), ¶ 3(1), in Davies, ed., *The Bicentennial Edition of the Works of John Wesley*, 9:70 (see chap. 4, n. 1).

What have you thought, said, or done, of which you doubt whether it be sin or not? Have you nothing you desire to keep secret?"[18] The purpose of this, of course, was not to pry into personal business, but simply to provide better accountability as a means to grow in sanctification. Band members were held to an even stricter accounting of the Methodist discipline and "General Rules."

Finally, two additional groups existed in early English Methodism for a period of time, as well.[19] First, those band members who were experiencing significant growth in sanctification (perhaps even Christian perfection) could request to be moved to a **select society**, which took the place of their band, and where the focus was on even greater intimate spiritual growth and accountability.[20] And for those who had "backslidden" in faith, Wesley established **penitent groups**, which—for a spiritual season—could take the place of one's class and which functioned in that context back then much like addiction recovery groups function today: to provide loving accountability for the purpose of renewing one's faith and restarting his or her sanctification journey after major spiritual failure.

So, each of the specific groups in the Methodist structure therefore served a specific purpose, and Wesley believed that where they were lacking, true faith would cease to be vital. In his *Journal*, he once wrote:

> I was more convinced than ever that the preaching like an apostle, without joining together those that are awakened and training them up in the ways of God, is only begetting children for the murderer. How much preaching has there been for these twenty years all over Pembrokeshire! But no regular societies, no discipline, no order or connection; and the consequence is that nine in ten of the once-awakened are now faster asleep than ever.[21]

---

18 John Wesley, "Rules of the Band Societies" (1738), final set of five rules, in Davies, 9:78.

19 Neither of these made the eventual journey to American Methodism, and because the classes and bands eventually took over their unique functions, these eventually died out in English Methodism, as well.

20 Select society confidentiality was such that Question 5 for the "Rules of the Select Societies" emphasizes, "Let nothing spoken in this Society be spoken again; no, not even to the members of it." Wesley, "Minutes of the First Annual Conference" (Thursday, June 28, 1744), "Rules of the Select Societies," Question 5, in Rack, ed., *The Bicentennial Edition of the Works of John Wesley*, 10:137 (see chap. 5, n. 11).

21 John Wesley, *Journal* (Thursday, August 25, 1763), in *The Bicentennial Edition of the Works of John Wesley*, vol. 21, *Journal and Diaries IV* (1755–1765), ed. W. Reginald Ward and Richard Heitzenrater (Nashville: Abingdon Press, 1992), 21:424.

A second prudential means of grace was the **Methodist discipline** utilized within the structure of Methodism itself.[22] In its original context, this discipline had nothing to do with bureaucratic rules and regulations for the *corporate* church but instead referred to simple rules for the development of one's *personal* spiritual holiness in life. Also known as the "general rules" of Methodism, this discipline involved a Christian doing three things:

> (1) *"Do No Harm"* (i.e., avoid sinful things)—for Wesley, this included things such as abstaining from swearing, drunkenness, extravagant dress, and "useless diversions, self-indulgence, and miserliness."
>
> (2) *"Do Good"* (i.e., engage in works of mercy)—for Wesley, this included not only taking care of the *physical needs* of others, such as caring for the poor, sick, distressed, and visiting those in prison, but also taking care of the *spiritual needs* of others by giving instruction, exhortation, and reproof.
>
> (3) *"Attend the ordinances of God"* (i.e., practice works of piety/the instituted means of grace). This rule was designed to help his Methodists understand that attending society and class meetings needed also to be supported by them practicing prayer, fasting, and "scripture searching" in their personal lives, but also by attending the Lord's Supper at their local Anglican church.

> **The "general rules" of Methodism**: a set of guidelines established by John Wesley as a tool of spiritual discipline and accountability by all Christians. These consisted of three basic "rules" that mirror Jesus's "Great Commandment": (1) Do no harm; (2) Do good; and (3) Attend the ordinances of God.

These three "general rules" of Methodism mirror Jesus's "Great Commandment," to "love the Lord your God with all your heart, and with all your soul, and with all your strength, and with all your mind; and your neighbor as yourself."[23] "Doing no harm" and "doing good" are two ways to "love our

---

22 An example of this Discipline can be found in Wesley, "The Nature, Design and General Rules of the United Societies," ¶¶ 4–6, in Davies, ed., *The Bicentennial Edition of the Works of John Wesley*, 9:72–74.

23 Luke 10:27 NRSV.

neighbor," while "attending the ordinances of God" are ways that we can "love the Lord" with all our hearts, souls, strength, and minds.[24]

In addition to its unique society structure and discipline, early Methodism also practiced several other prudential means of grace. The **songs and hymns** they used in worship gatherings (many of which were written by Charles Wesley) were very different from the musical forms found in the Anglican churches of the day. Nevertheless, this highlights how music styles can change from generation to generation, but that all can have the common theme of lifting up Jesus Christ. **Readings in the Christian library** comprised yet another prudential means of grace in early Methodism and can provide the same today. As one reads classic writings and works about influential men and women of God throughout Christian history, these can be sources for growth and development in sanctification in one's own life. In fact, by reading this book about the history and theology of John Wesley, you are, in fact, engaging in this particular means of grace. Additionally, Wesley believed that various types of **faith renewal services** could help both to affirm and reaffirm one in his or her faith walk from time to time. Examples of this means in Wesley's day included his extremely popular "covenant service,"[25] similar to our New Year's Eve watch night services, and today might include the service of baptismal renewal found in *The United Methodist Hymnal*.[26] Finally, once every quarter, each Methodist Society would host what was called a **love feast**—a celebration of Christian fellowship, singing, and testimony (no sermon)—for Methodists in good standing. A ticket provided by one's class leader was required in order to attend, and these very desirable events were a highlight for many society members' lives.

Because prudential means of grace, by definition, can change from one time and context to another, there is no limit to how many means can be classified in this category. Consequently, such means today might include things such as: Walk to Emmaus/Cursillo-type Christian retreats; worship

---

24 People have jokingly mentioned to me that only a Methodist preacher could take Jesus's *two* rules (i.e., love God; love your neighbor) and make them into *three*!

25 The first one was held in London in August 1755, with more than eighteen hundred people present.

26 "Baptismal Covenant IV: Congregational Reaffirmation of the Baptismal Covenant" in *The United Methodist Hymnal*, 50.

renewal, both contemporary and spirited traditional; in-depth Bible studies, such as *Disciple, Covenant, Alpha*,[27] and others; laity-focused ministries, such as Stephen Ministry; spiritual formation ministries and programs, such as *Companions in Christ*, The Upper Room, and others; and various styles and forms of contemporary Christian music.[28]

Cautions about the Means of Grace

Before we complete this chapter, it should be pointed out that Wesley offered at least three major **cautions** regarding the use and practice of the means of grace. All of these are found in the sermon we read earlier, and can be summarized as follows:

First, ***they are means, not ends***—they have no intrinsic power to save us in and by themselves. In the sermon, Wesley warned that "the use of all means whatever will never atone for one sin; . . . it is the blood of Christ alone, whereby any sinner can be reconciled to God; there being . . . no merit in any of [our] own works; not in uttering the prayer, or searching the Scripture, or hearing the word of God, or eating of that bread and drinking of that cup."[29] Later, he wrote that "the whole value of the means depends on their actual subservience to the end of religion; that, consequently, all these means, when separate from the end, are less than nothing and vanity."[30] His point in both of these, of course, is that our practice of the means of grace by themselves cannot save us, earn us favor with God, or get us into heaven. They are merely God-given tools to help us grow in our faith. As Wesley once summarized in his *Journal*, we should "neither neglect, nor rest in, the means of grace."[31]

---

27 See https://www.cokesbury.com/disciple-bible-studies; https://www.covenantbiblestudy.com/; and https://alphausa.org/about.

28 See https://www.stephenministries.org; https://www.cokesbury.com/search?q=companions+in+christ&pagenumber=1; https://www.upperroom.org/

29 Wesley, "The Means of Grace," § 2, ¶ 4, in Outler, ed., *Bicentennial Edition of the Works of John Wesley*, 1:382 (see chap. 3, n. 16). Read also § 1, ¶ 2, 1:378.

30 Wesley, § 2, ¶ 2, 1:381.

31 John Wesley, *Journal* (November 15, 1739), in *The Bicentennial Edition of the Works of John Wesley*, vol. 19, *Journal and Diaries II* (1738–1743), ed. W. Reginald Ward and Richard Heitzenrater (Nashville: Abingdon Press, 1992), 19:122.

Second, *these are the ordinary, but not the **only** means of grace*. In the sermon above, Wesley writes that

> it behoves us . . . always to retain a lively sense, that God is above all means. Have a care, therefore, of limiting the Almighty. He doeth whatsoever and whensoever it pleaseth Him. He can convey His grace either in or out of any of the means which He hath appointed.[32]

One may ask, for example, if God's presence can be experienced on a mountaintop? Or at a beach? Or playing golf? The answer, of course, is yes; we should not limit God. However, where have more people traditionally come to have an intimate relationship with God through Christ? On a mountain, beach, or golf course? Or at church? Thomas Langford explains Wesley's understanding in this way: "God may, in divine wisdom, work through *extraordinary* means. But in scripture, Christians are commanded to utilize the *ordinary* means."[33]

Finally, **the means of grace are not automatic**. In the sermon, Wesley writes that "all outward means whatever, if separate from the Spirit of God, cannot profit at all, cannot conduce, in any degree, either to the knowledge or love of God."[34] We are not guaranteed to have great religious experiences every time we pray, read the Bible, attend church, and so on. However, if we are disciplined in our practice of these, and trust in God's Spirit to work, then sooner or later we *will* experience God's presence and renewal through them.

The point to all of this is Wesley's belief that God does not simply save us and leave us to our own work to live the Christian life. Instead, we are supplied specific instruments—means of grace—by and through which we can first find, and then be nurtured as, Christians. With that in mind, then, let's turn in our next chapter to an exploration of the sacraments as examples of specific channels of God's grace.

---

32 Wesley, "The Means of Grace," § 5, ¶ 4 in Outler, ed., *Works*, 1:395.

33 Thomas A. Langford, *Practical Divinity* (Nashville: Abingdon Press, 1989), 45; emphasis added.

34 Wesley, "The Means of Grace," § 2, ¶ 3, in Outler, ed., *The Bicentennial Edition of the Works of John Wesley*, 1:382.

Discussion Questions

1. Which means of grace (instituted or prudential) discussed in this chapter have you found to be most useful in your own spiritual formation and development? Why?

2. How (like Wesley) have you experienced prayer to be the foundational means of grace upon and around which all the others are built?

3. On a scale of 1 to 10 (1=worst, 10=best), where would you place your relationship with God today? What would it take for your relationship to reach a 10? Are there specific means of grace that you read about that you feel would be helpful in accomplishing that?

4. If you are a Christian, how have you practiced the "General Rules" of Methodism ("do no harm, do good, attend the ordinances of God") in your own life of faith, even if you didn't call them by that name? What, do you think, are the value and importance of being able to have a discipline or structure by which one names and identifies the specific ways that one lives out one's Christian life?

5. What means of grace from this chapter's discussion might you feel God is inviting you to use more intentionally? What will you plan to do to ensure that this occurs?

CHAPTER 7

THE SACRAMENTS

As we turn our attention to a discussion of the Protestant sacraments of baptism and Holy Communion, it's important to know that Wesley's conception and practice of these was informed by his understanding of the function he believed that his movement played within the larger context of renewal in his own Church of England. As eminent Wesleyan scholar Albert Outler explains:

> It goes with Wesley's role in the [Methodist] Revival that he had scant interest in the speculative issues of sacramental doctrine and that he produced nothing distinctive in this domain of doctrine. This was not because of any indifference on his part or the lack of a stable perspective. On the contrary, it is just here that we may see yet once again Wesley's conception of his movement as an evangelical order within a catholic Church. It was his plain intention that his followers should depend on the Church, not only for the sacraments themselves but also for their doctrinal interpretation . . . . [Therefore], he felt no compulsion to do more than verify the central Anglican tradition with respect to "the means of grace."[1]

Still, even though Wesley did not produce any essentially *new* theology or practice regarding the sacraments, he did address their nature and meaning in a number of his writings.

Christian Baptism

Avoiding Two Extremes

Wesley's understanding and practice of Christian baptism, for instance, attempted to avoid at least two extremes that he felt misrepresented what the scriptures teach about this sacrament. On the one hand, Wesley wanted to avoid the notion that baptism is *only* an act of God that saves us *apart from* our response of faith. He believed that this view was commonly practiced

---

1 Albert Outler, ed., *John Wesley* (New York: Oxford University Press, 1964, 1980), 332.

CHAPTER 7

not only in his own Anglican tradition but also in the Roman Catholic tradition and other traditions that fixated almost exclusively on infant baptism. Of course, while the first part of the statement is true (baptism *is* an "act of God"), Wesley was concerned when recipients felt that they could experience full salvation apart from their own *personal* response of faith. As I mentioned in chapter 4, before entering ordained ministry, I attended law school. In one of my classes, I remember learning that a legal contract consists of an "offer" *plus* an "acceptance"—one without the other does not create a contract. Christian baptism, of course, is not a *contract* but a *covenant* with God. However, the principle is the same: God's offer of grace in baptism *without* our personal response and acceptance of that grace does not create a completed sacrament. So, to say that biblical baptism is "only an act of God that saves us *apart from* our response of faith" is incorrect because it implies that God does not want or need our response. To the contrary: God offers us salvation as a gift; yet, that gift must also be *intentionally received and opened* for it to be helpful to us.

On the other hand, a second misunderstanding that Wesley wanted to avoid is the notion that baptism is only an act of *human* obedience that we do *after* we are converted. He felt that this was the view practiced in most of the Anabaptist traditions of his day, which focused exclusively on the practice of adult or "believer's" baptism. For Wesley, baptism *can* be something done as an active and obedient response to one's conversion,[2] but he was concerned when a recipient forgets that even his or her *response* is only made possible by God's initiative in the first place. So, in trying to avoid the previous one, this view goes to the opposite extreme by making baptism solely a *human* action that God is not involved in at all.

By contrast, in keeping with the via media approach of his own Anglican tradition, Wesley's understanding and practice of Christian baptism chartered a middle course by setting out to avoid these two extremes. For him, baptism is an act of God that requires our human response of faith. That is: it is the outward sign of God's salvation given to all through Jesus's

---

2 For example, in Acts 2:38, Peter tells the crowd after they have been convicted of their sin to "repent, and be baptized . . . in the name of Jesus Christ so that your sins may be forgiven" (NRSV). The implication here is that baptism is a command of God that should be obeyed and carried out after we repent. And since repentance is something that requires a conscious decision of the will, then the idea here is that baptism is something that should be done only when one is older (*not* as infants).

death on the cross. However, for that prevenient, redemptive work to be truly beneficial in our lives, it must be consciously *appropriated*. As Wesleyan scholar Thomas Langford explains, "Baptism is the initiating representation of God's redeeming grace, but it is efficacious only when it is followed by actual repentance and conversion."[3] Wesley laid out this view in his 1756 sermon *A Treatise on Baptism*.

A Treatise on Baptism[4]
by John Wesley

Concerning baptism I shall inquire, *what* it is; what *benefits* we receive by it; whether our Savior designed it to remain *always* in his Church; and who are the proper subjects of it?

I.

1. What it is. It is the initiatory sacrament, which enters us into covenant with God. It was instituted by Christ, who alone has power to institute a proper sacrament, a sign, seal, pledge, and means of grace, perpetually obligatory on all Christians. We know not, indeed, the exact time of its institution; but we know it was long before our Lord's ascension. And it was instituted in the room of circumcision. For, as that was a sign and seal of God's covenant, so is this.

2. The matter of this sacrament is water; which, as it has a natural power of cleansing, is the more fit for this symbolical use. Baptism is performed by washing, dipping, or sprinkling the person, in the name of the Father, Son, and Holy Ghost, who is hereby devoted to the ever-blessed Trinity. I say, by washing, dipping, or sprinkling; because it is not determined in Scripture in which of these ways it shall be done, neither by any express precept, nor by any such example as clearly proves it; nor by the force or meaning of the word baptize.

3. That there is no express precept, all calm men allow. Neither is there any conclusive example. John's baptism in some

---

3 Langford, *Practical Divinity*, 46 (see chap. 6, n. 33).

4 John Wesley, *A Treatise on Baptism* (New York: N. Bangs and T. Mason, for the Methodist Episcopal Church, 1824).

things agreed with Christ's, in others differed from it. But it cannot be certainly proved from Scripture, that even John's was performed by dipping. It is true he baptized in Enon, near Salim, where there was "much water." But this might refer to breadth rather than depth; since a narrow place would not have been sufficient for so great a multitude. Nor can it be proved, that the baptism of our Savior, or that administered by his disciples, was by immersion. No, nor that of the eunuch baptized by Philip; though "they both went down to the water:" For that going down may relate to the chariot, and implies no determinate depth of water. It might be up to their knees; it might not be above their ankles.

4. And as nothing can be determined from Scripture precept or example, so neither from the force or meaning of the word. For the words baptize and baptism do not necessarily imply dipping, but are used in other senses in several places. Thus we read, that the Jews "were all baptized in the cloud and in the sea;" (1 Corinthians 10:2;) but they were not plunged in either. They could therefore be only sprinkled by drops of the sea-water, and refreshing dews from the cloud; probably intimated in that, "Thou sentest a gracious rain upon thine inheritance, and refreshedst it when it was weary." (Psalm 67:9) Again: Christ said to his two disciples, "Ye shall be baptized with the baptism that I am baptized with;" (Mark 10:38;) but neither he nor they were dipped, but only sprinkled or washed with their own blood. Again we read (Mark 7:4) of the baptisms (so it is in the original) of pots and cups, and tables or beds. Now, pots and cups are not necessarily dipped when they are washed. Nay, the Pharisees washed the outsides of them only. And as for tables or beds, none will suppose they could be dipped. Here, then, the word baptism, in its natural sense, is not taken for dipping, but for washing or cleansing. And, that this is the true meaning of the word baptize, is testified by the greatest scholars and most proper judges in this matter. It is true, we read of being "buried with Christ in baptism." But nothing can be inferred from such a figurative expression. Nay, if it held exactly, it would make as much for sprinkling as for plunging; since, in burying, the body is not plunged through the substance of the earth, but rather earth is poured or sprinkled upon it.

5. And as there is no clear proof of dipping in Scripture, so there is very probable proof of the contrary. It is highly probable,

the Apostles themselves baptized great numbers, not by dipping, but by washing, sprinkling, or pouring water. This clearly represented the cleansing from sin, which is figured by baptism. And the quantity of water used was not material; no more than the quantity of bread and wine in the Lord's supper. The jailer "and all his house were baptized" in the prison; Cornelius with his friends, (and so several households,) at home. Now, is it likely, that all these had ponds or rivers, in or near their houses, sufficient to plunge them all? Every unprejudiced person must allow, the contrary is far more probable. Again: Three thousand at one time, and five thousand at another, were converted and baptized by St. Peter at Jerusalem; where they had none but the gentle waters of Siloam, according to the observation of Mr. Fuller: "There were no water-mills in Jerusalem, because there was no stream large enough to drive them." The place, therefore, as well as the number, makes it highly probable that all these were baptized by sprinkling or pouring, and not by immersion. To sum up all, the manner of baptizing (whether by dipping or sprinkling) is not determined in Scripture. There is no command for one rather than the other. There is no example from which we can conclude for dipping rather than sprinkling. There are probable examples of both; and both are equally contained in the natural meaning of the word.

II.

1. What are the benefits we receive by baptism, is the next point to be considered. And the first of these is, the washing away the guilt of original sin, by the application of the merits of Christ's death. That we are all born under the guilt of Adam's sin, and that all sin deserves eternal misery, was the unanimous sense of the ancient Church, as it is expressed in the Ninth Article of our own. And the Scripture plainly asserts, that we were "shapen in iniquity, and in sin did our mother conceive us;" that "we were all by nature children of wrath, and dead in trespasses and sins;" that "in Adam all die;" that "by one man's disobedience all were made sinners;" that "by one man sin entered into the world, and death by sin; which came upon all men, because all had sinned." This plainly includes infants; for they too die; therefore they have sinned: But not by actual sin; therefore, by original; else what need have they of the death of Christ? Yea, "death reigned from Adam to Moses, even over those who had not sinned" actually

"according to the similitude of Adam's transgression." This, which can relate to infants only, is a clear proof that the whole race of mankind are obnoxious both to the guilt and punishment of Adam's transgression. But "as by the offense of one, judgment came upon all men to condemnation; so by the righteousness of one, the free gift came upon all men, to justification of life." And the virtue of this free gift, the merits of Christ's life and death, are applied to us in baptism. "He gave himself for the Church, that he might sanctify and cleanse it with the washing of water by the word;" (Ephesians 5:25, 26;) namely, in baptism, the ordinary instrument of our justification. Agreeably to this, our Church prays in the baptismal office, that the person to be baptized may be "washed and sanctified by the Holy Ghost, and, being delivered from God's wrath, receive remission of sins, and enjoy the everlasting benediction of his heavenly washing;" and declares in the Rubric at the end of the office, "It is certain, by God's word, that children who are baptized, dying before they commit actual sin are saved." And this is agreeable to the unanimous judgment of all the ancient Fathers.

2. By baptism we enter into covenant with God; into that everlasting covenant, which he hath commanded forever; (Psalm 111:9;) that new covenant, which he promised to make with the spiritual Israel; even to "give them a new heart and a new spirit, to sprinkle clean water upon them," (of which the baptismal is only a figure,) "and to remember their sins and iniquities no more;" in a word, to be their God, as he promised to Abraham, in the evangelical covenant which he made with him and all his spiritual offspring. (Genesis 17:7, 8) And as circumcision was then the way of entering into this covenant, so baptism is now; which is therefore styled by the Apostle, (so many good interpreters render his words,) "the stipulation, contract, or covenant of a good conscience with God."

3. By baptism we are admitted into the Church, and consequently made members of Christ, its Head. The Jews were admitted into the Church by circumcision, so are the Christians by baptism. For "as many as are baptized into Christ," in his name, "have" thereby "put on Christ;" (Galatians 3:27;) that is, are mystically united to Christ, and made one with him. For "by one Spirit we are all baptized into one body," (1 Corinthians 12:13,)

namely, the Church, "the body of Christ." (Ephesians 4:12) From which spiritual, vital union with him, proceeds the influence of his grace on those that are baptized; as from our union with the Church, a share in all its privileges, and in all the promises Christ has made to it.

4. By baptism, we who were "by nature children of wrath" are made the children of God. And this regeneration which our Church in so many places ascribes to baptism is more than barely being admitted into the Church, though commonly connected therewith; being "grafted into the body of Christ's Church, we are made the children of God by adoption and grace." This is grounded on the plain words of our Lord: "Except a man be born again of water and of the Spirit, he cannot enter into the kingdom of God." (John 3:5) By water then, as a means, the water of baptism, we are regenerated or born again; whence it is also called by the Apostle, "the washing of regeneration." Our Church therefore ascribes no greater virtue to baptism than Christ himself has done. Nor does she ascribe it to the outward washing, but to the inward grace, which, added thereto, makes it a sacrament. Herein a principle of grace is infused, which will not be wholly taken away, unless we quench the Holy Spirit of God by long-continued wickedness.

5. In consequence of our being made children of God, we are heirs of the kingdom of heaven. "If children," (as the Apostle observes,) "then heirs, heirs of God, and joint-heirs with Christ." Herein we receive a title to, and an earnest of, "a kingdom which cannot be moved." Baptism doth now save us, if we live answerable thereto; if we repent, believe, and obey the gospel: Supposing this, as it admits us into the Church here, so into glory hereafter.

III.

1. But did our Savior design this should remain always in his Church? This is the Third thing we are to consider. And this may be dispatched in a few words, since there can be no reasonable doubt, but it was intended to last as long as the Church into which it is the appointed means of entering. In the ordinary way, there is no other means of entering into the Church or into heaven.

2. In all ages, the outward baptism is a means of the inward; as outward circumcision was of the circumcision of the heart. Nor would it have availed a Jew to say, "I have the inward

circumcision and therefore do not need the outward too:" That soul was to be cut off from his people. He had despised, he had broken, God's everlasting covenant, by despising the seal of it. (Genesis 17:14) Now, the seal of circumcision was to last among the Jews as long as the law lasted, to which it obliged them. By plain parity of reason, baptism, which came in its room, must last among Christians as long as the gospel covenant into which it admits, and whereunto it obliges, all nations.

3. This appears also from the original commission which our Lord gave to his Apostles: "Go, disciple all nations, baptizing them in the name of the Father, of the Son, and of the Holy Ghost; teaching them. And lo! I am with you always, even unto the end of the world." Now, as long as this commission lasted, as long as Christ promised to be with them in the execution of it, so long doubtless were they to execute it, and to baptize as well as to teach. But Christ hath promised to be with them, that is, by his Spirit, in their successors, to the end of the world. So long, therefore, without dispute, it was his design that baptism should remain in his Church.

IV.

1. But the grand question is, Who are the proper subjects of baptism? grown persons only, or infants also? In order to answer this fully, I shall, First, lay down the grounds of infant baptism, taken from Scripture, reason, and primitive, universal practice; and, Secondly, answer the objections against it.

2. As to the grounds of it: If infants are guilty of original sin, then they are proper subjects of baptism; seeing, in the ordinary way, they cannot be saved, unless this be washed away by baptism. It has been already proved, that this original stain cleaves to every child of man; and that hereby they are children of wrath, and liable to eternal damnation. It is true, the Second Adam has found a remedy for the disease which came upon all by the offense of the first. But the benefit of this is to be received through the means which he hath appointed; through baptism in particular, which is the ordinary means he hath appointed for that purpose; and to which God hath tied us, though he may not have tied himself. Indeed, where it cannot be had, the case is different, but extraordinary cases do not make void a standing

rule. This therefore is our First ground. Infants need to be washed from original sin; therefore they are proper subjects of baptism.

3. Secondly. If infants are capable of making a covenant, and were and still are under the evangelical covenant, then they have a right to baptism, which is the entering seal thereof. But infants are capable of making a covenant, and were and still are under the evangelical covenant. The custom of nations and common reason of mankind prove that infants may enter into a covenant, and may be obliged by compacts made by others in their name, and receive advantage by them. But we have stronger proof than this, even God's own word: "Ye stand this day all of you before the Lord,—your captains, with all the men of Israel; your little ones, your wives and the stranger,—that thou shouldest enter into covenant with the Lord thy God." (Deuteronomy 29:10-12) Now, God would never have made a covenant with little ones, if they had not been capable of it. It is not said children only, but little children, the Hebrew word properly signifying infants. And these may be still, as they were of old, obliged to perform, in after time, what they are not capable of performing at the time of their entering into that obligation.

4. The infants of believers, the true children of faithful Abraham, always were under the gospel covenant. They were included in it, they had a right to it and to the seal of it; as an infant heir has a right to his estate, though he cannot yet have actual possession. The covenant with Abraham was a gospel covenant; the condition the same, namely, faith, which the Apostle observes was "imputed unto him for righteousness." The inseparable fruit of this faith was obedience; for by faith he left his country, and offered his son. The benefits were the same; for God promised "I will be thy God, and the God of thy seed after thee:" And he can promise no more to any creature; for this includes all blessings, temporal and eternal. The Mediator is the same; for it was in his Seed, that is, in Christ, (Genesis 22:18; Galatians 3:16,) that all nations were to be blessed; on which very account the Apostle says, "The gospel was preached unto Abraham." (Galatians 3:8) Now, the same promise that was made to him, the same covenant that was made with him, was made "with his children after him." (Genesis 17:7; Galatians 3:7) And upon that account it is called "an everlasting covenant." In this covenant children were also

obliged to what they knew not, to the same faith and obedience with Abraham. And so they are still; as they are still equally entitled to all the benefits and promises of it.

5. Circumcision was then the seal of the covenant; which is itself therefore figuratively termed the covenant. (Acts 7:8) Hereby the children of those who professed the true religion were then admitted into it, and obliged to the conditions of it; and when the law was added, to the observance of that also. And when the old seal of circumcision was taken off, this of baptism was added in its room; our Lord appointing one positive institution to succeed another. A new seal was set to Abraham's covenant; the seals differed, but the deed was the same; only that part was struck off which was political or ceremonial. That baptism came in the room of circumcision, appears as well from the clear reason of the thing, as from the Apostle's argument, where, after circumcision, he mentions baptism, as that wherein God had "forgiven us our trespasses;" to which he adds, the "blotting out the hand-writing of ordinances," plainly relating to circumcision and other Jewish rites; which as fairly implies, that baptism came in the room of circumcision, as our Savior's styling the other sacrament the passover, (Colossians 2:11-13; Luke 22:15,) shows that it was instituted in the place of it. Nor is it any proof that baptism did not succeed circumcision, because it differs in some circumstances, any more than it proves the Lord's supper did not succeed the passover, because in several circumstances it differs from it. This then is a Second ground. Infants are capable of entering into covenant with God. As they always were, so they still are, under the evangelical covenant. Therefore they have a right to baptism, which is now the entering seal thereof.

6. Thirdly. If infants ought to come to Christ, if they are capable of admission into the Church of God, and consequently of solemn sacramental dedication to him, then they are proper subjects of baptism. But infants are capable of coming to Christ, of admission into the Church, and solemn dedication to God. That infants ought to come to Christ, appears from his own words: "They brought little children to Christ, and the disciples rebuked them. And Jesus said, Suffer little children to come unto me, and forbid them not; for of such is the kingdom of heaven." (Matthew 19:13, 14) St. Luke expresses it still more strongly: "They brought

unto him even infants, that he might touch them." (18:15) These children were so little that they were brought to him; yet he says, "Suffer them to come unto me:" So little, that he "took them up in his arms;" yet he rebukes those who would have hindered their coming to him. And his command respected the future as well as the present. Therefore his disciples or Ministers are still to suffer infants to come, that is, to be brought, unto Christ. But they cannot now come to him, unless by being brought into the Church; which cannot be but by baptism. Yea, and "of such," says our Lord, "is the kingdom of heaven;" not of such only as were like these infants. For if they themselves were not fit to be subjects of that kingdom, how could others be so, because they were like them? Infants, therefore, are capable of being admitted into the Church, and have a right thereto. Even under the Old Testament they were admitted into it by circumcision. And can we suppose they are in a worse condition under the gospel, than they were under the law? and that our Lord would take away any privileges which they then enjoyed? Would he not rather make additions to them? This, then, is a Third ground. Infants ought to come to Christ, and no man ought to forbid them. They are capable of admission into the Church of God. Therefore, they are proper subjects of baptism.

7. Fourthly. If the Apostles baptized infants, then are they proper subjects of baptism. But the Apostles baptized infants, as is plain from the following consideration: The Jews constantly baptized as well as circumcised all infant proselytes. Our Lord, therefore, commanding his Apostles to proselyte or disciple all nations by baptizing them, and not forbidding them to receive infants as well as others, they must needs baptize children also. That the Jews admitted proselytes by baptism as well as by circumcision, even whole families together, parents and children, we have the unanimous testimony of their most ancient, learned, and authentic writers. The males they received by baptism and circumcision; the women by baptism only. Consequently, the Apostles, unless our Lord had expressly forbidden it, would of course do the same thing. Indeed, the consequence would hold from circumcision only. For if it was the custom of the Jews, when they gathered proselytes out of all nations, to admit children into the Church by circumcision, though they could not actually believe the law, or

obey it; then the Apostles, making proselytes to Christianity by baptism, could never think of excluding children, whom the Jews always admitted, (the reason for their admission being the same,) unless our Lord had expressly forbidden it. It follows, the Apostles baptized infants. Therefore, they are proper subjects of baptism.

8. If it be objected, "There is no express mention in Scripture of any infants whom the Apostles baptized," I would ask, Suppose no mention had been made in the Acts of those two women baptized by the Apostles, yet might we not fairly conclude, that when so many thousands, so many entire households, were baptized, women were not excluded? especially since it was the known custom of the Jews to baptize them? The same holds of children; nay, more strongly, on the account of circumcision. Three thousand were baptized by the Apostles in one day, and five thousand in another. And can it be reasonably supposed that there were no children among such vast numbers? Again: The Apostles baptized many families; nay, we hardly read of one master of a family, who was converted and baptized, but his whole family (as was before the custom among the Jews) were baptized with him: Thus the "jailer's household, he and all his; the household of Gaius, of Stephanas, of Crispus." And can we suppose, that in all these households, which, we read, were, without exception, baptized, there should not be so much as one child or infant? But to go one step further: St. Peter says to the multitude, "Repent and be baptized, every one of you, for the remission of sins. For the promise is to you, and to your children." (Acts 2:38, 39) Indeed, the answer is made directly to those who asked, "What shall we do?" But it reaches farther than to those who asked the question. And though children could not actually repent, yet they might be baptized. And that they are included, appears, (1.) Because the Apostle addresses to "every one" of them, and in "every one" children must be contained. (2.) They are expressly mentioned: "The promise is to you, and to your children."

9. Lastly. If to baptize infants has been the general practice of the Christian Church in all places and in all ages, then this must have been the practice of the Apostles, and, consequently, the mind of Christ. But to baptize infants has been the general practice of the Christian Church, in all places and in all ages. Of this we have unexceptionable witnesses: St. Austin for the Latin Church,

who flourished before the year 400; and Origen for the Greek, born in the second century; both declaring, not only that the whole Church of Christ did then baptize infants, but likewise that they received this practice from the Apostles themselves. (August. de Genesi, 1. 10, c. 23; Orig. in Rom. vi.) St. Cyprian likewise is express for it, and a whole Council with him. (Epist. ad Fidum.) If need were, we might cite likewise Athanasius, Chrysostom, and a cloud of witnesses. Nor is there one instance to be found in all antiquity, of any orthodox Christian who denied baptism to children when brought to be baptized; nor any one of the Fathers, or ancient writers, for the first eight hundred years at least, who held it unlawful. And that it has been the practice of all regular Churches ever since, is clear and manifest. Not only our own ancestors when first converted to Christianity, not only all the European Churches, but the African too and the Asiatic, even those of St. Thomas in the Indies, do, and ever did, baptize their children. The fact being thus cleared, that infant baptism has been the general practice of the Christian Church in all places and in all ages, that it has continued without interruption in the Church of God for above seventeen hundred years, we may safely conclude, it was handed down from the Apostles, who best knew the mind of Christ.

10. To sum up the evidence: If outward baptism be generally, in an ordinary way, necessary to salvation, and infants may be saved as well as adults, nor ought we to neglect any means of saving them; if our Lord commands such to come, to be brought unto him, and declares, "Of such is the kingdom of heaven;" if infants are capable of making a covenant, or having a covenant made for them by others, being included in Abraham's covenant, (which was a covenant of faith, an evangelical covenant,) and never excluded by Christ; if they have a right to be members of the Church, and were accordingly members of the Jewish; if, suppose our Lord had designed to exclude them from baptism, he must have expressly forbidden his Apostles to baptize them, (which none dares to affirm he did,) since otherwise they would do it of course, according to the universal practice of their nation; if it is highly probable they did so, even from the letter of Scripture, because they frequently baptized whole households, and it would be strange if there were no children among them; if the whole Church of Christ, for seventeen hundred years together,

baptized infants, and were never opposed till the last century but one, by some not very holy men in Germany; lastly, if there are such inestimable benefits conferred in baptism, the washing away the guilt of original sin, the engrafting us into Christ, by making us members of his Church, and thereby giving us a right to all the blessings of the gospel; it follows, that infants may, yea, ought to be baptized, and that none ought to hinder them. I am, in the Last place, to answer those objections which are commonly brought against infant baptism:—

V.

1. The chief of these is: "Our Lord said to his Apostles, 'Go and teach all nations, baptizing them in the name of the Father, the Son, and the Holy Ghost.' (Matthew 28:19) Here Christ himself put teaching before baptizing. Therefore, infants, being incapable of being taught, are incapable of being baptized." I answer, (1.) The order of words in Scripture is no certain rule for the order of things. We read in St. Mark 1:4: "John baptized in the wilderness, and preached the baptism of repentance;" and, verse 5, "They were baptized of him in Jordan, confessing their sins." Now, either the order of words in Scripture does not always imply the same order of things; or it follows, that John baptized before his hearers either confessed or repented. But, (2.) The words are manifestly mistranslated. For if we read, "Go and teach all nations, baptizing them,—teaching them to observe all things," it makes plain tautology, vain and senseless repetition. It ought to be translated, (which is the literal meaning of the words,) "Go and make disciples of all nations, by baptizing them." That infants are capable of being made proselytes or disciples has been already proved; therefore this text, rightly translated, is no valid objection against infant baptism.

2. Their next objection is: "The Scripture says, 'Repent and be baptized; believe and be baptized.' Therefore, repentance and faith ought to go before baptism. But infants are incapable of these; therefore they are incapable of baptism." I answer: Repentance and faith were to go before circumcision, as well as before baptism. Therefore, if this argument held, it would prove just as well, that infants were incapable of circumcision. But we know God himself determined the contrary, commanding them to be circumcised at eight days old. Now, if infants were capable

of being circumcised, notwithstanding that repentance and faith were to go before circumcision in grown persons, they are just as capable of being baptized; notwithstanding that repentance and faith are, in grown persons, to go before baptism. This objection, therefore, is of no force; for it is as strong against circumcision of infants as infant baptism.

3. It is objected, Thirdly, "There is no command for it in Scripture. Now, God was angry with his own people, because they did that which, he said, 'I commanded them not.' (Jeremiah 7:31) One plain text would end all the dispute." I answer, (1.) We have reason to fear it would not. It is as positively commanded in a very plain text of Scripture, that we should "teach and admonish one another with psalms, and hymns, and spiritual songs, singing to the Lord with grace in our hearts," (Ephesians 5:19,) as it is to honor our father and mother: But does this put an end to all dispute? Do not these very persons absolutely refuse to do it, notwithstanding a plain text, an express command? I answer, (2.) They themselves practice what there is neither express command nor clear example for in Scripture. They have no express command for baptizing women. They say, indeed, "Women are implied in 'all nations.'" They are; and so are infants too: But the command is not express for either. And for admitting women to the Lord's supper, they have neither express command nor clear example. Yet they do it continually, without either one or the other. And they are justified therein by the plain reason of the thing. This also justifies us in baptizing infants, though without express command of clear example. If it be said, "But there is a command, 'Let a man,' anqrwpov, 'examine himself, and so let him eat of that bread;' (1 Corinthians 11:28;) the word 'man,' in the original, signifying indifferently either men or women:" I grant it does in other places; but here the word "himself," immediately following, confines it to men only. "But women are implied in it, though not expressed." Certainly; and so are infants in "all nations." "But we have Scripture example for it: For it is said in the Acts, 'The Apostles continued in prayer and supplication with the women.'" True, in prayer and supplication; but it is not said, "in communicating:" nor have we one clear example of it in the Bible. Since, then, they admit women to the communion, without any express command or example, but only by consequence from

CHAPTER 7

> Scripture, they can never show reason why infants should not be admitted to baptism, when there are so many scriptures which by fair consequence show they have a right to it, and are capable of it. As for the texts wherein God reproves his people for doing "what he commanded them not;" that phrase evidently means, what he had forbidden; particularly in that passage of Jeremiah. The whole verse is, "They have built the high places of Tophet, to burn their sons and their daughters in the fire, which I commanded them not." Now, God had expressly forbidden them to do this; and that on pain of death. But surely there is a difference between the Jews offering their sons and daughters to devils, and Christians offering theirs to God. On the whole, therefore, it is not only lawful and innocent, but meet, right, and our bounden duty, in conformity to the uninterrupted practice of the whole Church of Christ from the earliest ages, to consecrate our children to God by baptism, as the Jewish Church were commanded to do by circumcision.

Two Parts: God's Initiative and Human Response

From this sermon, we can see Wesley's belief that there essentially are two parts to a correct biblical understanding and practice of Christian Baptism, *both* of which are required for effectual salvation. This can be illustrated in the following way (fig. 7.1):

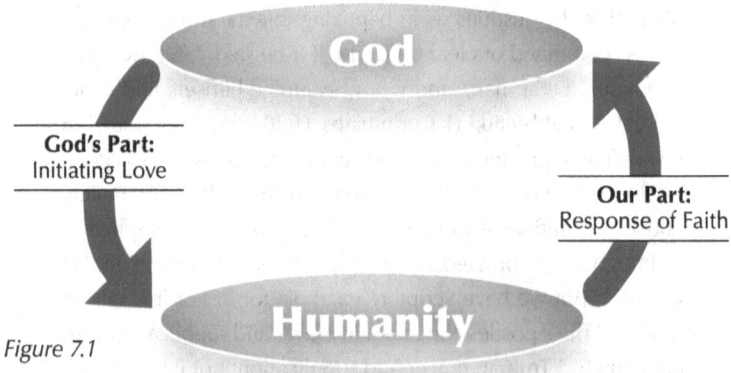

Figure 7.1

First of all, there is **God's part**—the **initiating action of love**. As Wesley explains at the beginning of his sermon, "It is the initiatory sacrament, which enters us into covenant with God."[5] Baptism, for him, is a tangible reminder of how God's prior love for us (i.e., prevenient grace) is specifically meant to *lead us to a personal faith commitment within the community of faith* (i.e., justification, new birth, and sanctification). Consequently, for Wesley, God's part of baptism involves several concepts:

First, baptism is *a sign of adoption*. Through it, we are spiritually adopted into God's family and made part of God's continuing story. As Wesley explains in his sermon above, "By baptism, we who were 'by nature children of wrath' are made the children of God,"[6] and we are made heirs to the kingdom of heaven, whereby "herein we receive a title to, and an earnest of, 'a kingdom which cannot be moved.'"[7] In this sense, then, in baptism we are given a new identity as a part of God's covenant family—spiritually, the old, broken self has passed away, and the new, whole life with God has come.[8] This is precisely why clergy only use a recipient's first and middle name during the practice of baptism—spiritually, one loses one's biological last name and takes on a new last name that is shared by anyone and everyone who has ever been or will be baptized.[9]

One of my favorite ways to talk about the adoptive nature of baptism is through one of the scenes in Walt Disney's original 1995 movie *Toy Story*. If you don't know the movie, it involves toys belonging to a boy named Andy who come to life when humans aren't present. In one memorable scene, the action hero Space Ranger toy named Buzz Lightyear stands in front of his fellow toys, lifts his foot, and notices that "AИDY" has been scribbled on the bottom of his boot. Then, pointing to the boot, he announces to his fellow toys, "It looks as though I've been accepted into your culture. Your chief, Andy, inscribed his name on me." One of the other toys exclaims, "With permanent ink, too!"[10] In many ways, this is a metaphor for God's initiating

---

5 Wesley, § 1, ¶ 1, p. 13.

6 Wesley, § 2, ¶ 4, p. 6.

7 Wesley, § 2, ¶ 5, p. 7.

8 2 Corinthians 5:17.

9 Whether that new name is "member of God's family," "child of God," "Christian," or something else, the wording used is merely a way to designate that those who have been baptized share the same spiritual family and identity.

10 *Toy Story*, directed by John Lasseter, performed by Tom Hanks, Tim Allen, et al., Walt Disney Pictures and Pixar Animation Studios, 1995, film.

work in Christian baptism: in and through it, we are accepted into God's covenant family (i.e., Buzz's "culture"), and God's name is "inscribed" on our hearts—"with permanent ink, too!" (i.e., God's love for us is always present).

However, in addition to being a sign of adoption, baptism is also *a sign of initiation* into a relationship both with God and with our fellow human beings in God's covenant community. In section 2 of the sermon above, speaking of God's covenant with Abraham, Wesley says, "As circumcision was then the way of entering into this covenant, so baptism is now."[11] In this sense, Wesley understood baptism to accomplish for the Christian what circumcision accomplished for those under the original Abrahamic covenant. Yet, baptism initiates us not only into a covenant with God, but also into union with other Christians—into the body of Christ itself, the church. In the same section of Wesley's sermon above, he remarks, "For 'as many as are baptized into Christ,' in his name, 'have' thereby 'put on Christ' . . . that is, are mystically united to Christ and made *one* with him [through] . . . the Church."[12] So, whenever someone is baptized, that individual begins a lifelong process of *living out* his or her Christian life in the context of a community of believers (i.e., "the church").

In addition to being a sign of adoption and initiation, baptism is also *a sign of anointing for ministry*. For Wesley, it was, in essence, the ordination and calling of every Christian to be a minister of Christ in the world. It's a reminder that all Christians have a task and responsibility to enact and share God's love in the world—a reminder (as in the "Cross of Faith" metaphor from chapter 5) that we are called to love not only God, but also our neighbors.

While understanding God's part and role in baptism was essential to Wesley, equally important is his emphasis on **our part**—the **response of faith**. In section 2, paragraph 5 of the sermon above, he wrote, "Baptism doth now save us, *if we live answerable thereto; if we repent, believe, and obey the gospel*."[13] In other words, for the spiritual work of baptism to be truly effectual, Wesley believed that there must be at some point a conscious response by *us*. For him, in fact, this *second* dimension (our response of faith) is the whole purpose and reason for the *first* dimension (God's initiating

---

11 Wesley, *A Treatise on Baptism*, § 2, ¶ 2, p. 6.

12 Wesley, § 2, ¶ 3, p. 6.

13 Wesley, § 2, ¶ 5, p. 7.

love). If in God's part of baptism, God says yes to us by conveying gifts of adoption, initiation, and anointing, then in our part of baptism, we say yes back to God in consciously *accepting* those gifts through faith. If in God's part we are *accepted* by God, in our part we *accept our acceptance*. If in God's part we are *claimed* as part of God's covenant family, in our part we *claim our place* in that family.

One of the ways Wesley's view accomplishes this is by making it clear that the purpose of baptism first and foremost is to convey justifying grace. For example, in speaking of the experience of new birth, in his commentary on Colossians 2:12, he wrote, "If we do not then experience this, our baptism has not answered the end of its institution."[14] In his sermon "The Marks of the New Birth," he asks:

> The question is not, what you was [sic] made in baptism; (do not evade;) but, What are you now? Is the Spirit of adoption now in your heart? To your own heart let the appeal be made. I ask not, whether you was [sic] born of water and of the Spirit; but are you now the temple of the Holy Ghost which dwelleth in you? I allow you was [sic] "circumcised with the circumcision of Christ;" (as St. Paul emphatically terms baptism;) but does the Spirit of Christ and of glory now rest upon you? Else "your circumcision is become uncircumcision."[15]

His point is that the authenticity of one's Christianity cannot be grounded merely in the experience of being baptized. No. If one does not *appropriate* Christ's justifying work through the experience of regeneration/new birth, then one's baptism is—in effect—incomplete. While Baptism is *not* the same thing as this, it is, nevertheless, always a *completion* of it.

In fact, while for Wesley, baptism is primarily Christological—that is, it aims to introduce and initiate people into Christ and his church through justifying grace—it nevertheless implies the presence and work of both prevenient and sanctifying grace as well. For example, in the baptism of those

---

14 Wesley, *John Wesley's Explanatory Notes on the New Testament*, commentary on Colossians 2:12, in Schoenhals, ed., *John Wesley's Commentary on the Bible*, 547 (see chap. 6, n. 7).

15 John Wesley, "The Marks of the New Birth," §4, ¶ 2, in Wesley, *The Works of the Reverend John Wesley, A.M.*, trans. John Emory (New York: T. Mason and G. Lane, 1840), 1:160.

who are not yet ready to take baptismal vows for themselves, such as infants and children, prevenient grace is certainly present in the life of the infant or child as a sign and seal of God's love even before he or she understands what that means. Justifying grace is present in that through baptism, God actually provides a form of regeneration/new birth for infants and children by forgiving and washing them of the actual spiritual dirtiness experienced by living in our broken, fallen world.[16] Sanctifying grace is present in the faith and lives of those of the biological family and the spiritual community of faith who are witnessing the baptism—it becomes for them a type of reaffirmation of baptism for their own lives!

Similarly, in the baptism of those who *are* taking vows for themselves (teens and adults), baptism is still a celebration of the prevenient grace of God that has already worked in their lives to bring them to a faith decision. Justifying grace is present through their justification in God's pardon of the *actual sin* that they've committed. Here again, sanctifying grace is also present as a form of baptismal reaffirmation in the faith and lives of those who are part of the recipient's family and community of faith as they witness the baptism. In this sense, then, while, for Wesley, the focus and motivation of Christian baptism is primarily Christological, all dimensions of his via salutis are present and at work in its practice.

Implications

Given Wesley's twofold understanding and practice of baptism, several important implications may be inferred. First, since God is always faithful to carry out the initiating part of baptism, then **we should not rebaptize**. To do so implies that God didn't "get it right" the first time. God's part of baptism, however, is *always* carried out fully and faithfully. Some will argue, of course, that they didn't understand what they were doing when they were baptized. Yet, is God limited by *our* lack of understanding? Of course not! God can and will work in love even if and when we don't fully understand the meaning of that work—and is it realistic, after all, to expect anyone of any age to fully understand that meaning anyway? Others will argue that they weren't "saved" when they were baptized. Yet, for Wesley, biblical baptism

---

16 For more about this, read generally Wesley, *A Treatise on Baptism*, § 2, ¶ 1, in Bangs, ed., 5–6.

is much more than something we do when we are converted. Additionally, such a statement reduces baptism to being merely a human act that doesn't involve God at all—which is the second misunderstanding shared earlier in this chapter. Instead, baptism is a sign of God's covenant promise of salvation with us, whether we feel or remember our conversion or not. In and through it, God is initiating salvation on our behalf and washing away our original sin *before* we knew that it needed to be washed away!

Still, even if God is always faithful, we humans are not. Therefore, **we Christians can and should renew our baptismal vows** from time to time. Married couples who renew their marriage vows are not getting married again—they are merely renewing *their part* of their marriage covenant. Renewing our baptismal covenants affords Christians the same opportunity—to be reminded of God's faithfulness as a motivation and encouragement for *us* to continue and renew our *own* faithfulness as we grow in sanctification.

> **Renewal of baptismal vows:** opportunities for individuals and entire congregations to use water in ways that can't be interpreted as baptism to reaffirm their faith to remind them of God's faithfulness as a motivation and encouragement to continue in their own faithfulness.

This was, in fact, the purpose and rationale behind early Methodism's various services of faith renewal that we learned about in chapter 6 (such as Wesley's "covenant services," watch night services, and the quarterly Methodist "love feast"). In that same spirit, our *United Methodist Hymnal* today contains several rituals by which both individuals and entire congregations can be reaffirmed in their baptismal faith,[17] using water in ways that can't be interpreted as baptism to remind recipients either of their own vows of faith, or of those made for them at their earlier baptism.

Baptism of Infants and Children

One vital implication to Wesley's understanding of the meaning and practice of baptism is his insistence that **infants and children** are biblically

---

17 *The United Methodist Hymnal*, 37 (for reaffirmation of an individual), 50-53 (for reaffirmation of an entire congregation).

proper recipients. Most of sections 4–5 in his sermon above are devoted to arguing this point. As stated earlier in this chapter, the essence of it is his belief—based on his interpretation of Colossians 2:11-12—that in Christian baptism, recipients (including infants and children) are initiated into God's covenant family in the same way that circumcision signaled the initiation of male infants and children into that same family under the covenant of Abraham. As he says in the very first paragraph of his sermon above, "[Baptism] was instituted in the room of circumcision. For, as that was a sign and seal of God's covenant, so is this."[18] The sermon then goes on to point out scriptures such as Acts 16:33 and 1 Corinthians 1:14-16, where the apostles baptized whole households, which certainly included infants and children.[19] For Wesley, then, baptism of infants and children is, at the very least, a sign of prevenient grace—of the fact that before a child is even aware of it, God loves that child and is willing and able to wash away his or her original sin. Like circumcision, baptism gives us an identity—it tells us *who* we are and *whose* we are, even (as in this case) before we understand or can articulate what any of that means.

> **Baptism of infants and children:** practiced as a sign of God's prevenient grace, the fact that God loves an infant or child and washes away that young one's original sin even before he or she is aware of it. Based on Colossians 2:11-12, where Paul implies that baptism is the Christian equivalent of male circumcision, as both initiate a recipient into God's covenant family. Also based on Acts 16:33 and 1 Corinthians 1:14-16, where whole households (which certainly included infants and children) were baptized.

Wesley makes it clear, however, that it is the responsibility of parents and sponsors in the church to ensure that children grow into and eventually claim their identity in the faith. In addition to the usual text of the sermon above, one version of the sermon manuscript contains the following addition from Wesley at its conclusion:

---

18   Wesley, *A Treatise on Baptism*, § 1, ¶ 1 in Bangs, ed., 3.

19   Read especially Wesley, § 4, ¶ 8, pp., 11–12.

THE SACRAMENTS

> In the ancient Church, when baptism was administered, there were usually two or more sponsors . . . for every person to be baptized. As these were witnesses, before God and the Church, of the solemn engagement those persons then entered into, so they undertook . . . to watch over those souls in a peculiar manner, to instruct, admonish, exhort and build them up in "the faith once for all delivered to the saints" (Jude 3). These were considered as a kind of spiritual parents to the baptized, whether they were infants or at man's estate.[20]

In other words, one role that the church plays in the life of a baptism recipient (especially an infant or child) is to help that recipient experience new birth for himself or herself. One implication of this today is that care should be taken *not* necessarily to baptize *every* infant brought to clergy for baptism, but only to baptize those whose spiritual support system (parents, family, and/or faith community) is strong enough to indicate that there is a good likelihood they will experience God's justifying grace for themselves at some point when they are older.

Modes of Baptism

Before completing our discussion of this sacrament, let me briefly highlight the **three modes of baptism** Wesley believed were found in scripture, and which he identifies in section 1, paragraphs 2-5 in his sermon above. First, there is *sprinkling*. Based on scriptures such as Ezekiel 36:25, Acts 9:17-19, and Hebrews 10:22, this method commonly symbolizes the washing away of original and (in the case of teens and adults) actual sin. Just as taking a physical shower washes one of physical dirtiness, so sprinkling reminds us that in baptism, we are washed of our spiritual dirtiness. This method was commonly used in the Church of England in Wesley's day, and is still perhaps the most popular method of baptism in Wesleyan communities of faith today.

A second method of baptism is *pouring* (which in his sermon Wesley sometimes calls "washing"). Based on scriptures such as Joel 2:28, Acts 2:4, and Titus 3:5-6, it symbolizes the pouring of God's Holy Spirit into the life of the recipient during baptism. Just as one might place his or her mouth

---

20 Addition to *A Treatise on Baptism,* taken from Wesley's *Serious Thoughts on Godfathers and Godmothers,* in Outler, ed., *John Wesley,* 331–32 (see chap. 7, n. 1).

under a running faucet to get a drink of water, so pouring reminds us that in baptism, our lives are placed under God's authority so that we might receive the Holy Spirit's empowering work. This method was also commonly used by the Anglican Church of Wesley's day, and is still used in many churches in the Wesleyan tradition today.

Finally, a third mode of baptism is *immersion* (sometimes called "dunking" today, and which in his sermon Wesley usually terms "dipping"). Based on scriptures such as Romans 6:2-11, it symbolizes death and resurrection—our dying to sin and being raised to a new life in Christ Jesus. Just as diving into and out of a pool on a hot, summer day brings refreshment and renewal to our physical bodies, so immersion reminds us that in baptism, God renews and gives new life to our spiritual bodies (i.e., our souls).

For Wesley, none of these modes of baptism was more "biblical" or of more value than the others. In the second paragraph of his sermon above, Wesley insists that "it is not determined in Scripture in which of these ways [baptism] shall be done, neither by any express precept, nor by any such example as clearly proves it; nor by the force or meaning of the word 'baptize.'"[21] Again, a mere three paragraphs later, he says that "the quantity of water used [in baptism] was not material; no more than the quantity of bread and wine in the Lord's supper."[22] Instead, just as "cleansing of sin," "receiving of the Holy Spirit," and "death and resurrection" are each equally important biblical themes, so sprinkling, pouring, and immersion are each equally valid modes of Christian baptism.

The Lord's Supper

If Christian baptism was instituted by Christ's example to be God's *initiating* sacrament of grace, then **the Lord's Supper** (also called **Holy Communion**, or the **Eucharist**) was instituted by Christ's words to be God's *continual* sacrament of grace. Wesley called this "the grand channel whereby the grace of [God's] Spirit [is] conveyed to the souls of all the children of God,"[23] and believed it to be the most powerful of all the means of grace

---

21 Wesley, *A Treatise on Baptism*, § 1, ¶ 2, in Bangs, ed., 3.

22 Wesley, 4–5.

23 John Wesley, "Upon Our Lord's Sermon on the Mount VI" (Sermon 26), § 3, ¶ 11, in Outler, ed., *The Bicentennial Edition of the Works of John Wesley*, 1:585.

available to Christians. Albert Outler explains that for Wesley, "the Lord's Supper is the paradigm of *all* 'the means of grace'—the chief actual means of actual grace and, as such, literally indispensable in the Christian life."[24]

Of course, as noted at the beginning of this chapter, since Wesley's Methodism was understood to be a renewal movement within the Anglican Church, devoted to preaching and teaching, the Lord's Supper was not generally included in early Methodist worship services. Instead, Wesley encouraged his Methodists to commune at their local Anglican parish whenever it was served. Wesley himself averaged communing once every four to five days, or at least once per week. To most Anglicans of the day, this seemed obsessive, as the Church of England required members to commune only three times per year.[25] Nevertheless, he wrote that "it is the duty of every Christian to receive the Lord's Supper as often as he can,"[26] and to partake "at every opportunity."[27] Early Methodists, in fact, caught hold of Wesley's understanding of this sacrament and flooded the local Anglican churches whenever it was served.

So, what was it about Wesley's understanding of its nature and practice that made the Lord's Supper so special? In 1787, he published a sermon titled "The Duty of Constant Communion"; it represented the culmination of a series of writings about this topic over the course of his ministry. In it, we find glimpses of his mature articulation of the nature, purpose, and practice of this sacrament.

The Duty of Constant Communion[28]
by John Wesley

The following discourse was written above five-and-fifty years ago, for the use of my pupils at Oxford. I have added very little, but retrenched much; as I then used more words than I

---

24 Outler, ed., *John Wesley*, 333; emphasis in original.

25 Wesley mentions this requirement in his sermon 101, "The Duty of Constant Communion," at § 2, ¶ 20, in Outler, ed., *The Bicentennial Edition of the Works of John Wesley*, 3:438.

26 Wesley, § 1, introduction, in Outler, 3:428.

27 Wesley, 3:439.

28 Wesley, 3:428–39.

do now. But, I thank God, I have not yet seen cause to alter my sentiments in any point which is therein delivered. J.W. 1788. "Do this in remembrance of me." Luke 22:19.

It is no wonder that men who have no fear of God should never think of doing this. But it is strange that it should be neglected by any that do fear God, and desire to save their souls; And yet nothing is more common. One reason why many neglect it is, they are so much afraid of "eating and drinking unworthily," that they never think how much greater the danger is when they do not eat or drink it at all. That I may do what I can to bring these well-meaning men to a more just way of thinking, I shall,

I. show that it is the duty of every Christian to receive the Lord's Supper as often as he can; and,

II. Answer some objections.

I.

I am to show that it is the duty of every Christian to receive the Lord's Supper as often as he can.

1. The First reason why it is the duty of every Christian so to do is, because it is a plain command of Christ. That this is his command, appears from the words of the text, "Do this in remembrance of me:" By which, as the Apostles were obliged to bless, break, and give the bread to all that joined with them in holy things; so were all Christians obliged to receive those signs of Christ's body and blood. Here, therefore, the bread and wine are commanded to be received, in remembrance of his death, to the end of the world. Observe, too, that this command was given by our Lord when he was just laying down his life for our sakes. They are, therefore, as it were, his dying words to all his followers.

2. A Second reason why every Christian should do this as often as he can, is, because the benefits of doing it are so great to all that do it in obedience to him; viz., the forgiveness of our past sins and the present strengthening and refreshing of our souls. In this world we are never free from temptations. Whatever way of life we are in, whatever our condition be, whether we are sick or well, in trouble or at ease, the enemies of our souls are watching to lead us into sin. And too often they prevail over us. Now, when we are convinced of having sinned against God, what surer way

have we of procuring pardon from him, than the "showing forth the Lord's death;" and beseeching him, for the sake of his Son's sufferings, to blot out all our sins

3. The grace of God given herein confirms to us the pardon of our sins, by enabling us to leave them. As our bodies are strengthened by bread and wine, so are our souls by these tokens of the body and blood of Christ. This is the food of our souls: This gives strength to perform our duty, and leads us on to perfection. If, therefore, we have any regard for the plain command of Christ, if we desire the pardon of our sins, if we wish for strength to believe, to love and obey God, then we should neglect no opportunity of receiving the Lord's Supper; then we must never turn our backs on the feast which our Lord has prepared for us. We must neglect no occasion which the good providence of God affords us for this purpose. This is the true rule: So often are we to receive as God gives us opportunity. Whoever, therefore, does not receive, but goes from the holy table, when all things are prepared, either does not understand his duty, or does not care for the dying command of his Saviour, the forgiveness of his sins, the strengthening of his soul, and the refreshing it with the hope of glory.

4. Let every one, therefore, who has either any desire to please God, or any love of his own soul, obey God, and consult the good of his own soul, by communicating every time he can; like the first Christians, with whom the Christian sacrifice was a constant part of the Lord's day service. And for several centuries they received it almost every day: Four times a week always, and every saint's day beside. Accordingly, those that joined in the prayers of the faithful never failed to partake of the blessed sacrament. What opinion they had of any who turned his back upon it, we may learn from that ancient canon: "If any believer join in the prayers of the faithful, and go away without receiving the Lord's Supper, let him be excommunicated, as bringing confusion into the church of God."

5. In order to understand the nature of the Lord's Supper, it would be useful carefully to read over those passages in the Gospel, and in the first Epistle to the Corinthians [1 Cor. 11], which speak of the institution of it. Hence we learn that the design of this sacrament is, the continual remembrance of the death of Christ,

by eating bread and drinking wine, which are the outward signs of the inward grace, the body and blood of Christ.

6. It is highly expedient for those who purpose to receive this, whenever their time will permit, to prepare themselves for this solemn ordinance by self-examination and prayer. But this is not absolutely necessary. And when we have not time for it, we should see that we have the habitual preparation which is absolutely necessary, and can never be dispensed with on any account or any occasion whatever. This is, First, a full purpose of heart to keep all the commandments of God; and, Secondly, a sincere desire to receive all his promises.

II.

I am, in the Second place, to answer the common objections against constantly receiving the Lord's Supper.

1. I say constantly receiving; for as to the phrase of frequent communion, it is absurd to the last degree. If it means anything less than constant, it means more than can be proved to be the duty of any man. For if we are not obliged to communicate constantly, by what argument can it be proved that we are obliged to communicate frequently yea, more than once a year, or once in seven years, or once before we die? Every argument brought for this, either proves that we ought to do it constantly, or proves nothing at all. Therefore, that indeterminate, unmeaning way of speaking ought to be laid aside by all men of understanding.

2. In order to prove that it is our duty to communicate constantly, we may observe that the holy communion is to be considered either, (1.) As a command of God, or, (2.) As a mercy to man.

First. As a command of God. God our Mediator and Governor, from whom we have received our life and all things, on whose will it depends whether we shall be perfectly happy or perfectly miserable from this moment to eternity, declares to us that all who obey his commands shall be eternally happy; all who not, shall be eternally miserable. Now, one of these commands is, "Do this in remembrance of me." I ask then, "Why do you not do this, when you can do it if you will? When you have an opportunity before you, why do not you obey the command of God?"

3. Perhaps you will say, "God does not command me to do this as often as I can:" That is, the words "as often as you can," are not added in this particular place. What then? Are we not

to obey every command of God as often as we can? Are not all the promises of God made to those, and those only, who "give all diligence;" that is, to those who do all they can to obey his commandments? Our power is the one rule of our duty. Whatever we can do, that we ought. With respect either to this or any other command, he that, when he may obey it if he will, does not, will have no place in the kingdom of heaven.

4. And this great truth, that we are obliged to keep every command as far as we can, is clearly proved from the absurdity of the contrary opinion; for were we to allow that we are not obliged to obey every commandment of God as often as we can, we have no argument left to prove that any man is bound to obey any command at any time. For instance: Should I ask a man why he does not obey one of the plainest commands of God, why, for instance, he does not help his parents, he might answer, "I will not do it now, but I will at another time." When that time comes, put him in mind of God's command again; and he will say, "I will obey it some time or other." Nor is it possible ever to prove that he ought to do it now, unless by proving that he ought to do it as often as he can; and therefore he ought to do it now, because he can if he will.

5. Consider the Lord's Supper, Secondly, as a mercy from God to man. As God, whose mercy is over all his works, and particularly over the children of men, knew there was but one way for man to be happy like himself; namely, by being like him in holiness; as he knew we could do nothing toward this of ourselves, he has given us certain means of obtaining his help. One of these is the Lord's Supper, which, of his infinite mercy, he hath given for this very end; that through this means we may be assisted to attain those blessings which he hath prepared for us; that we may obtain holiness on earth, and everlasting glory in heaven.

I ask, then, Why do you not accept of his mercy as often as ever you can? God now offers you his blessing;—why do you refuse it? You have now an opportunity of receiving his mercy;—why do you not receive it? You are weak:—why do not you seize every opportunity of increasing your strength? In a word: Considering this as a command of God, he that does not communicate as often as he can has no piety; considering it as a mercy, he that does not communicate as often as he can has no wisdom.

6. These two considerations will yield a full answer to all the common objections which have been made against constant communion; indeed to all that ever were or can be made. In truth, nothing can be objected against it, but upon supposition that, [at] this particular time, either the communion would be no mercy, or I am not commanded to receive it. Nay, should we grant it would be no mercy, that is not enough; for still the other reason would hold: Whether it does you any good or none, you are to obey the command of God.

7. However, let us see the particular excuses which men commonly make for not obeying it. The most common is, "I am unworthy; and 'he that eateth and drinketh unworthily, eateth and drinketh damnation to himself.' Therefore I dare not communicate, lest I should eat and drink my own damnation."

The case is this: God offers you one of the greatest mercies on this side heaven, and commands you to accept it. Why do not you accept this mercy, in obedience to his command? You say, "I am unworthy to receive it." And what then? You are unworthy to receive any mercy from God. But is that a reason for refusing all mercy? God offers you a pardon for all your sins. You are unworthy of it, it is sure, and he knows it; but since he is pleased to offer it nevertheless, will not you accept of it? He offers to deliver your soul from death: You are unworthy to live; but will you therefore refuse life? He offers to endue your soul with new strength; because you are unworthy of it, will you deny to take it? What can God himself do for us farther, if we refuse his mercy because we are unworthy of it?

8. But suppose this were no mercy to us; (to suppose which is indeed giving God the lie; saying, that is not good for man which he purposely ordered for his good;) still I ask, Why do not you obey God's command? He says, "Do this." Why do you not? You answer, "I am unworthy to do it." What? Unworthy to obey God? Unworthy to do what God bids you do? Unworthy to obey God's command? What do you mean by this? That those who are unworthy to obey God ought not to obey him? Who told you so? If he were even "an angel from heaven, let him be accursed." If you think God himself has told you so by St. Paul, let us hear his words. They are these: "He that eateth and drinketh unworthily, eateth and drinketh damnation to himself."

Why, this is quite another thing. Here is not a word said of being unworthy to eat and drink. Indeed he does speak of eating and drinking unworthily; but that is quite a different thing; so he has told us himself. In this very chapter we are told that by eating and drinking unworthily is meant, taking the holy sacrament in such a rude and disorderly way, that one was "hungry and another drunken." But what is that to you? Is there any danger of your doing so,— of your eating and drinking thus unworthily? However unworthy you are to communicate, there is no fear of your communicating thus. Therefore, whatever the punishment is, of doing it thus unworthily, it does not concern you. You have no more reason from this text to disobey God, than if there was no such text in the Bible. If you speak of "eating and drinking unworthily" in the sense St. Paul uses the words, you may as well say, "I dare not communicate, for fear the church should fall," as "for fear I should eat and drink unworthily."

9. If then you fear bringing damnation on yourself by this, you fear where no fear is. Fear it not for eating and drinking unworthily; for that, in St. Paul's sense, ye cannot do. But I will tell you for what you shall fear damnation;— for not eating and drinking at all; for not obeying your Maker and Redeemer; for disobeying his plain command; for thus setting at nought both his mercy and authority. Fear ye this; for hear what his Apostle saith: "Whosoever shall keep the whole law, and yet offend in one point, is guilty of all." (James 2:10)

10. We see then how weak the objection is, "I dare not receive [the Lord's Supper], because I am unworthy." Nor is it any stronger, though the reason why you think yourself unworthy is, that you have lately fallen into sin. It is true, our Church forbids those "who have done any grievous crime" to receive without repentance. But all that follows from this is, that we should repent before we come; not that we should neglect to come at all.

To say, therefore, that "a man may turn his back upon the altar because he has lately fallen into sin, that he may impose this penance upon himself," is talking without any warrant from Scripture. For where does the Bible teach to atone for breaking one commandment of God by breaking another? What advice is this,—"Commit a new act of disobedience, and God will more easily forgive the past!"

11. Others there are who, to excuse their disobedience, plead that they are unworthy in another sense, that they "cannot live up to it; they cannot pretend to lead so holy a life as constantly communicating would oblige them to do." Put this into plain words. I ask, Why do not you accept the mercy which God commands you to accept? You answer, "Because I cannot live up to the profession I must make when I receive it." Then it is plain you ought never to receive it at all. For it is no more lawful to promise once what you know you cannot perform, than to promise it a thousand times. You know too, that it is one and the same promise, whether you make it every year or every day. You promise to do just as much, whether you promise ever so often or ever so seldom.

If, therefore, you cannot live up to the profession they make who communicate once a week, neither can you come up to the profession you make who communicate once a year. But cannot you, indeed? Then it had been good for you that you had never been born. For all that you profess at the Lord's table, you must both profess and keep, or you cannot be saved. For you profess nothing there but this,—that you will diligently keep his commandments. And cannot you keep up to this profession? Then you cannot enter into life.

12. Think then what you say, before you say you cannot live up to what is required of constant communicants. This is no more than is required of any communicants; yea, of everyone that has a soul to be saved. So that to say, you cannot live up to this, is neither better nor worse than renouncing Christianity. It is, in effect, renouncing your baptism, wherein you solemnly promised to keep all his commandments. You now fly from that profession. You wilfully break one of his commandments, and, to excuse yourself, say, you cannot keep his commandments: Then you cannot expect to receive the promises, which are made only to those that keep them.

13. What has been said on this pretence against constant communion, is applicable to those who say the same thing in other words: "We dare not do it, because it requires so perfect an obedience afterwards as we cannot promise to perform." Nay, it requires neither more nor less perfect obedience than you promised in your baptism. You then undertook to keep the

commandments of God by his help; and you promise no more when you communicate.

14. A Second objection which is often made against constant communion, is, the having so much business as will not allow time for such a preparation as is necessary thereto. I answer: All the preparation that is absolutely necessary is contained in those words: "Repent you truly of your sins past; have faith in Christ our Saviour;" (and observe, that word is not here taken in its highest sense;) "amend your lives, and be in charity with all men; so shall ye be meet partakers of these holy mysteries." All who are thus prepared may draw near without fear, and receive the sacrament to their comfort. Now, what business can hinder you from being thus prepared—from repenting of your past sins, from believing that Christ died to save sinners, from amending your lives, and being in charity with all men? No business can hinder you from this, unless it be such as hinders you from being in a state of salvation. If you resolve and design to follow Christ, you are fit to approach the Lord's table. If you do not design this, you are only fit for the table and company of devils.

15. No business, therefore, can hinder any man from having that preparation which alone is necessary, unless it be such as unprepares him for heaven, as puts him out of a state of salvation. Indeed every prudent man will, when he has time, examine himself before he receives the Lord's Supper; whether he repents him truly of his former sins; whether he believes the promises of God; whether he fully designs to walk in His ways, and be in charity with all men. In this, and in private prayer, he will doubtless spend all the time he conveniently can. But what is this to you who have not time? What excuse is this for not obeying God? He commands you to come, and prepare yourself by prayer, if you have time; if you have not, however, come. Make not reverence to God's command a pretence for breaking it. Do not rebel against him for fear of offending him. Whatever you do or leave undone besides, be sure to do what God bids you do. Examining yourself, and using private prayer, especially before the Lord's Supper, is good; But behold! "to obey is better than" self-examination; "and to hearken," than the prayer of an angel.

16. A Third objection against constant communion is, that

it abates our reverence for the sacrament. Suppose it did; what then? Will you thence conclude that you are not to receive it constantly? This does not follow. God commands you, "Do this." You may do it now, but will not, and, to excuse yourself say, "If I do it so often, it will abate the reverence with which I do it now." Suppose it did; has God ever told you, that when the obeying his command abates your reverence to it, then you may disobey it? If he has, you are guiltless; if not, what you say is just nothing to the purpose. The law is clear. Either show that the lawgiver makes this exception, or you are guilty before him.

17. Reverence for the sacrament may be of two sorts: Either such as is owing purely to the newness of the thing, such as men naturally have for anything they are not used to; or such as is owing to our faith, or to the love or fear of God. Now, the former of these is not properly a religious reverence, but purely natural. And this sort of reverence for the Lord's Supper, the constantly receiving of it must lessen. But it will not lessen the true religious reverence, but rather confirm and increase it.

18. A Fourth objection is, "I have communicated constantly so long, but I have not found the benefit I expected." This has been the case with many well-meaning persons, and therefore deserves to be particularly considered. And consider this: First, whatever God commands us to do, we are to do because he commands, whether we feel any benefit thereby or no. Now, God commands, "Do this in remembrance of me." This, therefore, we are to do because he commands, whether we find present benefit thereby or not. But undoubtedly we shall find benefit sooner or later, though perhaps insensibly. We shall be insensibly strengthened, made more fit for the service of God, and more constant in it. At least, we are kept from falling back, and preserved from many sins and temptations: And surely this should be enough to make us receive this food as often as we can; though we do not presently feel the happy effects of it, as some have done, and we ourselves may when God sees best.

19. But suppose a man has often been at the sacrament, and yet received no benefit. Was it not his own fault? Either he was not rightly prepared, willing to obey all the commands and to receive all the promises of God, or he did not receive it aright, trusting in God. Only see that you are duly prepared for it, and

the oftener you come to the Lord's table, the greater benefit you will find there.

20. A Fifth objection which some have made against constant communion is, that "the Church enjoins it only three times a year." The words of the Church are, "Note, that every parishioner shall communicate at the least three times in the year." To this I answer, First, What if the Church had not enjoined it at all; is it not enough that God enjoins it? We obey the Church only for God's sake. And shall we not obey God himself? If, then, you receive three times a year because the Church commands it, receive every time you can because God commands it. Else your doing the one will be so far from excusing you for not doing the other, that your own practice will prove your folly and sin, and leave you without excuse.

But, Secondly, we cannot conclude from these words, that the Church excuses him who receives only thrice a year. The plain sense of them is, that he who does not receive thrice at least, shall be cast out of the Church: But they by no means excuse him who communicates no oftener. This never was the judgment of our Church: On the contrary, she takes all possible care that the sacrament be duly administered, wherever the Common Prayer is read, every Sunday and holiday in the year.

The Church gives a particular direction with regard to those that are in Holy Orders: "In all cathedral and collegiate Churches and Colleges, where there are many Priests and Deacons, they shall all receive the communion with the Priest, every Sunday at the least."

21. It has been shown, First, that if we consider the Lord's Supper as a command of Christ, no man can have any pretence to Christian piety, who does not receive it (not once a month, but) as often as he can. Secondly, that if we consider the institution of it, as a mercy to ourselves, no man who does not receive it as often as he can has any pretence to Christian prudence. Thirdly, that none of the objections usually made, can be any excuse for that man who does not, at every opportunity obey this command and accept this mercy.

22. It has been particularly shown, First, that unworthiness is no excuse; because though in one sense we are all unworthy, yet none of us need be afraid of being unworthy in St. Paul's

sense, of "eating and drinking unworthily." Secondly, that the not having time enough for preparation can be no excuse; since the only preparation which is absolutely necessary, is that which no business can hinder, nor indeed anything on earth, unless so far as it hinders our being in a state of salvation. Thirdly, that its abating our reverence is no excuse; since he who gave the command, "Do this," nowhere adds, "unless it abates your reverence." Fourthly, that our not profiting by it is no excuse; since it is our own fault, in neglecting that necessary preparation which is in our own power. Lastly, that the judgment of our own Church is quite in favour of constant communion. If those who have hitherto neglected it on any of these pretences, will lay these things to heart, they will, by the grace of God, come to a better mind, and never forsake their own mercies.

Threefold Meaning

In section 1, paragraph 2 of this sermon, Wesley identifies the three major purposes of the Lord's Supper: "[1] the forgiveness of our past sins and [2] the present strengthening and [3] refreshing of our souls."[29] This essential understanding was, in turn, based on the views of Daniel Brevint, dean of Lincoln College, Oxford University, which Wesley abridged and shared to explain his views:

> The Lord's Supper was chiefly ordained for a Sacrament (1) To represent the sufferings of Christ which are past, whereof it is a memorial. (2) To convey the first-fruits of these sufferings in present graces, whereof it is a means; and (3) to assure us of glory to come, whereof it is an infallible pledge.[30]

I will use this general structure to highlight Wesley's threefold description of the meaning of the Lord's Supper.

First, it is a **re-presentation from the past**—a remembrance of the

---

29 Wesley, 3:429, numbering mine. A general overview of Wesley's meaning can be found in the same sermon, § 1, ¶¶ 2–6, pp. 3:429–30.

30 Wesley's extract of Daniel Brevint, *The Christian Sacrament and Sacrifice*, § 2, ¶ 1, in J. Ernest Rattenbury, *The Eucharistic Hymns of John and Charles Wesley* (Akron, OH: OSL Publications, 2006), 158. See generally the background of this foundational understanding in Rattenbury, 12–15.

past suffering and death of Christ. "The design of this sacrament," Wesley says in the above sermon, "is, the continual remembrance of the death of Christ, by eating bread and drinking wine, which are the outward signs of the inward grace, the body and blood of Christ."[31] That is, the Lord's Supper directs our faith to the merits of Christ's death, by which alone we find and experience salvation. Wesley's view here is significantly different from both the Anabaptist and Roman Catholic understandings of this sacrament.[32]

In what is typically called the "memorial" view (also known as the Anabaptist view, generally derived from the teachings of Ulrich Zwingli, and from which comes most contemporary Baptist theology), the Lord's Supper is practiced as an intellectual reminder of Jesus's suffering and death on the cross two thousand–plus years ago, in obedience to Jesus's words to his disciples in Luke 22:19, "Do this in remembrance of me" (NRSV). However, the Greek word used there (*anamnesis*[33]) does not simply mean "to intellectually recall or think about something again" as we find with our English word "remember." Instead, it implies bringing into the present that which we are remembering—a reexperiencing of something from the past again in the present. So, Wesley believes that when Jesus says, "Do this in remembrance of me," he is doing more than inviting Christians to intellectually remember a historic act from the past. Instead, he is literally inviting us to experience the effects of that past sacrifice in our own lives today.

At the same time, Wesley's understanding is also not the same as the typical Roman Catholic view (called "transubstantiation"). In that view, when the ritual Words of Institution ("this is my body, given for you; this is my blood, shed for you") are shared, the bread mysteriously becomes the literal body of Jesus, and the wine mysteriously becomes the literal blood of Jesus, even though they still look (and taste) like bread and wine. For Wesley, however, in no way is Jesus sacrificed *again* in or through any part of the Lord's Supper,

---

31 Wesley, "The Duty of Constant Communion," § 1, ¶ 5, in Outler, ed., 3:430.

32 For this reason, it's sometimes been said that—regarding the meaning of Holy Communion—Wesley and his Methodists believe "more than the Baptists but less than the Catholics." While this cliché may be somewhat exaggerated, nevertheless there are parts of it that are certainly true.

33 Olive Tree Bible Software. "Enhanced Strong's Dictionary," Strong's Number g0364, Version 7.5.5, Build 1562 (July 2, 2019). It is from the term *anamnesis*, in fact, that we derive our English term *amnesia*. While *amnesia* references forgetting, *anamnesis* references its opposite: remembering.

literally or spiritually. Instead, Christ's sacrifice was done only *once* and can never be repeated. However, while that sacrifice occurred only once, the power of that onetime event can still be experienced today. Consider the astronomical example of Messier 25 (or, M25), a bright cluster of stars in the constellation Sagittarius. It can be viewed through most binoculars and small telescopes and is approximately two thousand light-years away from Earth. That means that the images we see of it in the night sky today have traveled for about two thousand years at 186,282 miles per second (the speed of light) before finally reaching us. In other words, the light we see *today* as M25 actually happened *in the past*—about the time Jesus lived. Yet, we are only now experiencing its effects. So it is with Wesley's understanding of the death and resurrection of Jesus celebrated in the Lord's Supper. Like the light from M25, it happened *once* for all time in the *past* about two thousand years ago, but its effects are only now being felt and experienced by those living today in the *present*. As Wesleyan scholar J. C. Bowmer summarizes, for Wesley, the Lord's Supper is "the extension of an act done in the past until its effects are a present power."[34]

This leads us into Wesley's second description of the Lord's Supper: that it is **a means of grace for the *present*.** In section 1, paragraph 3 of his sermon above, he says:

> The grace of God given herein confirms to us the pardon of our sins, by enabling us to leave them. As our bodies are strengthened by bread and wine, so are our souls by these tokens of the body and blood of Christ. This is the food of our souls: This gives strength to perform our duty, and leads us on to perfection.[35]

In other words, the Lord's Supper is something that conveys the fruits of Christ's past work into present forgiveness, grace, and power. You may remember from the previous chapter that in his sermon "The Means of Grace" he asked:

> Is not the eating of that bread, and the drinking of that cup, the outward, visible means, whereby God conveys into our souls all

---

34 J. C. Bowmer, in Colin W. Williams, *John Wesley's Theology Today* (Nashville: Abingdon Press, 1990), 160.

35 Wesley, "The Duty of Constant Communion", § 1, ¶ 3, in Outler, ed., 3:429.

> that spiritual grace, that righteousness, and peace, and joy in the Holy Ghost, which were purchased by the body of Christ once broken and the blood of Christ once shed for us?[36]

This, in fact, was the common Anglican understanding in Wesley's own day, known as the spiritual or "real presence" of Christ.

Again, unlike what is typically understood in the "memorial" view, Christ *is* truly present in the sacrament, but also unlike what is typically understood in the Roman Catholic view, that presence is not in a literal or physical form or way.[37] Additionally, Wesley did not believe Christ is forced *automatically* to be present in the bread and wine simply because the officiant recalls the ritual Words of Institution. Instead, Christ is present *by choice* through the presence of his Holy Spirit—hence the invitational "Prayer to the Holy Spirit" in many rituals of Holy Communion today. So, Jesus is present with us in this sacrament through his Holy Spirit, who is around us, in us, and in others, but not tied or limited to the literal Communion elements themselves.

In emphasizing Christ's presence in the Lord's Supper, however, Wesley also made it clear that participants must respond to that presence through the sacrifice of themselves. He once wrote:

> Too many who are called Christians, live as if under the gospel there were no sacrifice but that of Christ on the cross. And indeed, there is no other that can atone for sins or satisfy the justice of God. . . . But what is [also] necessary is to our having a share in that redemption. So that though the sacrifice of our ourselves cannot procure salvation, yet it is altogether needful to our receiving it.[38]

This is why *The United Methodist Hymnal* contains the following sentence in the ritual for Holy Communion: "In remembrance of these your mighty

---

36   Wesley, "The Means of Grace," § 3, ¶ 12, in Outler, ed., 1:389–90.

37   In addition to *transubstantiation*, another, similar view, called *consubstantiation* (held by Martin Luther) holds that though the Communion elements do not change into the actual body and blood of Christ, nevertheless Christ is still present both spiritually and physically in, with, and under the elements.

38   Wesley, *Hymns on the Lord's Supper*, in Williams, *John Wesley's Theology Today*, 163.

acts in Jesus Christ, we offer ourselves in praise and thanksgiving as a holy and living sacrifice, *in union with Christ's offering for us.*"[39]

A third and final way that Wesley viewed the Lord's Supper was as **a pledge and assurance of the future.**[40] In his "Duty of Constant Communion," above, he said that "through this means we may be assisted to attain those blessings which he hath prepared for us; that we may obtain holiness on earth, and everlasting glory in heaven."[41] For Wesley, the Lord's Supper conveyed, not only power from the past and grace in the present, but also an eschatological promise of the future—what he called a "pledge of heaven."

In addition, he believed that it provides us with a participation in the "communion of saints"—a tangible reminder that we don't share this sacrament only between ourselves and Christ, but also with all other children of God throughout time. Once when I was teaching a class on this subject, I had a student ask me, "Are you saying that Holy Communion is a place where time and infinity meet?" How profound! Yes, that is it exactly! When we celebrate the Lord's Supper, we are communing with God, who exists outside of time, with those who are physically present in the room with us now, and even with the spirits of those who have died and gone on to heaven ahead of us.

Finally, in this third view, Wesley also calls the Lord's Supper "heavenly food"—a foretaste of the heavenly feast/banquet in which all Christians will share one day. It's a taste of: the "great dinner" that Jesus talked about in Luke 14 (NRSV), where many are invited but few respond; the grand parties in Luke 15 given by the shepherd who left the ninety-nine sheep to find the one lost sheep; by the woman who searched her house to find the lost coin; and by the loving father upon the return of his prodigal son; and of the "marriage supper of the Lamb" described in Revelation 19 (NRSV).

Open Communion

In addition to this threefold understanding of the Lord's Supper, Wesley also made it clear that this is a sacrament meant for *everyone*—something that Methodist Christians since then have traditionally called **open Communion.**

---

39 *The United Methodist Hymnal*, 14; emphasis added.

40 See generally Williams, *John Wesley's Theology Today*, 65.

41 Wesley, "The Duty of Constant Communion," § 2, ¶ 5, in Outler, ed., 3:432.

Again, this differs from both the Reformed and Roman Catholic traditions, where the Lord's Supper is a covenant meal where only those who have been baptized (often only in that tradition) are invited to commune. The result in these traditions is usually to limit the practice of Communion only to those who are old enough to have completed a membership class of some sort (such as confirmation), and who are professing members of that particular Christian tradition, or in some cases only of that particular local church. Consequently, children, nonmembers, and non-Christians are not usually invited to commune. Yet, as discussed earlier, for Wesley, the Lord's Supper is both a sign and an expression of God's prevenient grace. Since that grace is given to *all*, and since our tradition is the only one *not* to require Christian baptism as a precondition, he believed that the Lord's Supper should be open equally to *all*, regardless of one's age, spiritual condition, or stage of faith.

> **Open Communion**: the Wesleyan way of describing the Lord's Supper as open to anyone and everyone, regardless of one's age, spiritual condition, or stage of faith.

Of course, one popular excuse given both in Wesley's day and today for not communing is the concern about *unworthiness*. Wesley specifically addressed this "most common" excuse in section 2, paragraphs 7–13 of his "Duty of Constant Communion," above. In response to the apostle Paul's warning about unworthy communing in 1 Corinthians 11:27-29, Wesley pointed out that "here is not a word said of being unworthy to eat and drink. Indeed, he does speak of eating and drinking unworthily; but that is quite a different thing."[42] In the Corinthian church, where the tradition was that members would bring their own bread and wine to share, evidently some were not sharing the bread, and getting drunk on the wine. In other words, the manner in which they were communing was rude and disorderly, and Paul's comments about "unworthiness" referenced that behavior, rather than any innate unworthiness of character.

Besides, if worthiness references our character, then *no one* could ever be worthy—all persons would *always* be "unworthy." Yet, since for Wesley the Lord's Supper is a sign and expression of prevenient grace, then it means

---

42 Wesley, § 2, ¶ 8, pp. 3:434.

that the sacrament is intentionally designed by God as a meal for unworthy people. For him, it is precisely *because* we are unworthy in our character that God sent Jesus to die on the cross for unworthy sinners like us in the first place! This is why—unlike expectations in the Anabaptist and Roman Catholic theological traditions—a Wesleyan view regarding Holy Communion inclusion believes only that "Christ our Lord invites to his table [1] all who love him, [2] who earnestly repent of their sin and [3] seek to live in peace with one another."[43] It truly is an "open table."

A Converting Ordinance

One final note about Wesley's understanding of the Lord's Supper that makes it different from a typical Reformed/Calvinist or Roman Catholic view is his belief that one could be *converted* by and through receiving it.[44] For most Christian traditions, the Lord's Supper functions as what is called a "confirming ordinance"—it strengthens and firms up the faith that they already possess. Wesley certainly agreed with this view. However, he was one of only a few Protestant theologians who believed that it also functions as a **converting ordinance**—a sacrament where people of all ages can experience God's grace for the first time, and perhaps even be moved to *respond* to that grace through conversion.

> **Converting ordinance**: the Wesleyan way of describing how the Lord's Supper conveys justifying grace that can lead to Christian conversion (rather than merely conveying sanctifying grace as a "confirming ordinance").

This is yet another reason for the Wesleyan practice of "open Communion," and for *not* limiting the sacrament's reception merely to "born-again" adults and/or church members—because someone might be converted while communing!

In sum, for Wesley the Lord's Supper was more than a mere symbol. It is an opportunity for anyone and everyone to meet Christ through the Holy

---

43 *The United Methodist Hymnal*, 12.

44 Read generally Williams, *John Wesley's Theology Today*, 164.

Spirit, and to receive all dimensions of God's grace. It is an aid to growth for the Christian, but also has the potential to convert people to Christ. In his *Journal*, Wesley summarized his view this way: "The Lord's Supper was ordained by God to be a means of conveying to men either preventing, or justifying, or sanctifying grace, according to their several necessities."[45] This means that for someone who is exploring or seeking faith for the first time, the invitation to the sacrament may act as a manifestation of prevenient grace. For someone who chooses to respond spiritually to that, it can act as a manifestation of justifying grace. To someone who is already converted and seeking to grow in his or her faith, it can act as a manifestation of sanctifying grace. Thus, all three stages or "movements" of God's grace function within this sacrament, just as all three also function in the sacrament of Christian baptism.

So, given all that we have discussed thus far, what can and does it all look like in our daily life of faith? How is and can a uniquely Wesleyan theology and practice of faith be lived out in today's world? This will be the subject of our next chapter.

Discussion Questions

1. Discuss your general understanding of the meaning and purpose of the sacraments and why Wesley felt that they are important in the life of a Christian. Has your view of the meaning of either of these sacraments changed in any substantive way from reading this chapter? If so, how and in what way?

2. Based on what has been shared in this chapter, what would you guess to be the major theological differences between the practice of infant *dedication* (found in Baptist and Anabaptist churches) and the practice of Christian *baptism* of infants (found in Wesleyan, Anglican, Lutheran, and Roman Catholic churches)?

3. Based on this chapter's points, discuss your understanding of the difference between viewing and practicing the Lord's Supper as (1) a

---

45 John Wesley, *Journal* (June 28, 1740), in Ward and Heitzenrater, eds., *The Bicentennial Edition of the Works of John Wesley*, 19:159 (see chap. 6, n. 31).

memorial; (2) transubstantiation; or (3) the spiritual presence of Christ. Why is it important that one distinguish between these views?

4. If you are a practicing Christian, describe a time when you experienced the Lord's Supper as a means of grace in the *present* (i.e., when you felt God's presence in a special and/or unique way through your partaking of this sacrament).

5. Have you ever known someone who was converted to Christianity through his or her participation in the Lord's Supper as an "open" sacrament? If so, how does/did that individual describe this in terms of the invitation he or she received to commune? If not, how do you conceive of the importance and value of the practice of "open Communion"/ the "open table" in enabling people to experience the Lord's Supper in this way?

| Part Four |

Toward a Uniquely Wesleyan Paradigm of Ministry

CHAPTER 8

CHARACTERISTICS OF A WESLEYAN LIFE AND MINISTRY

This book thus far has focused primarily on an in-depth exploration of the beliefs and theology of historic Wesleyan Christianity, framed by a general discussion of the life and times of John Wesley himself, and how these shaped those beliefs and theology. In my own experience both as a United Methodist pastor and teacher, however, I've found that in sharing these details, we often miss the big picture of how it all fits together—we are so busy focusing on the intricate branches of the "tree" that we miss the overall beauty of the "forest."

Consequently, as we conclude this book, what I'd like to offer are a few observations and suggestions about the nature and shape of a uniquely Wesleyan paradigm of ministry,[1] beginning with an overview of what I believe to be the essential **characteristics of a Wesleyan Christian life and ministry.** Such an overview is important because in today's context, people are rarely shaped by a single spiritual tradition or approach. Instead, our beliefs and practices are usually drawn from a smorgasbord of multiple spiritual traditions and practices, without fully comprehending the beauty of any one of them. While there is certainly value in appreciating and honoring multiple traditions, I believe that attempting to live life and spirituality out of them *all*, in fact, merely devalues them all. What I think is more helpful not only is to seek to *understand* and learn a single spiritual tradition of our choice and calling, but also for our spiritual *practice* to become immersed in it.

For this reason, understanding the essential characteristics of a Wesleyan Christian life and ministry—including the unique dimensions of both its theology and its practice—will enable not only those who are native to the Wesleyan/Methodist Christian tradition, but also those who are new to it, to understand and appreciate its uniqueness, rather than simply assuming

---

1 "Paradigm" simply means a "model," or "way to do things."

it to be defined by concepts and practices imported or derived from other traditions.[2]

The Unique Shape of Wesleyan Theology

With this in mind, let's begin by exploring the unique shape of Wesleyan *theology*: what are some of its defining characteristics, boundaries, and areas of focus? And what questions might help to prompt evaluation of our current life and/or ministry context in these regards?[3]

Here are the characteristics of a uniquely Wesleyan theology. It has:

1. a praxis orientation
2. distinctive beliefs about salvation
   a. three manifestations/"movements" of God's one grace;
   b. primary goal of salvation as the restoration of the imago Dei in our lives;
   c. integral relationship between divine grace and human response;
   d. Christian transformation and growth understood primarily in terms of process;
   e. Christian life understood primarily in terms of relationship;
   f. free will made possible by God's grace; and
   g. an acknowledgment of the broader eschatological context of salvation.

I contend that a uniquely and authentically Wesleyan theology is composed of at least two distinctive characteristics and criteria: (1) a singular praxis orientation; and (2) several distinctive beliefs about salvation.

---

2 As a pastor, I have many people in my local United Methodist church whose Christian experience has been shaped by traditions other than Methodism. As such, they often bring practices and beliefs of those former traditions into our church as assumptions about Methodist Christianity. Doing this, however, not only fails to recognize the differences and uniqueness that Wesleyan/Methodist Christianity brings to the table of ecumenical faith, but also denies its ability to shape and influence one in new and potentially transformative ways.

3 In this chapter, I include the questions for discussion and consideration in the midst of the chapter, rather than at the end.

(1) Praxis Orientation

Wesleyan theology is unique, first, because of its **praxis orientation.** It is grounded first and foremost in scripture; its theology and beliefs arise generally *out of* the practice of ministry; and its theology exists to serve that practice, rather than merely providing objective, systematic, scripturally ungrounded truth claims that then result in practice. As Henry Knight III explains, "Wesley did not develop a theology which he then applied; he participated in a range of practices which became both the source and object of his theological reflections."[4]

Consider, for example, what we learned in chapter 1 about how Wesley himself was both shaped by and a product of the spiritual context of his time. As I've shared throughout the book, many of Wesley's key theological concepts and understandings were developed as a result of his attempts to find practices of ministry that kept faith with scripture.

> Question for consideration: If you are active in a local Christian church, are you aware of how what your congregation believes is a result of the history they've experienced as a church? How would you explain this relationship to someone new to your church?

Not only does this mean that Wesleyan theology arises *out of* the foundation of scripture *through* the practice of ministry, but it also means that that practice, in turn, speaks back to, and helps shape, one's faithful interpretation of scripture (potentially resulting in new understandings of theology). In other words, praxis orientation means that there is an interplay, or "dance," that exists between scripture and tradition, shaping personal experience, and personal experience in turn raises questions and insights, which are taken back to help interpret scripture. It does *not* mean that the *authority* of scripture is ever set aside in favor of pure pragmatism or experience, merely

---

4 Henry H. Knight III, *The Presence of God in the Christian Life: John Wesley and the Means of Grace* (Metuchen, NJ: Scarecrow Press, 1992), 6. Randy Maddox offers the same observation: Wesley "did not develop explicit stances on . . . issues prior to engaging in doctrinal reflection. . . . [He] seldom provided extended articulations of his methodological assumptions. He postulated them in passing or exemplified them in the process of actual theological activity." Maddox, *Responsible Grace*, 26 (see chap. 3, n. 10). See also Maddox, 47.

that scripture can and should be interpreted and understood within the light and context of practice and experience.

Wesley's writings actually express this in his differentiation between what he called "speculative divinity" (objective theology that is unrelated to present context and concerns) and "practical divinity" (subjective theology that exists for the sole purpose of helping people find, experience, and grow in God's grace today).[5] Practical divinity preveniently brings people to God, enables them to experience justification/pardon and new birth/regeneration, empowers them to grow in discipleship through sanctification toward (and perhaps even in) Christian perfection, enables them through the church to engage in God's mission, and equips people to reflect on and understand existential questions of faith, like "why am I here?"; "what is the meaning of my life?"; "where is God in the midst of the complexities of my life situations?"; and so on. While such a practice may contain deep, objective concerns, their application is uniquely *practical*. That is what is meant by praxis orientation. Furthermore, not only should ministry be practical, but so should theology itself; hence, Wesley's bias toward "practical divinity"—theology that is truly helpful in the lives and faith of God's people.

> **Praxis orientation**: the interplay or "dance" in both doctrine and ministry between scripture, tradition, and personal experience; the idea that theology, grounded in scripture, arises out of, and exists to serve, *practice*, rather than the other way around.

Two prime examples of this are Wesley's defense of women serving as both class and band leaders and as informal lay preachers within the Methodist movement,[6] and his rationale for the "setting apart" of Thomas Coke and Francis Asbury in 1784 as co-superintendents of the work of Methodism

---

5 See generally, John Wesley, preface to *A Collection of Hymns for the Use of the People Called Methodist*, ¶ 4, in *The Bicentennial Edition of the Works of John Wesley*, vol. 7; *A Collection of Hymns for the Use of the People Called Methodist*, ed. Franz Hildebrandt, Oliver A. Beckerlegge, and James Dale (Nashville: Abingdon Press, 1983), 73–74.

6 Such as Sarah Crosby, Mary Bosanquet, and Sarah Mallet, all of whom fulfilled the role of lay preachers in early Methodism, even though Wesley was reticent to use the term "preacher" to describe them.

in America.[7] In both instances, the standard assumptions in his Church of England context should have prevented him from allowing or practicing either of these. However, he came to believe that these two were contemporary expressions of God's prudential means of grace, grounded in scripture, yet relevant to the missional and apostolic needs of his contemporary context. For him, the work of God's church was first and foremost about apostolic *mission*—being sent into the world as ambassadors for God, inviting others to a living relationship with the divine through Jesus. Praxis orientation in theology and ministry meant doing what needed to be done within *that* framework, to accomplish *that* biblical calling. It did *not* mean "anything goes," but did allow for a variety of belief and practice where *nonessentials* of faith were involved. As he once famously wrote, "As to all opinions which do not strike at the root of Christianity, we think and let think. So that whatsoever they are, whether right or wrong, they are no distinguishing marks of a Methodist."[8]

> If you are active in a local Christian church, are you (or your fellow members) more concerned with doing things the "correct" way, or with being open to what God (grounded in what God has done) is doing to reach people now in order to initiate and grow them in a relationship with Jesus Christ?

(2) Distinctive Beliefs about Salvation

As a result of its praxis orientation, an authentically Wesleyan theology of ministry also possesses various **distinctive concerns within its soteriological makeup**—how it talks about and understands the nature and meaning of salvation. In general, Albert Outler noted that "there is something quite distinctive in [Wesley's] particular configuration and synthesis of the great Christian themes: faith and good works, Scripture and tradition, God's sovereignty and human freedom, universal grace and conditional election, original

---

7 While Wesley would not use the terms "ordain" or "bishop" to describe what he had done ("set apart" and "superintendent" were the terms he used instead), within a few years these two men became known as the first two bishops of American Methodism.

8 John Wesley, "The Character of a Methodist" (1742), ¶ 1, in Davies, ed., *The Bicentennial Edition of the Works of John Wesley*, 9:34 (see chap. 4, n. 1).

CHAPTER 8

sin and Christian perfection."[9] In fact, Paul Wesley Chilcote built his entire book *Recapturing the Wesleys' Vision* around eight such themes.[10] While not all such themes are balanced equally in Wesleyan theology, nevertheless the attention given to the concept and practice of balance in the first place is significant. A further examination of several of these soteriological concerns will prove helpful in this regard.

First, Wesleyan theology understands and articulates essentially **three manifestations, or "movements," of God's one grace.** There is only *one* "grace of God." However to better understand how that one grace works in one's life, differing adjectives (*prevenient, justifying,* or *sanctifying*) are used to describe the particular spiritual function taking place at any given point in one's life. The titles given to my chapters 3–5 highlight the function of each of these: *prevenient grace* highlights the initiating work of God to spiritually clear the way for us to once again turn towards God by becoming a Christian; *justifying grace* highlights the pardoning and redeeming work of God to *make possible* our restoration with God; *sanctifying grace* highlights the empowering, equipping, and maturing work of God to bring to *actuality* that restoration by growing in salvation. Within these three major manifestations of grace, there are also various minor yet related ones. Examples include: conviction and repentance as subdimensions of prevenient grace; justification, new birth, and assurance as subdimensions of justifying grace; and Christian perfection as the *telos* (end goal) of sanctifying grace. Yet, even these minor works are merely small pieces of the three major works of grace as either prevenient, justifying, or sanctifying. As noted earlier, while these three terms are not unique in Christianity (or even in some traditions' ordo salutis), Wesley's articulation of them is.

In addition, in chapter 3, I also mentioned that, rather than viewing these three as separate and distinct stages, it is more helpful to think of them as

---

9 Albert C. Outler, *Evangelism and Theology in the Wesleyan Spirit* (Nashville: Discipleship Resources, 2000), 43. In fact, in many respects Wesley's theology is more than simply a "both/and" synthesis of oft-opposing polarities. As Henry Knight explains, Wesley was "not simply attempting to find a middle way between two extremes, but critically examining the common assumptions which underlie both positions. Wesley's own position is thus [often] not a compromise but a fresh conceptual approach." Knight, *The Presence of God in the Christian Life*, 7.

10 Paul Wesley Chilcote, *Recapturing the Wesleys' Vision: An Introduction to the Faith of John and Charles Wesley* (Downers Grove, IL: InterVarsity Press, 2004).

three movements within the context of *one* overall musical symphony, each with interrelated and interdependent themes found throughout the entirety of the piece, but nevertheless three distinct and unique variations of that one piece. In fact, these three movements also coincide roughly with the three dimensions of the classical Christian doctrine of the holy Trinity: God the Father/Creator describes God as the one who creates and initiates love (the work and function of prevenient grace); God the Son/Redeemer describes God as the one who redeems by forgiving and pardoning us of sin (the work and function of justifying grace); and God the Holy Spirit/Sustainer describes God as the one who sustains, empowers, equips, and grows us in love (the work and function of sanctifying grace).

Second, as I describe more extensively in both chapters 3 and 5, for Wesley, **the primary goal of salvation is restoration of the imago Dei in our lives.** The reason Jesus came to earth to live, die, and rise from the dead was to lay the spiritual foundation for our way back to being remade in God's image. Consequently, while prevenient grace is important in inviting and leading toward a renewed relationship with God, and while justifying grace is essential in making that relationship possible through justification (pardon), what these first two movements of grace primarily exist to do is to prepare and lead us into the third movement of sanctification, for which Christian perfection is the final objective. Consequently, the ultimate goal of salvation is not "getting into heaven," being "born again," or even being able to stand righteous before a holy God. These are important, and can be *part of* the process of salvation, but for Wesley, they are *not* its ultimate objective. No. That objective is for us as human beings to have the image of God restored in our lives so that we live in a perfect/mature love for God and others—what Wesley called "Christian perfection."

Third, Wesleyan theology also has a unique way of understanding the **integral relationship between divine grace and human response**—namely, that God's grace *makes possible* human response. As Geoffrey Wainwright explains, Wesley "acknowledg[ed] the primacy and priority of grace in all soteriology while calling also for the human response,"[11] and that for him, "there is no contradiction in saying 'God works; therefore do ye work,' but rather [a] close connection: 'For first, God works; therefore you can work.

---

11 Geoffrey Wainwright, *Methodists In Dialog* (Nashville: Abingdon Press, 1995), 101.

Secondly, God works; therefore you must work.'"[12] For Wesley, all that we as humans do (including works of faith) is, in fact, merely the result of God's grace, which both invites and enables our response. According to Randy Maddox:

> [Wesley's] fundamental conviction about the inherent relation of grace and responsibility [is that] our very capacity for growth in Christ-likeness (new birth) is contingent upon God's gracious pardoning prevenience (initial justification), while the continuance of God's acceptance (final justification) becomes contingent upon our responsive growth in Christ-likeness (sanctification).[13]

Consequently, while an authentic Wesleyan theology will certainly emphasize the importance of both divine grace and human response, it also is clear that the former makes possible the latter.

This stress on the primacy of grace does *not* mean Wesley adhered to a typical interpretation of the classic Protestant doctrine of justification "sola fide" (by faith alone). As mentioned in chapter 1, Wesley took the traditional meaning and modified it because, for him, there was always a degree to which at least some human response *is* a condition of salvation. While Christian faith certainly is a response, for him the *living out* of that faith is as essential as its possession alone. After all, God does invite, initiate, and enable our salvation through grace. Yet, just as a primed water pump must be physically pumped for water to issue out, so Wesley believed that God's initiating grace towards us must be appropriated and exercised through faith and works in order to experience the benefits of that grace. Thus, while his theology certainly fits the traditional Protestant concept of justification "by faith alone," what he actually practiced was nonetheless more akin to justification "by faith, with works as a necessary response." Maddox describes this in terms of "a dance in which God always takes the first step, but we must participate responsibly, lest the dance stumble or end."[14]

Fourth, in an authentically Wesleyan theology, **Christian transformation**

---

12 Wainwright, 102. See generally 100–105.

13 Maddox, *Responsible Grace*, 172.

14 Maddox, 151.

and growth are understood primarily in terms of *process*.[15] As Theodore Runyon explains, for Wesley, "grace is not simply one generous act by a judge but a process involving the constant presence, recognized or unrecognized, of the Spirit drawing the person into a relationship that will sustain and reinforce on the way."[16] In Reformed/Calvinist traditions, salvation is typically understood to be a onetime spiritual event or encounter designed to bring sinners to stand righteous before a just God. For Wesley, however, it is an *ongoing* pattern and *process* of generosity from God that's designed to restore the imago Dei within each of us. In the former, the goal of salvation is justification, with sanctification merely being its aftereffect. In Wesley's view, however, the goal is sanctification that moves us toward Christian perfection, with justification merely being the door to it. So then, salvation is not merely about a *destination*, but also about a *journey*—there is never a point where one can say he or she has "arrived" as a Christian. Instead, one is continuously appropriating more and more aspects of salvation, on its way towards a specific goal.

For Wesley, that goal, of course, was Christian perfection—perfect love of God and neighbor. While Eastern Christianity also contains this emphasis (in fact, much of Wesley's understanding came from his readings of Eastern patristic writers), it is unique to Wesley within Western Protestant Christian spirituality. Of course, instantaneous, single-moment spiritual events still have their place, even for Wesley; but only within the larger framework of *process*.[17] As Maddox explains, "While Wesley indeed allowed for mo-

---

15 See generally, Maddox, 151–54. He points out there that this understanding is actually more consistent with Eastern Christianity (which primarily views Christian life and growth in terms of *process*) than with Western Christianity, which primarily views this life in terms of a *state* or *status* to be achieved.

16 Theodore Runyon, *The New Creation: John Wesley's Theology Today* (Nashville: Abingdon Press, 1998), 29.

17 An example of this theme is found in Wesley's sermon "The Scripture Way of Salvation," where he stated that "from the time of our being 'born again,' the *gradual* work of sanctification takes place." Wesley, "The Scripture Way of Salvation," § 1, ¶ 8, in Outler, ed., *Works*, 2:160; emphasis added. Elsewhere, he asked if sanctification is "gradual or instantaneous? It is both the one and the other. From the moment we are justified, there may be a gradual sanctification, a growing in grace, a daily advance in the knowledge and love of God. And if sin cease before death, there must, in the nature of the thing, be an instantaneous change; there must be a last moment wherein it does exist, and a first moment wherein it does not." John Wesley, "Minutes of Several Conversations Between Rev. Mr. Wesley and Others" (1744–1789), Question 56, Answer (7) in Jackson, ed., *The Works of John Wesley*, 8:328–29.

CHAPTER 8

mentary [e.g., instantaneous] transitions in the Christian life, he integrally related these transitions to gradual growth in response to God's grace, both preceding and following the transition."[18]

> If you are active in a local Christian church, do its ministries of outreach and/or spiritual invitation and initiation emphasize only events (such as revivals, altar calls, crusades, and other experiences geared to evoke singular transformation), or do they also include experiences and opportunities for gradual and processive transformation (such as seeker-type groups where participants can explore faith before conversion)?

A fifth characteristic of uniquely Wesleyan theology is that the **Christian life is understood primarily in terms of *relationship*.** As mentioned previously, for Wesley, salvation consists not of a fixed *state* to be achieved, but of a network of living, ongoing, vital *relationships* that must be initiated, nurtured, and maintained. Of course, the primary focus of this characteristic is our relationship with God, whom Wesley views as being our "divine parent"—a view that stood in sharp contrast with the predominant Reformed/Calvinist model in his time, where God was viewed essentially as a "divine monarch."[19] Yet, the relational character of Wesleyan theology goes beyond our relationship with God—it also informs our relationships with ourselves, with others,[20] and with the created order. Thus, for Wesley, while salvation is God-centric, it is not God-*exclusive*.

A sixth characteristic of authentic Wesleyan theology is that it understands humanity's relationship with God as a product of **free will made possible by God's grace.** As highlighted in chapter 1, it is distinctively Arminian (as opposed to Reformed/Calvinist) theology. In this view, humans are not puppets in God's hands—this is *not* a theology of irresistible grace (i.e., "once saved, always saved"). As Maddox explains, Wesley "construed

---

18 Maddox, *Responsible Grace*, 154.

19 See generally, Maddox, 56. Also Runyon, *The New Creation*, 13, 82, 218.

20 As Henry Knight explains, "For Wesley, to fail to love one's neighbor indicates a deficiency in our love for God, and therefore that we have not been recreated by God's love for us." Knight, *The Presence of God in the Christian Life*, 4.

God's power or sovereignty fundamentally in terms of empowerment, rather than control or overpowerment. . . . God's grace works powerfully, but not irresistibly, in matters of human life and salvation; thereby empowering our response-ability, without overriding our responsibility."[21] The result is the tendency within the Wesleyan tradition to emphasize the *immanence* (i.e., closeness) of God, rather than the *transcendence* (i.e., sovereignty) of God.

In fact, even within the Christian life, Wesley believed that God gave humans free will to reject or ignore God's grace in the Christian life, even though to continually do so would weaken and—if done so long enough—perhaps even void our relationship with God. Yet, as Runyon noted, in the Wesleyan understanding, even "free will is not natural . . . but supernatural, a divine gift to restore the fallen creature to responsibility and agency."[22] Consequently, Wesleyan theology does prioritize the availability of human free will, but stresses that even *it* is made possible by the gracious gift of God's grace.

Finally, authentic Wesleyan theology also **acknowledges the larger eschatological context of salvation.** That is: it does not separate individual salvation from the larger goal of renewal of all creation. Runyon affirmed that in the Wesleyan tradition, "when we deal with the earth and its resources, and when we deal with our fellow creatures, we are dealing with God. For Wesley, therefore, sanctifying faith can in no wise be divorced from care for the environment."[23] In today's context, such a focus is sometimes referred to as "environmental theology." For Wesley, however, it is merely a recognition that God's gracious initiative of grace is meant not only for humans, but also for the created order itself, and that individual salvation cannot be divorced from one's responsibility toward and with both others and creation. In this sense, then, personal salvation is never private salvation, and the considerations of social salvation (such as social justice ministry and environmentalism) cannot exist without equal concern for individual spirituality. As shared earlier, Wesley is famously quoted as saying that "the gospel of Christ knows of no religion, but social; no holiness but social holiness."[24]

---

21 Maddox, *Responsible Grace*, 55.

22 Runyon, *The New Creation*, 16.

23 Runyon, 207.

24 Wesley, preface to *Hymns and Sacred Poems*, ¶ 5 in Chilcote and Collins, eds., *The Bicentennial Edition of the Works of John Wesley*, 13:39 (see chap. 3, n. 17).

CHAPTER 8

For him, then, the personal and the social dimensions of salvation are thus integrally related and essential to a proper understanding of what it means to be "saved." I believe this is an especially important distinction in today's pop-culture Christianity, where faith is often diluted to become merely a private transaction between God and us, with the role of others and of the community of faith being de-emphasized or erased altogether. So, the notion of the essentially social nature of Christianity and the Christian gospel is an important defining characteristic of uniquely Wesleyan theology.

> If you are active in a local Christian church, to what extent do its ministries address social concerns and justice? If you are the pastor, do you preach about the importance of these? Or do you only preach about "personal salvation"? In other words, how do you help congregants understand and experience how salvation involves something greater than one's personal life?

The Unique Shape of Wesleyan Practice

In addition to having a unique shape to its *theology*, a truly Wesleyan life and ministry is also composed of several distinctive characteristics and criteria within its *practice* of ministry. These include the following:

1. Tensional emphases

    a. evangelism *and* social justice

    b. inward-focused *and* outward-focused spirituality

    c. individualism *and* community

    d. Methodism as a church *and* as a renewal movement

    e. "head" *and* "heart"

    f. Christianity as both a product of culture *and* a prophetic response to it

2. Christian life as an "embodied apologetic"

3. Use of means of grace

4. Evangelism and the church's broader eschatological mission

5. A "catholic spirit"

It is characterized by the presence of (1) a series of tensional emphases; (2) Christian life as an "embodied apologetic"; (3) the open acknowledgment and use of prudential means of grace; (4) an emphasis upon evangelism and the eschatological mission of the church; and (5) its "catholic spirit."

(1) Tensional Emphases

As we learned from the practices of Wesley and the early Methodists, an authentically Wesleyan practice of ministry has always been characterized, first and foremost, by a series of what I'm calling **tensional emphases**—that is: a both/and, rather than an either/or, approach. In this sense, "tensional" does not mean watered down, but merely something that holds seemingly *opposite* concepts and/or practices together in constructive equilibrium or balance, *without* the need to synthesize either into a compromise.

> **"Tensional" emphasis**: the ability to hold and value seemingly opposite concepts and/or practices together in constructive equilibrium without the need to synthesize either into a compromise; an ability to have and practice a "both/and" approach (versus an "either/or" approach).

In practical terms, for the following items, visualize a balancing scale between *two* unique items, rather than a reconstituted single item—it is *not* a joining of thesis and antithesis to create a new "synthesis," but a maintenance of thesis and antithesis in *balance*. In addition, while you'll note that the individual constituent elements within each of the emphases below is not usually unique, their juxtaposition and partnership with their perceived opposite usually is.

For one, an authentically Wesleyan practice of ministry always combines equal concern for both **evangelism**[25] *and* **social justice**—a balance

---

25 That is, ministries of spiritual invitation and initiation—those that invite and/or initiate people into Christian faith for the first time.

between word and deed. [26] As Outler explained, in the Wesleyan tradition,

> the essence of faith is personal and inward, but the evidence of faith is public and social. . . . Evangelism must issue in visible social effects or else its fruits will fade and wither. . . . The Word made audible must become the Word made visible, if [people's] lives are ever to be touched by the "Word made flesh."[27]

Among other things, this means that for Wesley, biblical salvation includes more than just the individual, but also the social structures around that individual. In the words of David Lowes Watson, "Salvation in the Wesleyan perspective is not only for persons, but also for institutions, social systems, and for cities and nations."[28]

> If you are active in a local Christian church, do you hear as much emphasis on issues of social justice and social salvation as on personal salvation from the pulpit, in small groups, and in other settings?

A second tensional emphasis is closely connected with the first: a balance between **inward-focused *and* outward-focused spirituality.**[29] This has often been described as a balance between being people of *prayer* and being people of *work*.[30] Another way to talk about this is as one possessing a dual emphasis upon both "works of piety" (those spiritual activities that foster a better inward relationship with God, such as Wesley's instituted means of grace), and "works of mercy" (those activities that foster and support good works toward others, such as many of Wesley's prudential means of grace). As we've already learned, the early Methodist society,

---

26 For a review of how these two tensions have often been pulled apart in contemporary Christianity, and an excellent argument for their re-fusion, see generally Ronald J. Sider, *One Sided Christianity? Uniting the Church to Heal a Lost and Broken World* (Grand Rapids: Zondervan, 1993).

27 Outler, *Evangelism and Theology in the Wesleyan Spirit*, 22.

28 David Lowes Watson, cited in M. Douglas Meeks, *The Portion of the Poor* (Nashville: Kingswood Books, 1995), 126.

29 The former can also be described as "contemplative/meditative" spirituality, while the latter can also be described as "social/active" spirituality.

30 See generally, Wainwright, "*Ora et Labora*: Benedictines and Wesleyans at Prayer and Work," in *Methodists in Dialog*, 89–106.

class, and band structures were the immediate context for this balance in Wesley's day. Within them, we find examples of activities that engendered both personal piety (such as the group prayer, accountability, and devotional/study functions) *and* missional outreach (such as group collections for the poor, and the early Methodists' visitation of those sick and in prison).

> If you are active in a local Christian church, does it offer opportunities for people to be involved not only in inward ministries of spiritual formation and prayer (those that address the spiritual well-being of one's inner soul), but also in active ministries of missional outreach (those that address the physical well-being of others)?

A third important tensional emphasis in Wesleyan praxis is the balance between **individualism *and* community.** In today's North American culture, privatized, individualistic faith reigns supreme in pop spirituality—its focus is usually on what is best for *me*, rather than what is best for my community as a *whole*. Of course, this phenomenon merely mirrors our culture itself, where marketing is all about the individual (consider the **i**Phone, **i**Pad, and the myriad of other products customizable to the individual's preferences). No wonder, then, that sermons, Bible studies, and church events and program offerings often cater to the felt needs of *individuals* to the extent that *corporate* needs and concerns either are downplayed or overlooked altogether. As Runyon noted, in this context, "Christian faith is reduced to what takes place within the individual and his or her personally experienced awareness of God."[31] Yet, while Wesley's practice of ministry did address the physical and spiritual needs of the individual, that practice was not reduced to in-dividual*ism*. Instead, in early Methodism, individual salvation was worked out within the context of Wesley's small group structure (i.e., the societies, classes and bands), so that the corporate *groups* became the birthing places for *personal* faith. Indeed, in many ways, this third manifestation of tensional emphases is merely another way of describing the first two.

---

31 Theodore Runyon, *The New Creation*, 102.

CHAPTER 8

> In your own understanding, is God's church merely a collection of individuals who have separately experienced personal salvation? OR do you understand it to be truly a "community of faith" in which connection to your fellow faith-journeyers is as important as your individual, personal journey?

A fourth tensional emphasis found in Wesleyan praxis is the constant tension between it being what I'm calling **an ecclesiola in ekklesia (church within Church)** *and* **being an ekklesia (Church)**—in other words, between being a *movement within* an institution, and being the institution itself. In its earliest days in England, Methodism was, of course, clearly the former. Yet, once it was transported across different times and cultures, it had to take on more and more elements of the latter, thereby often losing the unique elements it possessed as the former. The result has often been intense debate over the role and function of Wesleyan Christianity within the universal body of Christ: Is it best understood as a renewal movement? Or as an institutional church? One's answer to this often determines the focus of one's ministry practice. For example, if one understands it as the former, then creative, innovative, "outside the box" ministry practices can be more easily fostered and supported. However, if one understands it as the latter, then there tends to be a bias toward "tradition" and "the way we've always done things" in one's practice of ministry. Of course, Wesley himself struggled with this tension in his approach to the issue of schism with the Church of England. Although he consistently resisted any attempts to formally separate Methodism from the established church, forces within Methodism itself often had schismatic tendencies that Wesley's descendants found it difficult (and at times, impossible) to overcome.

Although the tension between movement and institution will always exist to some degree within a truly Wesleyan practice of ministry, the two need not be mutually exclusive. For example, Wesley himself advocated the use of many traditional practices associated with the established Anglican *ekklesia*, such as use of the traditional Anglican liturgy, lectionary, church year, Articles of Religion, formal prayers, a typical Anglican view of the Eucharist, and (when in Anglican pulpits) "pastoral preaching" characteristic of any typical Anglican pastor of his day.[32] At the same time, in his ministry Wesley also utilized a number of practices consistent with an *ecclesiola in ecclesia* identity, many of which were quite innovative for that day and time. Among these were his occasional altering of the traditional Anglican liturgy, the use of lay preachers and other laity (especially women) in leadership, modifications to the Articles of Religion, an un-Anglican emphasis on the regular practice of the Lord's Supper,[33] his use of extemporaneous prayers, altered hymns, and most important, his use of field preaching to reach the masses.[34] This mixture of traditional and innovative ministry practices illustrates how a uniquely Wesleyan praxis can actually *live in the tension* between *ecclesiola in ecclesia* and *ekklesia*. As Albert Outler once expressed it, Methodism is an "'evangelical order of witness and worship, discipline and nurture' that needs 'a catholic church' within which to function."[35]

> If you are active in a local Christian church, in what ways does it practice a balance of both the new things of God *and* the traditional ways of doing things? How does it maintain an intentional (if uneasy) balance between the needs of "spiritual renewal" and institutional needs (organizational, structural, denominational)?

A fifth tensional emphasis in an authentically Wesleyan practice of ministry is a balance between **head *and* heart.** While Wesley himself was a highly educated Oxford don, and clearly valued formal education (i.e., an emphasis on religion of the head), he also insisted that he and his Methodists preachers be bilingual in learning to speak the language of the most common commoner. Consider, for example, Wesley's comments in the preface to his *Sermons on Several Occasions*:

---

32 See generally, Maddox, *Responsible Grace*, 201–8.

33 Remember from chapter 7 that Wesley's sermon "The Duty of Constant Communion" encouraged Christians to receive the Lord's Supper whenever possible, rather than merely the three times a year required by the Church of England.

34 See generally, Maddox, *Responsible Grace*, 208–13.

35 Outler, cited in Wainwright, *Methodists in Dialog*, 105.

CHAPTER 8

> I design plain truth for plain people: Therefore, of set purpose, I abstain from all nice and philosophical speculations; from all perplexed and intricate reasonings; and, as far as possible, from even the show of learning, unless in sometimes citing the original Scripture. I labour to avoid all words which are not easy to be understood, all which are not used in common life; and, in particular, those kinds of technical terms that so frequently occur in Bodies of Divinity; those modes of speaking which men of reading are intimately acquainted with, but which to common people are an unknown tongue.[36]

For him, both intellectual integrity *and* personal passion were essential to a uniquely Wesleyan practice of ministry.

> If you are active in a local Christian church, how does it balance its emphases on head and heart religion in its ministries? In its Christian formation experiences? In its small group offerings? In the foci of its sermons?

A final tensional emphasis in uniquely Wesleyan practice is in viewing **Christianity as both a product of culture *and* as a response to it**. On the one hand, recall from chapters 1 and 2 how Wesley's theology and ministry practice were drastically shaped by the events and circumstances of his eighteenth-century English culture and by his own upbringing. Additionally, while Wesley felt that the church should engage culture both as the *Christian community* (with its own uniquely Christian voice), and according to the universal common standards set by society itself, he nevertheless also utilized cultural techniques inherent in the day and time to advance the gospel. Two simple examples of this are Wesley's use of contemporary marketing tools, such as pamphlets and tracts, in his spreading of the gospel, and his use of new technologies, such as incandescent gas lighting, to offer evening evangelistic services.

On the other hand, early Methodism was not only *shaped by* its surrounding culture, but also acted to critique and reshape *it*, as well. For example, while the early Methodist class structure was not established

---

36 John Wesley, preface to *Sermons on Several Occasions*, ¶ 3, in Albert Outler, ed., *The Bicentennial Edition of the Works of John Wesley: Sermons I* (1–33) (Nashville: Abingdon Press, 1984), 104.

primarily to offer a prophetic voice within English society, it had the effect of doing just that by critiquing various social issues, such as human rights, slavery and the slave trade, rights of the poor, women's rights, stewardship of the natural world (today's environmentalism), and ecumenism.[37] There is, furthermore, strong evidence that the class system itself was in many ways directly responsible for the widespread distribution and reading of Wesley's "Thoughts upon Slavery." This pamphlet was, in turn, an important document whose message began to change English attitudes regarding the slave trade.[38] This shaping of society was felt even in the arena of public leadership. For instance, Runyon observed:

> The leaders of the labor movement in nineteenth-century Britain were largely Methodist local preachers and class leaders, natural leaders experienced in speaking, personal evangelism, organization, and leadership skills, which they applied to recruiting and organizing unions.[39]

Of course, in an authentically Wesleyan practice of ministry, being countercultural is never an end in itself. Instead, Christian community exists primarily to engender initiation and nurture growth within the *Christian* life. However, the fringe benefit of that initiation and growth is a community of Christian faith that looks and acts and lives fundamentally *differently* from the rest of society—primarily through the enactment of Christian love for one another and the world. As Outler explained, "What the [Methodist] Revival did was to sponsor a very different kind of revolution—an actual transformation of social morals and manners."[40] While this may perhaps exaggerate the point, it is certainly true that one of the hallmarks of Wesleyan Christianity has been its ability to be seen as both a *product* of culture and a *response* to it.

> If you are active in a local Christian church, to what extent does it balance being involved in a community

---

37 See generally, Runyon, *The New Creation*, 193–215.

38 See Warren Thomas Smith, *John Wesley and Slavery* (Nashville: Abingdon Press, 1986), 98.

39 Runyon, *The New Creation*, 187.

40 Outler, *Evangelism and Theology in the Wesleyan Spirit*, 25.

with being a prophetic voice in its community? How is it shaped by its community? And how does it challenge the status quo of its community?

(2) Christian Life as Embodied Apologetic

In 1995, author Kevin Graham Ford was among the first to identify the pressing need for contemporary Christians to provide what he called an **"embodied apologetic"** for Christianity.[41] Instead of using rational debate and proof texts to intellectually convince people of the logic of Christianity and Christian faith claims, he argued that Christians need to influence others toward faith through their very *lives*—what is also sometimes called *lifestyle apologetics*. Not only is this need still valid in North American culture today, but for Wesley and the early Methodists, such a method was practiced as the *primary* means by which to persuade others toward Christian faith.

While it is true that Wesley did occasionally use rationally grounded debate,[42] he tended to use it only in written form, and even then, only sparingly. Runyon described the more common approach utilized when confronted by a skeptic: "Wesley did not respond with rational arguments.... Instead, [he] invited the skeptic to attend the meeting of a local [Methodist] society, to become a member of a class, which proved to be the best apologetic method, because it invited a skeptic to be open to a new community of experience."[43] It was in these communal experiences that most conversions happened. While there used to be a presumption in American Christianity that intellectual believing leads to a desire to belong to God's community (the church), in both Wesley's and today's culture, it is the other way around: *belonging* to (and serving in) a Christian community leads to *believing* in the God of that community. Thus, an authentic practice of Wesleyan life and

---

41   See Kevin Graham Ford, *Jesus for a New Generation* (Westmont, IL: InterVarsity Press, 1995), 175.

42   Examples include his extensive intellectual arguments in John Wesley, *An Earnest Appeal to Men of Reason and Religion* (1743) in Gerald R. Cragg, ed., *The Bicentennial Edition of the Works of John Wesley*, vol. 11, *The Appeals to Men of Reason and Religion and Certain Related Other Letters* (Nashville: Abingdon Press, 1989), 37–94; and John Wesley, "A Farther Appeal to Men of Reason and Religion" (1745), pts 1–3, in Cragg, 11:95-325; and the rational nature of the content of the arguments in many of his letters when he was responding to accusations of "enthusiasm."

43   Runyon, *The New Creation*, 158.

ministry is characterized by experiencing the Christian life as an "embodied apologetic" through the lifestyles of one's community of faith.

> If you are active in a local Christian church, does it have groups and experiences that are not only open to but friendly toward spiritual seekers/searchers? Or does its groups require one to be a church member before they are allowed to participate?

(3) Use of Means of Grace

For Wesley and the early Methodists, the practice of the first two characteristics (tensional emphases, and Christian life as an "embodied apologetic") did not merely happen *ex nihilo* (out of nothing). Instead, they were enabled and nurtured by and through the use of the **means of grace** that were discussed in chapter 6. An authentically Wesleyan practice of faith today should do no less. Maddox notes that in the Wesleyan tradition, through these means, we are "progressively empowered and responsibly nurtured along the Way of Salvation,"[44] while Knight notes that "the means of grace enable and invite a distinctive relationship with God and provide a way for that relationship to grow and deepen over time."[45]

Not only did these provide ways to balance out the tensional Christian practices mentioned earlier, but also provided specific ways that the early Methodists could become a counterculture that influenced others toward faith through their lifestyle. As Knight explains, for Wesley, "to fail to 'use' the means of grace was to fail to maintain a continuing relationship with God, and thereby to not progress in the Christian life."[46] While nearly all Christian traditions use what Wesley called the *instituted means of grace*, uniquely Wesleyan ministry especially relies on an openly acknowledged use of various *prudential* means—those prudent for a particular time, context, and situation. In Wesley's day, these, of course, included the innovative ministry practices mentioned above. However, by far the most important prudential means were: (1) the creation and use of the early

---

44 Maddox, *Responsible Grace*, 192.
45 Knight, *The Presence of God in the Christian Life*, 174–75.
46 Knight, 44.

Methodist society structure; and (2) the early Methodist emphasis on a disciplined life.

First, since for Wesley, the nature of true Christianity is communal and social as much as it is personal and individual, his creation of the **Methodist societies, classes, bands, select societies, and penitent groups** specifically enabled this to happen. In fact, as Knight observes, "the small groups . . . became centers for nurturing faith, enabling persons to experience the presence of God in the means of grace of the church."[47] Wesley himself once stated:

> I am more and more convinced, that the devil himself desires nothing more than this, that the people of any place should be half-awakened, and then left to themselves to fall asleep again. Therefore I determine, by the grace of God, not to strike one stroke in any place where I cannot follow the blow.[48]

His creation of the Methodist society structure provided the desired follow-up so that Christian growth and development were not merely *haphazard* but were instead *intentional* and *structured*.

> If you are active in a local Christian church, what kind of "discipleship system" does it have to intentionally move people from being seekers of Christian faith to becoming deeply committed Christians? Does your church have one? Can you articulate its process to people who might ask?

Second, it was expected that anyone who was a part of these groups would also adhere to a certain Methodist **discipline** for spiritual development. For Wesley, like the organizational structure itself, this was a prudential means of grace that not only leads one *toward* sanctification, but also assists one's Christian growth *in it* by providing accountability, fellowship, and an outlet for works of mercy. While there were numerous ways to describe this discipline, you may remember from chapter 2 that its fundamentals were highlighted in Wesley's own description of the "General Rules of the United

---

47 Knight, 35.

48 Wesley, *Journal* (Sunday, March 13, 1743), in Ward and Heitzenrater, eds., *The Bicentennial Edition of the Works of John Wesley*, 19:318 (see chap. 6, n. 29).

Societies" of Methodism: "Any person determined to save his soul may be united with [the Methodists]. But this desire must be evidenced by three marks: avoiding all known sin; doing good after his power; and attending all the ordinances of God."[49] All of this highlights how Wesleyan practice always includes tools for expectation and accountability for those within it.

So, authentically Wesleyan ministry practice includes the open and unabashed use of both the instituted means of grace, and various prudential means, especially including the use of small group structures and formations for the purpose of mutual, disciplined accountability within Christian community.

> If you are active in a local Christian church, what kind of accountability structures are in place there? Does it hold its members accountable to some kind of expectations (such as the United Methodist membership vows) in the same way that early Methodism held its members accountable to its three general rules? What kind of expectations does it have that members live the twenty-first-century equivalent of a disciplined lifestyle?

(4) Evangelism and the Church's Eschatological Mission

A fourth element of distinctively Wesleyan ministry practice is its emphasis on **evangelism** (outwardly focused attention for the purpose of first-time spiritual initiation) and what I'm calling the **eschatological mission of the church**. For Wesley, making disciples for the kingdom of God represented the first of two great purposes for the existence of the church as an institution in general, and for the existence of church order in particular. To him, the church exists first and foremost to be *sent* into mission. Only then does it exist for the building up and maturing of its own fellowship. In other words, truly Wesleyan practice of ministry is not so much focused *internally* on itself, but instead possesses an *outward* focus. While this kind of outward

---

49 Wesley, "On God's Vineyard," § 3, ¶ 1, in Outler, ed., 3:511. See also Wesley, "The Nature, Design, and General Rules of the United Societies," ¶¶ 4–6, in Davies, ed., *The Bicentennial Edition of the Works of John Wesley: The Methodist Societies*, 9:70–73 (see chap. 4, n. 1).

focus (evangelism) is not unique to Wesleyan spirituality, its stress upon the *eschatological* context and goal is. What I mean by this is that—as explained previously—salvation in the Wesleyan tradition is not only about making a *personal* commitment to God through Christ, but also about one's relationships with self, others, and all of the created order. As David Lowes Watson summarizes, from a Wesleyan perspective, "the good news of salvation is not merely for persons, but [also] for institutions, for systems, and for cities and nations."[50] In other words, it has an *eschatological* (i.e., an outward, communal, future-focused) orientation to it.

> If you are active in a local Christian church, to what extent does it engage in evangelism—outward activity that intentionally invites, welcomes, and incorporates people into Christian faith? More than that, though, how ecologically aware is your congregation? How does its leadership help members understand their responsibility to be good stewards of their city or community? Of the earth itself?

(5) Catholic Spirit

A fifth and final element of a uniquely Wesleyan *practice* of ministry is that it maintains a **"catholic spirit"** in its view of and interactions with other people of Christian faith. In 1771, a sermon of the same name was published in which Wesley identifies this perspective and gives examples of how it can be lived out in his day and time.

Catholic Spirit[51]
by John Wesley

"And when he was departed thence, he lighted on Jehonadab the son of Rechab coming to meet him, and he saluted him, and said to him, Is thine heart right, as my heart is with thy heart?

---

50 Watson, cited in Meeks, ed., *The Portion of the Poor*, 126.

51 John Wesley, "Catholic Spirit," in Outler, ed., *The Bicentennial Edition of the Works of John Wesley*, 2:81–95.

And Jehonadab answered: It is. If it be, give me thine hand." 2 Kings 10:15.

1. It is allowed even by those who do not pay this great debt, that love is due to all mankind, the royal law, "Thou shalt love thy neighbour as thyself," carrying its own evidence to all that hear it: and that, not according to the miserable construction put upon it by the zealots of old times, "Thou shalt love thy neighbour," thy relation, acquaintance, friend, "and hate thine enemy;" not so; "I say unto you," said our Lord, "Love your enemies, bless them that curse you, do good to them that hate you, and pray for them that despitefully use you, and persecute you; that ye may be the children," may appear so to all mankind, "of your Father which is in heaven; who maketh his sun to rise on the evil and on the good, and sendeth rain on the just and on the unjust."

2. But it is sure, there is a peculiar love which we owe to those that love God. So David: "All my delight is upon the saints that are in the earth, and upon such as excel in virtue." And so a greater than he: "A new commandment I give unto you, That ye love one another: as I have loved you, that ye also love one another. By this shall all men know that ye are My disciples, if ye have love one to another" (John 13:34, 35). This is that love on which the Apostle John so frequently and strongly insists: "This," saith he, "is the message that ye heard from the beginning, that we should love one another" (1 John 3:11). "Hereby perceive we the love of God, because he laid down his life for us: and we ought," if love should call us thereto, "to lay down our lives for the brethren" (verse 16). And again: "Beloved, let us love one another: for love is of God. He that loveth not, knoweth not God; for God is love" (4:7, 8). "Not that we loved God, but that he loved us, and sent his Son to be the propitiation for our sins. Beloved, if God so loved us, we ought also to love one another" (verses 10, 11).

3. All men approve of this; but do all men practise it? Daily experience shows the contrary. Where are even the Christians who "love one another as he hath given us commandment?" How many hindrances lie in the way! The two grand, general hindrances are, first, that they cannot all think alike and, in consequence of this, secondly, they cannot all walk alike; but in several smaller points their practice must differ in proportion to the difference of their sentiments.

4. But although a difference in opinions or modes of worship may prevent an entire external union, yet need it prevent our union in affection? Though we cannot think alike, may we not love alike? May we not be of one heart, though we are not of one opinion? Without all doubt, we may. Herein all the children of God may unite, notwithstanding these smaller differences. These remaining as they are, they may forward one another in love and in good works.

5. Surely in this respect the example of Jehu himself, as mixed a character as he was of, is well worthy both the attention and imitation of every serious Christian. "And when he was departed thence, he lighted on Jehonadab the son of Rechab coming to meet him; and he saluted him, and said to him, Is thine heart right, as my heart is with thy heart? And Jehonadab answered, It is. If it be, give me thine hand."

The text naturally divides itself into two parts:—First, a question proposed by Jehu to Jehonadab: "Is thine heart right, as my heart is with thy heart?" Secondly, an offer made on Jehonadab's answering, "It is:" "If it be, give me thine hand."

I.

1. And, first, let us consider the question proposed by Jehu to Jehonadab, "Is thine heart right, as my heart is with thy heart?"

The very first thing we may observe in these words, is, that here is no inquiry concerning Jehonadab's opinions. And yet it is certain, he held some which were very uncommon, indeed quite peculiar to himself; and some which had a close influence upon his practice; on which, likewise, he laid so great a stress, as to entail them upon his children's children, to their latest posterity. This is evident from the account given by Jeremiah many years after his death: "I took Jaazaniah and his brethren and all his sons, and the whole house of the Rechabites, . . . and set before them pots full of wine, and cups, and said unto them, Drink ye wine. But they said, We will drink no wine: for Jonadab," or Jehonadab, "the son of Rechab, our father" (it would be less ambiguous, if the words were placed thus: "Jehonadab our father, the son of Rechab," out of love and reverence to whom, he probably desired his descendants might be called by his name), "commanded us, saying, ye shall drink no wine, neither ye, nor your sons for ever. Neither shall ye build house, nor sow seed; nor plant vineyard, nor have any: but all your days ye shall dwell in tents. . . . And we have obeyed, and done according to all that Jonadab our father commanded us" (Jer. 35:3-10).

2. And yet Jehu (although it seems to have been his manner both in things secular and religious, to drive furiously) does not concern himself at all with any of these things, but lets Jehonadab abound in his own sense. And neither of them appears to have given the other the least disturbance touching the opinions which he maintained.

3. It is very possible, that many good men now also may entertain peculiar opinions; and some of them may be as singular herein as even Jehonadab was. And it is certain, so long as we know but in part, that all men will not see all things alike. It is an unavoidable consequence of the present weakness and shortness of human understanding, that several men will be of several minds in religion as well as in common life. So it has been from the beginning of the world, and so it will be "till the restitution of all things."

4. Nay, farther: although every man necessarily believes that every particular opinion which he holds is true (for to believe any opinion is not true, is the same thing as not to hold it); yet can no man be assured that all his own opinions, taken together, are true. Nay, every thinking man is assured they are not, seeing *humanum est errare et nescire*: "To be ignorant of many things, and to mistake in some, is the necessary condition of humanity." This, therefore, he is sensible, is his own case. He knows, in the general, that he himself is mistaken; although in what particulars he mistakes, he does not, perhaps he cannot, know.

5. I say "perhaps he cannot know;" for who can tell how far invincible ignorance may extend or (that comes to the same thing) invincible prejudice—which is often so fixed in tender minds, that it is afterwards impossible to tear up what has taken so deep a root. And who can say, unless he knew every circumstance attending it, how far any mistake is culpable? Seeing all guilt must suppose some concurrence of the will; of which he only can judge who searcheth the heart.

6. Every wise man, therefore, will allow others the same liberty of thinking which he desires they should allow him; and will no more insist on their embracing his opinions, than he would

have them to insist on his embracing theirs. He bears with those who differ from him, and only asks him with whom he desires to unite in love that single question, "Is thy heart right, as my heart is with thy heart?"

7. We may, secondly, observe, that here is no inquiry made concerning Jehonadab's mode of worship; although it is highly probable there was, in this respect also, a very wide difference between them. For we may well believe Jehonadab, as well as all his posterity, worshipped God at Jerusalem: whereas Jehu did not: he had more regard to state-policy than religion. And, therefore, although he slew the worshippers of Baal, and "destroyed Baal out of Israel," yet from the convenient sin of Jeroboam, the worship of the "golden calves," he "departed not" (2 Kings 10:29).

8. But even among men of an upright heart, men who desire to "have a conscience void of offence," it must needs be, that, as long as there are various opinions, there will be various ways of worshipping God; seeing a variety of opinion necessarily implies a variety of practice. And as, in all ages, men have differed in nothing more than in their opinions concerning the Supreme Being, so in nothing have they more differed from each other, than in the manner of worshipping him. Had this been only in the heathen world, it would not have been at all surprising: for we know, these "by" their "wisdom knew not God;" nor, therefore, could they know how to worship him. But is it not strange, that even in the Christian world, although they all agree in the general, "God is a Spirit; and they that worship him must worship him in spirit and in truth;" yet the particular modes of worshipping God are almost as various as among the heathens.

9. And how shall we choose among so much variety? No man can choose for, or prescribe to, another. But every one must follow the dictates of his own conscience, in simplicity and godly sincerity. He must be fully persuaded in his own mind and then act according to the best light he has. Nor has any creature power to constrain another to walk by his own rule. God has given no right to any of the children of men thus to lord it over the conscience of his brethren; but every man must judge for himself, as every man must give an account of himself to God.

10. Although, therefore, every follower of Christ is obliged, by the very nature of the Christian institution, to be a member

of some particular congregation or other, some Church, as it is usually termed (which implies a particular manner of worshipping God; for "two cannot walk together unless they be agreed"); yet none can be obliged by any power on earth but that of his own conscience, to prefer this or that congregation to another, this or that particular manner of worship. I know it is commonly supposed, that the place of our birth fixes the Church to which we ought to belong; that one, for instance, who is born in England, ought to be a member of that which is styled the Church of England, and consequently, to worship God in the particular manner which is prescribed by that Church. I was once a zealous maintainer of this; but I find many reasons to abate of this zeal. I fear it is attended with such difficulties as no reasonable man can get over. Not the least of which is, that if this rule had took [sic] place, there could have been no Reformation from Popery; seeing it entirely destroys the right of private judgement, on which that whole Reformation stands.

11. I dare not, therefore, presume to impose my mode of worship on any other. I believe it is truly primitive and apostolical: but my belief is no rule for another. I ask not, therefore, of him with whom I would unite in love, Are you of my church, of my congregation? Do you receive the same form of church government, and allow the same church officers, with me? Do you join in the same form of prayer wherein I worship God? I inquire not, "Do you receive the supper of the Lord in the same posture and manner that I do nor whether, in the administration of baptism, you agree with me in admitting sureties for the baptized, in the manner of administering it; or the age of those to whom it should be administered?" Nay, I ask not of you (as clear as I am in my own mind), whether you allow baptism and the Lord's supper at all. Let all these things stand by: we will talk of them, if need be, at a more convenient season, my only question at present is this, "Is thine heart right, as my heart is with thy heart?"

12. But what is properly implied in the question I do not mean, What did Jehu imply therein? But, What should a follower of Christ understand thereby, when he proposes it to any of his brethren?

The first thing implied is this: Is thy heart right with God? Dost thou believe his being and his perfections? His eternity, immensity, wisdom, power; his justice, mercy, and truth? Dost thou believe that he now "upholdeth all things by the word of his power" and that he governs even the most minute, even the most noxious, to his own glory, and the good of them that love him? Hast thou a divine evidence, a supernatural conviction, of the things of God? Dost thou "walk by faith not by sight," looking not at temporal things, but things eternal?

13. Dost thou believe in the Lord Jesus Christ, "God over all, blessed for ever"? Is he revealed in thy soul? Dost thou know Jesus Christ and him crucified? Does he dwell in thee, and thou in him? Is he formed in thy heart by faith? Having absolutely disclaimed all thy own works, thy own righteousness, hast thou "submitted thyself unto the righteousness of God," which is by faith in Christ Jesus? Art thou "found in him, not having thy own righteousness, but the righteousness which is by faith"? And art thou, through him, "fighting the good fight of faith, and laying hold of eternal life"?

14. Is thy faith *energoumenh di agaphs*,—filled with the energy of love? Dost thou love God (I do not say "above all things," for it is both an unscriptural and an ambiguous expression, but) "with all thy heart, and with all thy mind, and with all thy soul, and with all thy strength"? Dost thou seek all thy happiness in him alone? And dost thou find what thou seekest? Does thy soul continually "magnify the Lord, and thy spirit rejoice in God thy Saviour"? Having learned "in everything to give thanks, dost thou find "it is a joyful and a pleasant thing to be thankful"? Is God the centre of thy soul, the sum of all thy desires? Art thou accordingly laying up thy treasure in heaven, and counting all things else dung and dross? Hath the love of God cast the love of the world out of thy soul? Then thou art "crucified to the world;" thou art dead to all below; and thy "life is hid with Christ in God."

15. Art thou employed in doing, "not thy own will, but the will of him that sent thee,"—of him that sent thee down to sojourn here awhile, to spend a few days in a strange land, till, having finished the work he hath given thee to do, thou return to thy Father's house? Is it thy meat and drink "to do the will of thy Father which is in heaven"? Is thine eye single in all things? Always fixed on him? Always looking unto Jesus? Dost thou point at him in whatsoever thou doest in all thy labour, thy business,

thy conversation aiming only at the glory of God in all, "whatsoever thou doest, either in word or deed, doing it all in the name of the Lord Jesus; giving thanks unto God, even the Father, through him?"

16. Does the love of God constrain thee to serve him with fear, to "rejoice unto him with reverence"? Art thou more afraid of displeasing God, than either of death or hell? Is nothing so terrible to thee as the thought of offending the eyes of his glory? Upon this ground, dost thou "hate all evil ways," every transgression of his holy and perfect law; and herein "exercise thyself, to have a conscience void of offence toward God, and toward man"?

17. Is thy heart right toward thy neighbour? Dost thou love as thyself, all mankind, without exception? "If you love those only that love you, what thank have ye"? Do you "love your enemies"? Is your soul full of good-will, of tender affection, toward them? Do you love even the enemies of God, the unthankful and unholy? Do your bowels yearn over them? Could you "wish yourself" temporally "accursed" for their sake? And do you show this by "blessing them that curse you, and praying for those that despitefully use you, and persecute you"?

18. Do you show your love by your works? While you have time, as you have opportunity, do you in fact "do good to all men," neighbours or strangers, friends or enemies, good or bad? Do you do them all the good you can; endeavouring to supply all their wants; assisting them both in body and soul, to the uttermost of your power? If thou art thus minded, may every Christian say, yea, if thou art but sincerely desirous of it, and following on till thou attain, then "thy heart is right, as my heart is with thy heart."

II.

1. "If it be, give me thy hand." I do not mean, "Be of my opinion." You need not: I do not expect or desire it. Neither do I mean, "I will be of your opinion." I cannot, it does not depend on my choice: I can no more think, than I can see or hear, as I will. Keep you your opinion; I mine; and that as steadily as ever. You need not even endeavour to come over to me, or bring me over to you. I do not desire you to dispute those points, or to hear or speak one word concerning them. Let all opinions alone on one side and the other: only "give me thine hand."

2. I do not mean, "Embrace my modes of worship," or, "I will embrace yours." This also is a thing which does not depend either on your choice or mine. We must both act as each is fully persuaded in his own mind. Hold you fast that which you believe is most acceptable to God, and I will do the same. I believe the Episcopal form of church government to be scriptural and apostolical. If you think the Presbyterian or Independent is better, think so still, and act accordingly. I believe infants ought to be baptized; and that this may be done either by dipping or sprinkling. If you are otherwise persuaded, be so still, and follow your own persuasion. It appears to me, that forms of prayer are of excellent use, particularly in the great congregation. If you judge extemporary prayer to be of more use, act suitable to your own judgement. My sentiment is, that I ought not to forbid water, wherein persons may be baptized; and that I ought to eat bread and drink wine, as a memorial of my dying Master: however, if you are not convinced of this, act according to the light you have. I have no desire to dispute with you one moment upon any of the preceding heads. Let all these smaller points stand aside. Let them never come into sight "If thine heart is as my heart," if thou lovest God and all mankind, I ask no more: "give me thine hand."

3. I mean, first, love me: and that not only as thou lovest all mankind; not only as thou lovest thine enemies, or the enemies of God, those that hate thee, that "despitefully use thee, and persecute thee;" not only as a stranger, as one of whom thou knowest neither good nor evil, —I am not satisfied with this,—no; "if thine heart be right, as mine with thy heart," then love me with a very tender affection, as a friend that is closer than a brother; as a brother in Christ, a fellow citizen of the New Jerusalem, a fellow soldier engaged in the same warfare, under the same Captain of our salvation. Love me as a companion in the kingdom and patience of Jesus, and a joint heir of his glory.

4. Love me (but in a higher degree than thou dost the bulk of mankind) with the love that is long-suffering and kind; that is patient,—if I am ignorant or out of the way, bearing and not increasing my burden; and is tender, soft, and compassionate still; that envieth not, if at any time it please God to prosper me in his work even more than thee. Love me with the love that is not provoked, either at my follies or infirmities; or even at my acting

(if it should sometimes so appear to thee) not according to the will of God. Love me so as to think no evil of me; to put away all jealousy and evil-surmising. Love me with the love that covereth all things; that never reveals either my faults or infirmities,—that believeth all things; is always willing to think the best, to put the fairest construction on all my words and actions,—that hopeth all things; either that the thing related was never done; or not done with such circumstances as are related; or, at least, that it was done with a good-intention, or in a sudden stress of temptation. And hope to the end, that whatever is amiss will, by the grace of God, be corrected; and whatever is wanting, supplied, through the riches of his mercy in Christ Jesus.

5. I mean, Secondly, commend me to God in all thy prayers; wrestle with him in my behalf, that he would speedily correct what he sees amiss, and supply what is wanting in me. In thy nearest access to the throne of grace, beg of him who is then very present with thee, that my heart may be more as thy heart, more right both toward God and toward man; that I may have a fuller conviction of things not seen, and a stronger view of the love of God in Christ Jesus; may more steadily walk by faith, not by sight; and more earnestly grasp eternal life. Pray that the love of God and of all mankind may be more largely poured into my heart; that I may be more fervent and active in doing the will of my Father which is in heaven, more zealous of good works, and more careful to abstain from all appearance of evil.

6. I mean, Thirdly, provoke me to love and to good works. Second thy prayer, as thou hast opportunity, by speaking to me, in love, whatsoever thou believest to be for my soul's health. Quicken me in the work which God has given me to do, and instruct me how to do it more perfectly. Yea, "smite me friendly, and reprove me," whereinsoever I appear to thee to be doing rather my own will, than the will of him that sent me. O speak and spare not, whatever thou believest may conduce, either to the amending my faults, the strengthening my weakness, the building me up in love, or the making me more fit, in any kind, for the Master's use.

7. I mean, Lastly, love me not in word only, but in deed and in truth. So far as in conscience thou canst (retaining still thy own opinions, and thy own manner of worshipping God), join with me

in the work of God; and let us go on hand in hand. And thus far, it is certain, thou mayest go. Speak honourably wherever thou art, of the work of God, by whomsoever he works, and kindly of his messengers. And, if it be in thy power, not only sympathize with them when they are in any difficulty or distress, but give them a cheerful and effectual assistance, that they may glorify God on thy behalf.

8. Two things should be observed with regard to what has been spoken under this last head: the one, that whatsoever love, whatsoever offices of love, whatsoever spiritual or temporal assistance, I claim from him whose heart is right, as my heart is with his, the same I am ready, by the grace of God, according to my measure, to give him: the other, that I have not made this claim in behalf of myself only, but of all whose heart is right toward God and man, that we may all love one another as Christ hath loved us.

III.

1. One inference we may make from what has been said. We may learn from hence, what is a catholic spirit.

There is scarce any expression which has been more grossly misunderstood, and more dangerously misapplied, than this: but it will be easy for any who calmly consider the preceding observations, to correct any such misapprehensions of it, and to prevent any such misapplication.

For, from hence we may learn, first, that a catholic spirit is not speculative latitudinarianism. It is not an indifference to all opinions: this is the spawn of hell, not the offspring of heaven. This unsettledness of thought, this being "driven to and fro, and tossed about with every wind of doctrine," is a great curse, not a blessing, an irreconcilable enemy, not a friend, to true catholicism. A man of a truly catholic spirit has not now his religion to seek. He is fixed as the sun in his judgement concerning the main branches of Christian doctrine. It is true, he is always ready to hear and weigh whatsoever can be offered against his principles; but as this does not show any wavering in his own mind, so neither does it occasion any. He does not halt between two opinions, nor vainly endeavour to blend them into one. Observe this, you who know not what spirit ye are of: who call yourselves men of a catholic spirit, only because you are of a muddy understanding; because your mind is all in a mist; because you have no settled, consistent principles, but are for jumbling all opinions together. Be convinced, that you have quite missed your way; you know not where you are. You think you are got into the very spirit of Christ; when, in truth, you are nearer the spirit of Antichrist. Go, first, and learn the first elements of the gospel of Christ, and then shall you learn to be of a truly catholic spirit.

2. From what has been said, we may learn, secondly, that a catholic spirit is not any kind of practical latitudinarianism. It is not indifference as to public worship, or as to the outward manner of performing it. This, likewise, would not be a blessing but a curse. Far from being an help thereto, it would, so long as it remained, be an unspeakable hindrance to the worshipping of God in spirit and in truth. But the man of a truly catholic spirit, having weighed all things in the balance of the sanctuary, has no doubt, no scruple at all, concerning that particular mode of worship wherein he joins. He is clearly convinced, that this manner of worshipping God is both scriptural and rational. He knows none in the world which is more scriptural, none which is more rational. Therefore, without rambling hither and thither, he cleaves close thereto, and praises God for the opportunity of so doing.

3. Hence we may, thirdly, learn, that a catholic spirit is not indifference to all congregations. This is another sort of latitudinarianism, no less absurd and unscriptural than the former. But it is far from a man of a truly catholic spirit. He is fixed in his congregation as well as his principles. He is united to one, not only in spirit, but by all the outward ties of Christian fellowship. There he partakes of all the ordinances of God. There he receives the supper of the Lord. There he pours out his soul in public prayer, and joins in public praise and thanksgiving. There he rejoices to hear the word of reconciliation, the gospel of the grace of God. With these his nearest, his best-beloved brethren, on solemn occasions, he seeks God by fasting. These particularly he watches over in love, as they do over his soul; admonishing, exhorting, comforting, reproving, and every way building up each other in the faith. These he regards as his own household; and therefore, according to the ability God has given him, naturally cares for them, and provides that they may have all the things that are needful for life and godliness.

4. But while he is steadily fixed in his religious principles in what he believes to be the truth as it is in Jesus; while he firmly adheres to that worship of God which he judges to be most acceptable in his sight; and while he is united by the tenderest and closest ties to one particular congregation, —his heart is enlarged toward all mankind, those he knows and those he does not; he embraces with strong and cordial affection neighbours and strangers, friends and enemies. This is catholic or universal love. And he that has this is of a catholic spirit. For love alone gives the title to this character: catholic love is a catholic spirit.

5. If, then, we take this word in the strictest sense, a man of a catholic spirit is one who, in the manner above-mentioned, gives his hand to all whose hearts are right with his heart: one who knows how to value, and praise God for, all the advantages he enjoys, with regard to the knowledge of the things of God, the true scriptural manner of worshipping him, and, above all, his union with a congregation fearing God and working righteousness: one who, retaining these blessings with the strictest care, keeping them as the apple of his eye, at the same time loves—as friends, as brethren in the Lord, as members of Christ and children of God, as joint partakers now of the present kingdom of God, and fellow heirs of his eternal kingdom—all, of whatever opinion or worship, or congregation, who believe in the Lord Jesus Christ; who love God and man; who, rejoicing to please, and fearing to offend God, are careful to abstain from evil, and zealous of good works. He is the man of a truly catholic spirit, who bears all these continually upon his heart; who having an unspeakable tenderness for their persons, and longing for their welfare, does not cease to commend them to God in prayer, as well as to plead their cause before men; who speaks comfortably to them, and labours, by all his words, to strengthen their hands in God. He assists them to the uttermost of his power in all things, spiritual and temporal. He is ready "to spend and be spent for them;" yea, to lay down his life for their sake.

6. Thou, O man of God, think on these things! If thou art already in this way, go on. If thou hast heretofore mistook the path, bless God who hath brought thee back! And now run the race which is set before thee, in the royal way of universal love. Take heed, lest thou be either wavering in thy judgement, or

straitened in thy bowels: but keep an even pace, rooted in the faith once delivered to the saints, and grounded in love, in true catholic love, till thou art swallowed up in love for ever and ever!

* * *

{**Note:** For the sake of space, I have not included Charles Wesley's hymn "Catholic Love," which was originally included here in some published versions of this sermon.}

Obviously, the term "Catholic" here has nothing to do with the Roman Catholic Christian tradition, but instead to a spirit of love and respect that Wesley believes all Christians are to manifest towards others who are part of the *universal* (i.e., catholic) church of Jesus Christ. Today, much has been written about the meaning of Wesley's "Catholic spirit": How far does (and should) it go in defining orthodox Christian doctrine and practice? and to what extent can it be used to justify and/or encourage ecumenical and even inter-*faith* dialogue and endeavors? The answers are not entirely clear.

> **"Catholic Spirit"**—The title of one of Wesley's sermons, but more importantly, the ability to honor and respect beliefs and practices of others that differ from one's own for the sake of, and resulting out of, Christian love.

On the one hand, it must be remembered that Wesley was writing this within a context where the established Church of England was the predominant voice and standard against which all religious views and practices were measured. While Roman Catholic and Dissenter/non-Conformist voices and practices were certainly present, these were usually ostracized and looked on with contempt and suspicion by the establishment. So, while Wesley's intent was certainly to broaden the field of dialogue and respect within his specific cultural context, the extent to which he intended a sense of Catholic spirit to be applied to ministry partnerships across the varied *Christian* traditions within English culture is debatable. Here it seems to mean that, at the very least, we have mutual fellowship with fellow *Christians* and find ways to do partner ministries with them, even if we disagree about specific doctrine and practice. Likewise, while it's clear that Wesley wrote and intended that this sermon's themes be applicable to relationships between *Christians*, the question might be raised today as to whether or not its *principles* might also be applied or help to shape the nature of Christian inter-*faith* dialogue and activity (i.e., between Christians and members of other world *religions*). Consequently, because the concepts and practices of this sermon can be seriously debated, opposing sides of theological discussion and interpretation today have often used its points to justify their respective views.

From the text, however, at least two things *are* nevertheless clear. First, Catholic spirit does *not* mean "anything goes" regarding fundamental doctrine, practice, or faith form. In Wesley's words in Section 3 of the sermon above, it is not an "indifference to all opinions," whether that be in the form of what he called "speculative latitudinarianism" (an apathy regarding doctrine), "practical latitudinarianism" (an apathy regarding fundamental Christian practices), or an "indifference to all congregations" (an apathy regarding ecclesial form or discipline). [52] As an example, in Section 2, Paragraph 1 of the sermon, he writes,

> "If it be, give me thy hand." I do not mean, "Be of my opinion." You need not: I do not expect or desire it. Neither do I mean, "I will be of your opinion." I cannot, it does not depend on my choice: I can no more think, than I can see or hear, as I will. Keep you your opinion; I mine; and that as steadily as ever. You need not even endeavour to come over to me, or bring me over to you. I do not desire you to dispute those points, or to hear or speak one word concerning them. Let all opinions alone on one side and the other: only "give me thine hand."[53]

Obviously, for him there are some "opinions" (and practices and faith forms) that are fundamental and must be protected and preserved, even while maintaining a gracious spirit that allows for others to practice and believe differently while still claiming them as fellow sisters and brothers in Christian faith.

Still, exactly *what* these were—and still are—is a further point of debate, because a second thing the sermon does is to set forth a gracious generosity and respect towards—and a humility about—those who believe and practice faith differently. In this sense, by offering common ministry as a bridge

---

52 Wesley, "Catholic Spirit," § 3, ¶¶ 1–3 in Outler, ed., *Works*, 2:92–94.

53 Wesley, "Catholic Spirit," § 2, ¶ 1 in Outler, ed., *Works*, 2:89.

towards mutual honor and respect, it provides needed caution against the tyranny of either/or ways of thinking, living, and believing. Recall that in Paragraph 4 of the Intro, Wesley says,

> Although a difference in opinions or modes of worship may prevent an entire external union, yet need it prevent our union in affection? Though we cannot think alike, may we not love alike? May we not be of one heart, though we are not of one opinion? Without all doubt, we may. Herein all the children of God may unite, notwithstanding these smaller differences. These remaining as they are, they may forward one another in love and in good works.[54]

One example illustrates this concept and practice very well. The story is told that a staunch Calvinist once asked George Whitefield whether or not John Wesley would be found in heaven. Since the man knew that the two great evangelists had grown apart over theological differences since their early ministry together, he expected Whitefield to respond adamantly in the negative. Instead, Whitefield responded, "I fear not, he will be so near the throne, and we shall be at such a distance, that we shall hardly get a sight of him."[55] Here, then, is an example of Wesley's Catholic spirit manifested in the words and actions of one of his most staunch theological opponents, but who was also one of his close friends.

It is this same spirit of generous respect that he encourages his Methodists to follow, as well. In Section 3, Paragraph 4 of his sermon, Wesley shares what he believes it means for a Christian to practice Catholic spirit:

> While he is steadily fixed in his religious principles in what he believes to be the truth as it is in Jesus; while he firmly adheres to that worship of God which he judges to be most acceptable in his sight; and while he is united by the tenderest and closest ties to one particular congregation,—his heart is enlarged toward all mankind, those he knows and those he does not; he embraces with strong and cordial affection neighbours and strangers, friends and enemies. This is catholic or universal love. And he

---

54 Wesley, "Catholic Spirit," Intro, ¶ 4 in Outler, ed., *Works*, 2:82.

55 Whitefield, cited in Donald Bloesch, *The Future of Evangelical Christianity: A Call for Unity Amid Diversity* (Colorado Springs: Helmers and Howard, 1988), 95.

that has this is of a catholic spirit. For love alone gives the title to this character: catholic love is a catholic spirit.[56]

So, opposite to what we often find in today's world, Wesley believes that Christians (especially what we would call *Wesleyan* Christians) have a responsibility to practice a spirit of generous respect towards others. Knight summarizes this view in the following way:

> What we believe about predestination, Christian perfection, infant baptism, and the like is of great importance, for it involves our being faithful to Christ in proclaiming, teaching, and living the faith. But it should not prevent us from honoring that same faithfulness in Christians who hold contrary opinions, yet who nonetheless remain our sisters and brothers in Christ.[57]

> If you are active in a local Christian church, in what way(s) does your church practice a "generous spirit" towards those who believe or practice faith and/or spirituality differently? In what ecumenical and/or inter-faith endeavors are they involved?

In conclusion, there is certainly a distinctive and unique shape to an authentically Wesleyan life and ministry which can be identified by the presence of both the theological and the practical characteristics described in this chapter. One certainly does not need to believe or practice them all flawlessly in order to live out of a uniquely Wesleyan paradigm. However, faithfulness to that tradition does require us not only to be aware of their presence, but also to do one's best to honor them both in our discourse and practice of faith and ministry.

In addition, as Christians today increasingly experiment with and use newer ministry paradigms and practices, what I have proposed here is a way for twenty-first-century Christians who choose to do so to operate out of a *Wesleyan* approach that both faithfully maintains the unique shape of that theology and practice, but also which seeks to creatively translate that shape into ministry that is relevant to one's cultural context.

---

56 Wesley, "Catholic Spirit", § 3, ¶ 4 in Outler, ed., *Works*, 2:94.

57 Henry H. Knight III, "Consider Wesley: Wesley on a 'Catholic Spirit,'" *Catalyst*, April 1, 2009, https://www.catalystresources.org/consider-wesley-45/.

If you are active in a local Christian church in the Wesleyan tradition, of the TWO uniquely Wesleyan theological characteristics and the FIVE uniquely Wesleyan practical characteristics, which one(s) does your church (or do you) most need to be reminded of today? Why?

CHAPTER 9

CONCLUSION

For John Wesley, biblical Christianity did not consist only in the thinking of or believing in certain things, but also in the practicing and doing of certain things and of living in a certain way.[1] Consequently, in the past eight chapters, I've sought to share what I consider to be that which is fundamental about the nature and practice of a uniquely Wesleyan form of Christianity. To do this, we've read nine of Wesley's sermons and tried to interpret these and other primary source materials within their original contexts in order to more fully understand the essence of their meaning. We've learned a bit about Wesley's own life, and how he was both shaped by, and helped to shape, the culture around him. We've explored how both of those gave rise to the DNA of what we today call Wesleyan/Methodist Christianity and identified some of the defining characteristics both of its theology and practice. And along the way, within the text itself as well as through the chapter discussion questions, I've attempted to suggest a few practical implications for how all of this can be lived out in today's world.

As we conclude this book, then, it's my hope that through all of these, you have been both enlightened and better equipped to understand what it means both to be and to live as a Wesleyan Christian in today's world. If you began as a long-time Methodist (of whatever brand that might be),[2] my hope has been that these readings have strengthened your understanding of who you *already are* as a Wesleyan Christian. If you are someone who is new to this tradition, my hope has been that these readings have perhaps confirmed for you why you chose to *become* a Wesleyan Christian. If you have been reading this book as a Christian from outside of this tradition who was seeking to know more about it,

---

1 In his book, *The New Creation*, 147 (see chap. 8, n. 16), Theodore Runyon refers to these two focal points as *orthodoxy* (right belief) and *orthopraxy* (right practice).

2 I.E., United Methodist, African Methodist Episcopal (AME), African Methodist Episcopal Zion (AMEZ), Christian Methodist Episcopal (CME), Congregational Methodist, Independent Methodist, Salvation Army, Church of the Nazarene, Church of God (Cleveland, TN), or some other brand of Wesleyanism/Methodism.

then my hope has been that you have gained better insight into both the commonalities *with* and differences *between* your own tradition and this one. Finally, if you have been reading from outside of Christianity itself—either as a person from another world religion, or even as a person who claims no specific spiritual faith at all—then my hope has been that there have been parts about Wesleyan Christianity that have intrigued you enough to want to explore this way of engaging and experiencing life and spirituality in more depth.

Regardless of your starting point, however, my goal—as stated in the Introduction—has not been to create or replicate "good little Methodists," but merely to help all readers to better understand what it means to be a great *Christian* who chooses to live out their Christianity in a uniquely *Wesleyan* way—that is: to make the case for the understanding and a living of Christianity the Wesleyan way. This is even more important in today's culture where, as has been the case throughout Methodist history, there is a tendency to try to apply either/or solutions to both/and problems—a practice that is not usually faithful to a uniquely Wesleyan paradigm of Christian ministry. In fact, the use of this practice within the tradition itself is currently resulting in the significant theological and practical challenges within many of its brands (United Methodism, in particular). However, it's my belief that if we begin with the essentials of theology and practice from this book in mind, then regardless of how one approaches the various issues causing those challenges, faithfulness to the essence of Christianity as understood through the lens of Wesleyanism not only can be honored, but can provide helpful resources to address the practical needs of twenty-first-century culture.

In conclusion, let me remind us that the story and impact of Wesleyan Christianity is unfinished. If you are either currently in or considering becoming part of this tradition, then please remember that you and I are the ones who will be adding the next chapter(s) to pass on to future generations. What John Wesley's brother Charles expresses in Verses 1-2 of one of his hymns regarding *individual* responsibility can also be applied to the *corporate* responsibility of all Wesleyan Christians:

> A Charge to keep I have, a God to glorify;
> A never-dying soul to save, and fit it for the sky.

> To serve the PRESENT age, my calling to fulfill;
> Oh, may it all my powers engage to do my Master's Will! [3]

My hope and prayer is that God will bless you in your journey to discover and live a faithful life as a Christian in the Wesleyan way.

---

3 Verses 1–2 of Charles Wesley's hymn "A Charge to Keep I Have," in *The United Methodist Hymnal* (Nashville: The United Methodist Publishing House, 1989), 413, emphasis added.

APPENDIX

THE CULTURAL CONTEXT OF WESLEY'S ENGLAND AND EARLY METHODISM'S RESPONSE

This book sets forth the fundamental tenets of a uniquely Wesleyan theology and practice of ministry. Yet, from where do these come? Put another way, do the historical, theological, and experiential beliefs and practices of John Wesley and the early Methodists give us clues today not only as to what these tenets look like, but were there forces at work in the cultural context of that day and time which gave rise to that theology and practice of ministry? In Chapter One, I set forth how the *spiritual context* of the day affected these. While in my estimation this was the *most* important influence on the shaping of these, in this appendix I want to describe another important source that influenced them—the *sociological and cultural context* of eighteenth-century England—and how Wesley's Methodism responded to that context in a way that profoundly impacted British society of the day. To understand this, it will first be helpful to give a brief overview of eighteenth-century English culture in general.

Overview of Eighteenth-Century English Culture

Known variously as the "Augustan Age"[1] and the "Georgian Age,"[2] eighteenth-century English culture was one filled with contrast, inconsistency, and social ambiguity. As Roy Porter remarks, "English society was disparate, fluid, and spangled with contrasts and anomalies. No single scientific terminology captures that complexity in its entirety."[3] At the same time, William

---

1 "The 'Augustan Age' of British civilization [was] a gathering from other ruins of the opulence that once was Rome–Rome at its height–and an emulation of that very Roman decadence out of which . . . Christianity had struggled to survive, rise, and reach northward to England" [David Lyle Jeffrey, ed., *A Burning and a Shining Light: English Spirituality in the Age of Wesley* (Grand Rapids, MI: William B. Eerdmans Publishing Co, 1987), 1].

2 Named after the reigns of Kings George I (1714–26), George II (1727–59), and George III (1760–89).

3 Roy Porter, *English Society in the Eighteenth Century* (rev. ed.) (London: Penguin Books, 1990), 5; See generally Porter, Chapter 1, "Contrasts," 7–47.

APPENDIX

Willcox notes that "the people of eighteenth-century Britain lived in a paradoxical society in which elegance in architecture, furniture, and sometimes in manners went hand-in-hand with widespread callousness and cruelty, a clamorous and abusive press, and intermittent riots."[4] Thus we find an eighteenth-century England that is at once both publicly smug and secure concerning their current situation, yet privately apprehensive and anxious about the future. Given this general condition of society, then, what were the specific cultural, philosophical, and social challenges of eighteenth-century England? While I believe that there are various similarities with contemporary American society, let me highlight three "shifts" taking place in that day and time that stand out as defining for eighteenth-century England.

Shift #1: The Industrial Revolution (A Technology Shift)

First, just as contemporary culture is experiencing a technology shift known as the "Information Age" (defined by electronic and social media technology), eighteenth-century England experienced the beginnings of what would come to be called the Industrial Revolution, or "Industrialization," which can be best viewed as an example of a type of technology shift, because it deals with a shift in the way society views and uses technology. As William Willcox explains, "Industrial Revolution . . . is [merely] a capsule description of the process whereby new methods of production and new sources of power [e.g., new industrial technologies] enabled a given worker to produce an ever greater quantity of goods and through which a largely agricultural society transformed itself into one composed primarily of producers of manufactured goods and providers of services."[5]

As with most technological "revolutions," the cultural changes resulting

---

4 William B. Willcox and Walter L. Arnstein, *A History of England, Volume Three: The Age of Aristocracy (1688–1830)* (Fourth Edition) (Lexington, MA: D. C. Heath and Co., 1983), 60. Indeed, in *English Society in the Eighteenth Century*, Porter traces three overarching themes found in eighteenth-century English culture: (1) the essential strength and resilience of the *status quo* social hierarchy through (2) continual adaptiveness to various social, economic, and cultural challenges of that century, and (3) the futile attempt of this hierarchy to create cultural consensus within this increasingly divergent society. He suggests that the paradoxes of that century's social upheaval resulted from the pointless attempt to impose such a consensus upon that society. While these three main points run throughout his book, this fundamental thesis is best summarized at Porter, 340–345.

5 Willcox, 168. See generally Patrick Rooke, *The Industrial Revolution* (New York: The John Day Company, 1971), 10–12.

from industrialism, though significant, were not immediate.[6] Consequently, an exact beginning and ending date for this phenomenon is difficult to establish with certainty, but most historians place the crux of its activity between 1760 and 1830. At first, industrialization was often viewed as a savior from the former medieval, backwards, and largely agricultural English society. Yet, as it progressed, its consequences revealed a more sinister side.[7] Indeed, J.H. Plumb says that "profound changes in the economic life of the country must necessarily disturb its whole social structure, and the Industrial Revolution was no exception."[8] As Roy Porter notes, through industrialization, "the Georgians created vast problems they left for others to solve."[9]

For example, while it is true that communication-technologies did not fuel the eighteenth-century English Industrial Revolution as they do today's Information-age revolution, they nevertheless were greatly impacted by it. For one, the cheap availability of mass printed books, newspapers, magazines, and tracts[10] meant that those who desired to stay "on top of" the new industrial technologies (or for that matter, "on top of" any topic of importance) were required to be literate. Similar to a lack of computer skills today, eighteenth-century illiteracy would often lead to economic hardship and

---

6   "What was revolutionary was not an initial cataclysm but rather the magnitude of the consequences, . . . the cumulative outcome of millions of individual actions throughout the [economic and cultural] system" [Porter, 313; See also Celia Bland, *The Mechanical Age: The Industrial Revolution in England* (New York: Celia Bland, 1995), 4; Willcox, 182].

7   "Until the end of the [eighteenth] century, the face of industrialization was found more impressive than horrifying" (Porter, 333; See generally Porter, 332-339). For example, "in the early days of the Industrial Revolution it was relatively easy for a modest man . . . to start up a business of enormous expansive potential without having to own much capital" (Porter, 322). Nevertheless, by the early nineteenth-century, "what most men felt was not that new doors had been thrown open but that old rights had been taken away . . . . What was lost by factories and enclosure was the independence, variety and freedom which small producers had enjoyed: an enforced asceticism" [Christopher Hill, *Reformation to Industrial Revolution: A Social and Economic History of Britain, 1530–1780* (London: Weidenfeld and Nicolson, 1967), 218]. See also William Gibson, *Church, State, and Society: 1760–1850* (New York: St. Martin's Press, 1994), 90.

8   J.H. Plumb, *England in the Eighteenth Century (1714–1815)* (Baltimore, MD: Penguin Books, 1950), 84.

9   Porter, 360. Historian Derek Jarrett parallels this when he states that "by making themselves the richest nation on earth [through industrialization,] the English created in their own country problems which could no longer be solved by the old easy-going methods of local management" (Jarrett, cited in Porter, 360).

10 See generally Porter, 234-235; Also Hill, 25–27, 180.

poverty, all resulting from the lack of a basic business skill. Consequently, while it was actually invented several centuries before (and merely exploited by industrial technology), mass-print communication proved to be both a blessing and curse to that era's fundamentally pre-literate English society.

Shift #2: The Enlightenment (A Philosophical Shift)

A second cultural dimension shift that impacted eighteenth-century English society in a drastic way was the philosophical mindset of what has come to be known as the Western Enlightenment, or the "Age of Reason."[11] It was a period which reacted against many of the medieval philosophical emphases of paradox, mystery, the divine, and the supernatural[12] by putting in their place what B.W. Young calls "the notion of [rationalist] empiricism as [a] guiding philosophy, [and] a pragmatic ideal which acted as the foundation of all but the most obscurantist and mystically inclined argument."[13]

Although at first espoused mostly by early intellectuals such as John Locke, Isaac Newton, and Francis Bacon, and later expounded by figures such as Edward Hume, David Gibbon, and Adam Smith, by the eighteenth-century, Plumb says that "[Enlightenment] curiosity, the thirst for knowledge and for rational explanation . . . had begun to seep down through society, . . . [resulting in] an attitude of increasing empiricism [that] had by this time begun to permeate the lower strata of English society."[14] It is interesting to note that while the Enlightenment marked the beginning of the "modern" era, today's "postmodernism" rejects its tenets and signals its demise.

---

11 For general background and origins, see Willcox, 77–78.

12 It is true that not ALL medieval theology or practice focused upon "paradox, mystery, the divine, and the supernatural"—consider, for example, the strong Aristotelian stress upon human reason one finds in the writings of Thomas Aquinas. However, while Aquinas's influence impacted the elite of European society, a more widespread emphasis upon human reason cannot be discerned in the *general population* until the Enlightenment period. Consequently, my reference here to Medieval paradox, mystery, etc. is a reference to *populist* (as opposed to academic) Christianity.

13 B.W. Young, *Religion and Enlightenment in Eighteenth-Century England: Theological Debate from Locke to Burke* (Oxford: Clarendon Press, 1998), 83. For example, J.H. Plumb notes that "Freedom, Liberty, Right, Reason, Necessity, these were the great girders of abstraction upon which [Enlightenment thinkers] built their treatises of philosophic liberalism" (Plumb, *England*, 134).

14 J.H. Plumb, *In the Light of History* (Boston: Houghton Mifflin Co., 1973), 14, 17. "The ideas of Newton and Locke lost many of their radical implications and became the

As Plumb explains, one result of this new philosophical mindset was that "the Western sky was studded with brilliant stars [e.g., persons] who had, or seemed to have, freed themselves from the myth-ridden universe of their ancestors . . . . [They] no longer looked to God for any answers, . . . and even if we allow that most of the philosophes believed in God, it was a highly generalized deism to which most of them subscribed; more a polite bow to the unknown than an act of faith."[15] Thus, the "Age of Reason" sought to look forward to the future by shedding any vestige of populist medieval paradox, mystery, and "enthusiasm" that generally characterized the preceding "Age of Faith."[16]

Shift #3: Social Fragmentation (A Community-Relationship Shift)

A third cultural dimension shift to reshape eighteenth-century English society was a drastic change in the way that communities related to one another (what I'm calling a "community-relationship shift"), characterized by a shift from generally cohesive agricultural communities to the beginnings of a socially fragmented urban one.[17] Porter explains that "disorder pockmarked Georgian England,"[18] and that as "urban society became more anonymous, . . . fears of crime grew, and toleration of disorder . . . diminished."[19] The result was "an edge to life in the eighteenth century

---

    conventional wisdom of the day" (Willcox, 78). "Reason was no longer the propaganda of a family of philosophers, it had become the weapon of a social class" (Plumb, *Light*, 24).

15 Plumb, *Light*, 3–4. See also Willcox, 80. Of course, Plumb has noted the irony that "the closer we look at the great protagonists of a rational approach to humanity, the more we find a great deal of oddity, much prejudice and a penchant for the irrational, . . . [such as the] numerous examples of credulity and superstition in [even] the most sophisticated and intellectual circles" (Plumb, *Light*, 5). Furthermore, he goes on to trace the beginnings of a general move *away from* Enlightenment thought (e.g., the genesis of what would eventually become POST-modern thought) also to the early eighteenth-century (See generally Plumb, *Light*, 6–12).

16 "[While] the eyes of earlier generations had been trained on the past, . . . the eighteenth-century focused its gaze far more upon the present—and then forward into the future" (Porter, 275).

17 See generally Porter, Chapter 2, "The Social Order," 48–97; Also Porter, 13–15, 286, 310.

18 Porter, 103.

19 Porter, 141. See generally Duncan Taylor, *Fielding's England* (New York: Roy Publishers, Inc., 1966), Chapter 7 ("In Trouble"), 208–229.

which is hard for us to recapture" today,[20] and which Willcox identifies as a "restlessness [that] ran through much of society, although it did not always appear on the surface."[21] Again, it is interesting to note how this social fragmentation parallels today's similar fragmentation in a remarkable way. One major difference is simply the fact that while eighteenth-century England's social fragmentation resulted largely from a shift from agricultural to industrial society, today's version of this has resulted largely from the shift from industrial to post-industrial/Information age society noted in the first shift above.

Responses of Wesley's Methodism to English Cultural Context

Given this general overview of the cultural context of eighteenth-century English society, how did Wesley's Methodism respond? Put another way, what were a few of the ways that Wesley's Methodism addressed the sociological and cultural challenges of that day? To answer this, one must recall that "it was . . . to an England which was largely desperately poor and hopeless, materially and spiritually, or genteelly indifferent to the claims of the Christian revelation, and within a Church and nation where enthusiasm was a term of abuse, that . . . Wesley [was] ordained to preach the Gospel and administer the Sacraments."[22] Consequently, his ecclesiological approach recognizes that often only radical strategies will effectively address the radical needs resulting from the drastic cultural shifts of his day.[23] What, then, were a few of these responses?

---

20 Plumb, *England*, 95.

21 Willcox, 73. See also Willcox, 81. One example of this "edge" and "restlessness" was "the fantastic gambling and drinking, the riots, brutality and violence, and everywhere and always a constant sense of death" (Plumb, *England*, 95). Willcox notes this, as well: "Never did so large a number of English men and women find it so easy to drown their sorrows as during the 1720s, 1730s, and 1740s—the so-called 'gin age'" (Willcox, 57).

22 Horton Davies, *Worship and Theology in England: From Watts and Wesley to Martineau, 1690–1900* (Grand Rapids, MI: William B. Eerdmans Press, 1996), 144.

23 As Jeffrey notes, "the England of [the] day [of Wesley] was . . . [for him] as Rome itself was for St. Jerome or St. Augustine—a den of iniquity so vast and so rationalized in its habits and appetites that only a call to radical purity could make clarity of the confusion" (Jeffrey, 10).

Response #1: Christianity Both Shaped by Culture and a Response to It

One general overarching response to culture found in early Methodism is the tension felt between Christianity as *shaped by* culture, and Christianity as a *response to it*. While in many respects it addressed challenges resulting from all three primary cultural shifts, it should be noted that this very tension was in contrast with the prevailing Anglican attitude, which tended to merely reflect the dominant culture around it, and was often viewed as synonymous with it.[24] As William Gibson notes, "Methodism . . . was a living religious movement, which changed and was changed by the social contexts in which it took root."[25] On the one hand, Wesley's Methodism could probably not have taken shape without the unconscious assistance and inadvertent protection of the Anglican Establishment.[26] At the same time, as Porter notes, "Methodism became the century's most fertile new national organization . . . [and] challenged the Establishment more than any contemporary political movement, because it had the power to generate enduring self-respect and self-government among its converts."[27]

In fact, Wesley's own theology and ministry exemplify this tension as they represent *both* his acceptance/use of contemporaneous philosophies *and* his radical critique against them.[28] As Geoffrey Wainwright notes, "philosophically, Wesley . . . both was affected by and responded to the Enlightenment in its English form, characterized as it was by a Lockean

---

24 Referring to the Anglican Establishment, Porter states that "religion in Georgian England rubber-stamped social, power and property relations, generally ingrained already" (Porter, 183).

25 Gibson, 80. See generally Wellman J. Warner, *The Wesleyan Movement in the Industrial Revolution* (New York: Longmans, Green, and Co, 1930), 273; Also Jeffrey, 23, 206.

26 Indeed, E.P. Thompson's *The Making of the English Working Class* suggests that it was Methodism that developed the social and psychological attitudes which promoted acceptance of the establishment (See generally Gibson, 76; Also Warner, Chapter 9, "The Contribution of Wesleyanism to the New Social Values," 271–282).

27 Porter, 177–178. Porter also suggests that another reason for this is "because Methodist ministers escaped the obloquy of being parasitic tithe-gatherers" (Porter, 178).

28 "[Wesley] could not, of course, escape the influences of the theology and intellectual climate of his own age . . . . [His] formidable programme [sic] of reading which he executed on horseback or in his coach . . . meant that he was aware of current trends in several branches of science and philosophy" [Anthony Armstrong, *The Church of England, the Methodists, and Society, 1700-1850* (Totowa, NJ: Rowman and Littlefield, 1973), 81].

APPENDIX

empiricism and a Deistic worldview."[29] Consider, for example, his employment of reason as a source of theological authority. In true Enlightenment fashion, Wesley constantly refers to it in his writings. However, a more careful reading will reveal that his *use* of the term differs drastically and often refers to something entirely different from how it is used by many Anglicans in general, and by Deists in particular. [30]

Another way to describe this first response is to say that early Methodism lived in a constant tension between its connection to the Established Church of England *ekklesia*, and its self-given identity as an *ecclesiola in ecclesia* in that system—a characteristic of Wesleyan practice that I identify in Chapter eight. The very nature of this tension enabled it to generate creative responses to the eighteenth-century cultural shifts that were unavailable to traditional Anglicanism. These are exemplified in the remaining responses below.

Response #2: Attention to New Industrial Regions

A second creative response of Methodism (which grew out of the tensions of the first one) was its attention to the needs of the burgeoning populations found in the new industrial regions. In contrast to the Established Church's inability (or unwillingness) to cope with these needs, Wesley's Methodism intentionally sought to address them. An important element in this success was his employment of an itinerant system by which preachers rotated, giving mobility to his evangelical revival, and providing the new industrial regions with preachers and opportunities for spiritual nourishment.[31] This,

---

29 Wainwright, 122.

30 The Anglicans spoken of here are the "Latitudinarian" and "Unitarian" Anglicans (also known as "Anti-dogmatists"), who accepted the tenets of the Enlightenment to such a great degree that they often tossed aside traditional "dogmatic" Christian doctrines and practices in favor of a "latitude" of unorthodox belief, thought, and practice. See generally Theodore Runyon, *The New Creation* 14-15, 72-74, 157-158, 164-165; also Maddox, *Responsible Grace*, 40–42 (see chap. 3, n. 10). As another example of this tension in Wesley, in referring to the doctrine of "Christian perfection," Wainwright states that "historically, we may suspect Wesley of sharing too far in the individualistic and voluntaristic view of humanity characteristic of the Enlightenment" (Wainwright, 149). Furthermore, as he explores what has come to be known as the "Wesleyan quadrilateral," Wainwright also goes on to compare and contrast each dimension of the quadrilateral as used by Wesley with its meaning and use by the culture at large in Wesley's own day and time. See Wainwright, 124–137; Also Armstrong, 82; Tracy (generally).

31 At the same time, it should be pointed out that "in communities that were settled, and under the domination of squire and parson, the Methodists had little response" (Armstrong,

too, contrasted with the traditional Anglican method of having only one parson for a geographic area.[32] As a result, by 1784, three hundred and fifty-six Methodist chapels had been built in places where there had been practically no Anglican churches whatsoever.[33]

Response #3: Innovative Liturgical Forms and Styles

Although it was not utilized exclusively within the new industrial regions described above, a third response—innovative liturgical forms and styles—was one of the key ways that Wesley's Methodism was able to address the needs caused by industrialization. What were some of these liturgical innovations? Let us explore at least three.

The first innovation was **Methodism's ability to creatively blend elements from several traditions**.[34] For example, many liturgical scholars have noted how eighteenth-century Methodist worship generally combined classical Anglicanism's stress on tradition, Eucharist, formality, and uniformity with the Puritan and non-conformist emphases upon scripture, didactic worship, informality and impromptu intimacy.[35] This fusion has prompted Horton Davies to assert that "the essence of [eighteenth-century] Methodist worship . . . was the combination of the advantages of liturgical forms and of free prayers."[36]

---

91). It is easy to draw the conclusion, then, that though the itinerant system worked well in the new industrial regions, it was less effective in established Anglican communities.

32 Of the inefficiency of the traditional Anglican system, Wesley once wrote: "Be their talents ever so good, they will ere long grow dead themselves, and so will most of them that hear them . . . [I cannot] believe it was ever the will of our Lord that any congregation should have one teacher only. We have found by a long and constant experience that a frequent change of teacher is best" [Wesley, *Works*, Volume 13, "Second Letter to the Rev. Samuel Walker" (1756), 199].

33 See generally Plumb, *England*, 90, 93.

34 In this regard, this first "liturgical innovation" is "innovation" merely in a broad sense, for Methodism did not, in fact, introduce any singular new worship forms or styles. Instead, it merely borrowed already-existing elements from diverse traditions and combined them in styles and ways not previously used before.

35 See generally Davies, 19-34; Also Davies, Chapter 8, "The Methodist Union of Formal and Free Worship," 184-209. One example can be seen in Wesley's understanding of public prayer as a combination of both Anglican and Puritan elements: "[While] Anglicans conceived of common prayer as chiefly characterized by uniformity, dignity, comprehensiveness, order, and tradition, . . . Puritans and Nonconformists thought of public prayer as distinguished by spontaneity, simplicity, intimacy, particularity, and flexibility" (Davies, 29).

36 Davies, 184.

APPENDIX

A second innovation grew out of the fact that the eighteenth-century English "public domain was growing increasingly secular. The Church's once overwhelming place in communal life was being eroded."[37] Consequently, there was a growing need for ways to reach these increasingly "secular" persons. To accomplish this, Wesley's Methodism employed what today would be termed **seeker-oriented methods, events and services**. At least two of these became hallmarks of early Methodism.

First, since Porter notes that "Georgian social life gravitated out of doors, . . . trades were carried on in yards, open-fronted workshops, and booths looking out on to the world, . . . [and] people did their business, discussed their politics, and took their pleasures in the open air, in public spaces, . . ."[38] there were great opportunities for such spaces to become forums for the proclamation of the Christian gospel. Wesley's answer to this opportunity (albeit reluctantly at first) was what we referred to in Chapter Two as "field preaching," whereby he and his Methodist preachers would preach in the streets, squares, pastures, coal mines, and wherever they could draw a crowd.[39]

A second Methodist seeker-oriented event was their use of evening preaching services. Since these did not generally occur in an Established church building, their informal format enabled them to "provide a lighter diet than the strong meat of the Gospel for those who were often making their first contacts with the Christian faith."[40] Here again, it is important to note that this form of innovative service did not originate with the Methodists—they had initially been introduced by the "Old Dissent"

---

37 Porter, 226. In like manner, Anglican Bishop Joseph Butler bewailed in 1761, "the number of those who call themselves unbelievers increases, and with their number, their zeal. The deplorable distinction of our age is an avowed scorn of religion in some and a growing disregard of it in the generality" (Butler, cited in Porter at 279). Wesley himself once rhetorically asked, "What is the present characteristic of the English nation? It is ungodliness. This is at present the characteristic of the English nation. Ungodliness is our universal, our constant, our peculiar character, . . . a total ignorance of God is almost universal among us" [John Wesley, "An Estimate of the Manners of The Present Times" (1782), in Thomas Jackson, ed., *The Works of John Wesley: Thoughts, Addresses, Prayers, Letters* (Third Edition) (Grand Rapids, MI: Baker Book House, 1979), 11:159].

38 Porter, 225.

39 See generally Davies, 146–150.

40 Davies, 108.

Presbyterians and Independents. However, Methodism borrowed the idea and popularized their usage in a way that the originators had not ever done.[41]

A third Methodist liturgical innovation was their **use of hymns**, which contrasted sharply with the traditional Anglican practice of singing only metrical psalms.[42] Once again, Methodism borrowed this "innovation" from Puritanism, which first introduced hymns as an alternative way to communicate creeds.[43] Davies notes that, in its communication of doctrine, Methodist hymns have functioned in much the same manner.[44] Thus, one way that Wesley's Methodism was able to respond to the cultural shifts of eighteenth-century England was through their various innovative liturgical forms and styles.

Response #4: Use of Lay Preachers and Women

A fourth response by Wesley's Methodism was its use of lay preachers and women in key ministry and leadership roles.[45] It is true that such usage was at first justified by Wesley only on the basis of Methodism being an "emergency order," raised up by God to address the specific spiritual crisis confronting eighteenth-century English society. It is also true that this usage of laypersons (who very often had little formal education) disqualified all of Methodism in the eyes of much of the English middle and upper class. Nevertheless, at the same time it also sent a clear—even if (at first) unintentional—signal to the otherwise neglected lower classes of English society: "Methodism offers the Christian gospel for YOU."

What made this usage even more innovative was the way that these lay persons came to be leaders. As Warner explains, "the [Methodist]

---

41 See generally Davies, 108, 111; Also Armstrong, 75–76.

42 See generally Armstrong, 76-80; Also Jeffrey, 55; Davies, 201; Taylor, 120–125. Indeed, in response to this Methodist challenge, Archbishop Secker of Canterbury was reported to have written: "something must be done to put our psalmnody on a better footing; the Sectarists [i.e., Methodists] gain a multitude of followers by their better singing" (Secker, cited in Armstrong at 80).

43 See Davies, 34.

44 According to him, the Wesleyan hymns "came to be the sung creeds of the Methodists" (Davies, 201).

45 See generally Armstrong, 113–114; Warner, 258–267.

APPENDIX

movement's leaders were not imposed upon it from above."[46] Instead, "by an intensely democratic process [e.g., the apprenticing of persons with leadership potential], the movement produced its own leaders."[47] He also goes on to assert his contention that "the extent to which women were accorded positions of leadership in [the] early period [of Methodism] was [one] of the factors which added to the vitality of the movement."[48]

Response #5: Small-Group Ministry

A fifth response was the creation of various small group accountability structures, such as Wesley's Societies, Classes, Bands, Select Societies, and Penitent Societies that I described in Chapter Six.[49] This was a response that most specifically addressed needs and challenges arising from industrialization and its resulting social fragmentation. For example, through these small-group structures, many lower-class men and women, who generally had few outlets for social advancement (if any) in the rest of English society, were given opportunities to advance themselves both economically and socially[50]—indeed, there is great evidence to suggest that this, indeed, is what took place.[51] To combat the growing anonymity and social fragmentation of the industrial world, many found in these groups a place of identity and belonging once again. In fact, there is evidence that the Methodist Classes even functioned as a seeker-oriented, family-type support group for those who wanted to examine Christianity before making a public commitment.[52]

---

46 Warner, 258.

47 Warner, 266.

48 Warner, 264.

49 See generally Armstrong, 66–70; Also Paul W. Chilcote, *She Offered Them Christ: The Legacy of Women Preachers in Early Methodism* (Nashville: Abingdon Press, 1993).

50 As Plumb explains, throughout the rest of English culture, "there was little scope for ambitious men and women with a social conscience. All doors were closed to them, . . . but Wesley['s Society structure] provided an organization in which they could fulfil their need for power and their sense of duty" (Plumb, *England*, 95; See generally, Armstrong, 92-94; Also Warner, 248; Runyon, 193–215).

51 Consider, for example, the fact that "the leaders of the labor movement in nineteenth-century Britain were largely Methodist local preachers and class leaders, natural leaders experienced in speaking, personal evangelism, organization, and leadership skills, which they applied to recruiting and organizing unions" (Runyon, 187; See also Maddox, 246; Runyon, 193).

52 See Runyon, 158.

Once again, Wesley was not the originator of the small-group idea. As noted in Chapter One, this honor belongs instead to the German-Pietists, who conceived the *ecclesiola in ecclesia* concept as a way to renew and revitalize an established *ekklesia* from within. Establishment Anglicanism may have then borrowed this innovation in its creation of Society groups such as the S.P.C.K., the S.P.G. and the S.R.M.[53] Wesley, in turn, may have thus appropriated at least a portion of the small-group concept from his own Anglican heritage (in addition to borrowing from Patristic, Moravian, and Pietist writers and practices), and then maximized its organization and popularized its usage to reach the spiritual needs of the increasingly socially fragmented population of eighteenth-century England.[54]

Response #6: Return to Traditional Anglican Theological and Practical Orthodoxy

All of the first five responses listed above led Wesley and the early Methodists to a sixth: a return to classical Anglican theological and practical orthodoxy. First of all, whether consciously sought out or not, Wesley's theology in many ways signified a fundamental reinstatement of more classical Anglican theology as outlined in the "Book of Homilies" and the "Thirty-Nine Articles of Religion." Examples of this theological return include, among others, Wesley's emphasis upon the traditional Anglican doctrines of Original Sin, Justification by Faith, new birth/Regeneration, and a belief in the Holy Spirit as an active agent of salvation.[55]

It should be remembered that while such emphases were consistent with Anglicanism from one-hundred to one-hundred-fifty years before, in the eighteenth-century they were precisely in opposition to the prevailing anti-dogmatism found in Latitudinarian and Unitarian Anglicanism of the time. The result was that for many of these theological emphases (especially his emphasis upon "new birth" and the activity of the Holy

---

53 Respectively, the "Society for Promoting Christian Knowledge" (SPCK, founded in 1699), the "Society for the Propagation of the Gospel" (SPG, founded in 1701), and the "Society for the Reformation of Manners" (also founded in 1699).

54 See generally Armstrong, 51.

55 See generally Davies, 150–155. Several notable exceptions to the general notion that Wesley's theology marks a return to "classic" Anglican theology include his dominant Arminianism, and his emphasis upon both Christian perfection and prevenient grace.

Spirit), Wesley and the early Methodists were accused of "enthusiasm."[56] Thus, the theological component of this return to Anglican orthodoxy signaled a specific response to the philosophical challenge of Enlightenment thought.

Furthermore, regarding Wesley's return to traditional Anglican practice, it is helpful to notice how early Methodism—like classical Anglicanism—stressed the interplay between scripture, tradition, and personal experience in the defining of theological content. While classical Anglicanism articulated this as a preference "for pragmatic application rather than speculative insight,"[57] Wesley's Methodism likewise emphasized that it was more concerned with "practical divinity" than with "speculative divinity"[58]—something I highlighted in Chapter Eight. Another example of this return is Wesley's high view of the mystery of the Eucharist.[59] Against the prevailing philosophical tide of the Enlightenment, Wesley's view "made the Methodist movement as much a sacramental as an evangelical revival, and, in this respect, . . . the forerunner of the Oxford or Tractarian Movement of the nineteenth century [which also] . . . spurred the revival of the Sacrament in both Anglican and Dissenting Churches of all parties."[60] Again, this high view of the Sacrament was of course not really "new," but represented fundamental rejection of Enlightenment philosophy and a return to a more classical Anglican theological and practical orthodoxy.

Response #7: Appropriation of Eighteenth-Century Technology

Finally, in critique of and response to the dehumanizing use of technology by industrialism, Wesley's Methodism sought a creative appropriation of

---

56 For example, "the assertion that the Holy Spirit is the agent in conversion was regarded in those days not as a commonplace of theology but as an affront to reason" (Davies, 69).

57 Stephen Sykes and John Booty, *The Study of Anglicanism* (London: Fortress Press, 1988), 326.

58 See generally John Wesley, Preface to *A Collection of Hymns for the Use of the People Called Methodist*, ¶ 4 in Franz Hildebrandt, Oliver A. Beckerlegge, and James Dale, eds., *The Bicentennial Edition of the Works of John Wesley: A Collection of Hymns for the Use of the People Called Methodist* (Nashville: Abingdon Press, 1983), 7:73-74.

59 See generally Davies, 208-209.

60 Davies, 209; see generally Sykes, 277-278. Also Armstrong, 110.

eighteenth-century technology that placed technology in the service of *meeting* human need, rather than *exploiting* it – which was how it tended to be used in the early stages of the Industrial Revolution. For example, utilizing mass print technologies that had recently made books, magazines and newspapers accessible to the general public, Wesley made his message and theology more open to "the masses" by the publishing of his letters, journal, and many of his sermons. His *Arminian Magazine*, *Primitive Physick*, and various religious and health-related tracts are all additional examples of his use of the communication-technology of mass print to spread the message and hope of Methodism throughout England. In addition, to combat the illiteracy that put so many at economic disadvantage in industrial society, Wesley not only made sure that the costs of his various publications were kept to a minimum (so the poor could afford them), but also offered literacy classes and even a Course of Study (for his lay preachers) so that more people might participate in the new literate communication-paradigm of that day. Finally, some scholars have even suggested that the early Methodists were able to offer many of the "seeker"-type services listed above precisely because of their appropriation and use of the recently discovered new technology of incandescent gas lighting for evening meetings.[61]

Conclusion

Consequently, given the three primary eighteenth-century English cultural dimension shifts of Industrialization, Enlightenment, and Social Fragmentation, we find that Wesley's Methodism answered with at least seven unique responses that positively addressed this context and reached many new people with the gospel: (1) a tensional understanding of Christianity as both shaped by culture and as a response to it; (2) attention to the new industrial regions; (3) employment of various innovative liturgical forms and styles; (4) use of lay preachers and women in ministry; (5) emphasis upon small-group ministry; (6) a return to traditional Anglican theological and practical orthodoxy; and (7) a creative appropriation of eighteenth-century technology.

---

61 See Davies, 108, 111, 201; also Taylor, 32.

INDEX

"acts of piety" and "acts of mercy," 22, 114–16, 152–53, 173
Aldersgate experience, 2–27, 104
Anabaptist views, 184, 219, 224
Arminius, Jacob, and Arminianism, 11–12, 238–39
Assurance. *See also* Witness of the Spirit, 27, 67, 99, 104–7, 114, 234

backsliding, 116, 118–22
bands, in early Methodist Societies, 9, 37-38, 175–76, 250, 286–87
Baptism, 13–14, 78, 171, 183–206, 223, 225; as Christian form of circumcision 185, 188–98, 203–4; meaning 184–85, 198–202; modes of 205–6; baptismal renewal/reaffirmation (vs. re-baptism), 202–3; of infants and children, 203–5
Böhler, Peter, 26
Brevint, Daniel, 218

Calvin, John, and Calvinism, 10–12, 74, 77–78, 109, 234, 237–38; Wesley as a "hairs breadth" from it, 11
"catholic spirit," 252–68
"Christian perfection," 17–18, 118, 122–47, 172, 234–35, 237
Church of England, 12–14, 21–25, 39, 174, 183, 205, 207, 233, 244–45, 265, 282
circumcision. *See* Baptism as Christian form of

classes, in early Methodist Societies, 8–9, 34, 37–38, 174–76, 243, 250, 286–87
Communion, Holy. *See* Lord's Supper, The
conscience, human, as sign of Prevenient Grace 64, 75, 77–78
Conversion 15, 22, 27, 99, 102, 106, 109–17, 175, 184–85, 234; Instantaneous vs. Gradual, 111; consisting of Justification, New Birth and Assurance 113, 234
conviction. *See* Repentance, of believers, 69–72, 78–79, 82, 85–86, 107, 112, 116–17, 234

Eastern spirituality. *See* Fathers of the Church, 18, 237
Ecumenical Spirit. *See* "Catholic Spirit"
election, divine. *See* Predestination, 11, 77–78, 120–21, 233
enlightenment, The, 278–82
Epworth, 21–23, 28–29
Eucharist. *See* Lord's Supper, The
"evangelical humility." *See* repentance, of believers, 116–17
experience, Christian, 8, 14–15, 110, 112, 152, 231–32, 248, 288

faith: definition and characteristics of, 56–57, 63–73, 80–82, 87–99, 110, 113–16, 119–22, 239–40; degrees of, 80–82, 116–18; fullness of, 122–47; goal of 122–47; potential for loss of, 118–22;

relationship with good works, 8, 17, 24, 26, 65, 69-71, 93-94, 233, 242, 261, 267; *Sola Fide* (by Faith Alone), 7–8, 13, 236; of a Servant vs. Faith of a Son, 81–82
Fall, the, and original Sin, 46–59, 61
fasting, 70, 153, 171–72, 177,
Fathers of the Church, influence on Wesley of, 17–18, 188, 195
field preaching, 27–29, 38, 245, 284
forgiveness, 64, 91–92, 99–101, 103–5. *See also* pardon
fragmentation, social, 279–80, 286–87
free will, 11–12; natural free will denied, 81, 239;
provided by Grace, 238–39. *See* predestination

Georgia, mission to and in, 24–26
"General Rules" of Methodism, 37, 175–78, 250–51
Gibbon, Edward, 278
God, sovereignty of, 10–12, 239
grace, conceptions of, 145–47, 234–40; growth in, 109–47; means of, 151–81; "preventing"/prevenient, 45–82; repentance in, 116–18; justifying, 85–107; sanctifying, 109–47; perfecting, 122–47

Herrnhut. *See* Moravians, 9
holiness, 18, 33, 59, 111, 123; as goal of Christian life, 122–24; personal vs. social, 172, 239
Holy Club, 22–24, 32
Holy Communion. *See* Lord's Supper, The
Holy Spirit, 66, 85, 101, 205, 221, 235, 287; work of 66, 85, 101, 287; witness of 99, 104-107; fruits of the 114–16
Hopkey, Sophie, 25
humanity: in its "original state," 45–46; in its "natural state"(the human dilemma), 46–59; in its "evangelical state" (salvation), 86–87, 110

imago Dei, 45–46, 60–62, 77, 87, 103, 107, 109–10, 122, 235,
Industrial Revolution, 276–78, 289

judgement, 48, 78-81, 89–92, 100
Justification, 99–101, 235; relationship to Sanctification 111–12

Kempis, Thomas à, 17, 22
Knight, Henry, III, 112, 231, 234, 238, 249–50, 268

Law, William, 22
Lord's Supper, the, 153–70, 206–25; a "Converting Ordinance" and a "Confirming Ordinance," 224–25; "Open Communion," 222–24. *See also* Holy Communion; Eucharist
Luther, Martin, 7–9, 221

Maddox, Randy, 32, 75, 118, 231, 236–39, 245, 249, 282, 286
"Marcarius the Egyptian," 18
means of grace, 151–81; instituted, 152–72; prudential, 173–78
Methodism, 173–78; First Annual Conference, 39; and Church of England, 35, 39
moral law, 78–79, 95
Moravians, influence on Wesley, 10, 26
mysticism, 16–17, 26

292

new birth. *See* Regeneration, 99, 101–4, 107, 121, 201

Oglethorpe, George, 24
Oxford University, 16–17, 22–23, 33
Ordo Salutis. See Also Salvation; *Via Salutis* 15, 74, 234
Outler, Albert, C., 18, 183, 207, 233, 242, 245, 247

pardon. *See* Forgiveness; Grace; Justification; Sin, 64, 91, 99, 105, 209
patristic influences. *See* fathers of the Church
Paul, St., 35, 90, 97, 110, 114, 118, 122–23, 135, 201, 204, 212–13,
penitent groups, in early Methodist Societies, 119, 121, 174, 176, 250, 286
perfection, Christian (perfect love). *See* Sanctification 122–47
Pietism, 9
prayer, 153, 156–58, 160–61, 165, 170
preachers, early Methodist (use of laity and women), 8, 34–35, 38–39, 232, 245, 247, 282, 284–86
predestination. *See* Calvinism; free will, 10–12, 77–78
Primitive Physic(k), 31–32

Quadrilateral, Wesleyan, 8, 13, 282

Reformation, Protestant, 7–12
"real presence." *See* Communion, Holy; Eucharist; Lord's Supper, The, 221

regeneration. *See* new birth, 99, 101–4, 201–2
repentance: *see* conviction, 78–82; of believers, see evangelical humility, and conviction, 116–17

Roman Catholics, 13, 16–17, 219, 221–22, 224

sacraments. *See* Baptism; Communion, Holy; Lord's Supper, The, 183–225
salvation: defined, 59–62; *Ordo Salutis* vs. *Via Salutis* (process of) 15, 74–75; possible loss of?, 120–22
sanctification, 109–22; gradual vs. instantaneous, 65, 73, 109–14; as a process, 109–14
scripture, and experience, 231–33; primacy of, for Wesley (*Homo unius libri*), 8
Select Societies, in early Methodist Societies, 176, 250, 286
sin: actual vs. original, 59, 99, 102; in believers, 110, 116–18; conception of, 46–59; conviction of, 78–80; forgiveness of, 99–101; Original, 46–59. *See also* Fall, the; grace; repentance
slavery, 25, 247
small group ministry, 9, 14, 16, 37, 172–76, 243, 251, 286–87
Society for Prompting of Christian Knowledge (SPCK), 14, 287
Spangenberg, Augustus, 26
synergism, divine, 118

Taylor, Jeremy, 22
"Tensional" theology and ministry practice, 241–48
"Transubstantiation." *See*

Communion, Holy; Eucharist; Lord's Supper, The

Via Media. See Church of England
Via Salutis. See Ordo Salutis; Salvation, vi, 15, 43–47

Wesley, Charles, 23, 58, 178,
Wesley, John, 21–41, a "brand plucked from the burning" 22; Aldersgate experience, 26–27; Ecumenical spirit 252–69; "the world as my parish," 29
Wesley, Samuel, Sr., 14, 21–22
Wesley, Susanna, 21–22
Whitefield, George, 10, 23, 28, 32, 267
witness of the Spirit. *See* Assurance, 10, 99, 104–7, 114
women, in early Methodist ministry, 38, 232, 245, 285–86
works, the place of, in Christian life, 7–8, 17, 24, 26–27, 68–71, 73, 94, 114–16, 153, 157, 164, 177, 179, 235–36, 242

Zinzendorf, Count Ludwig von, 9–10
Zwingli, Ulrich, 10, 74, 219

www.ingramcontent.com/pod-product-compliance
Lightning Source LLC
Chambersburg PA
CBHW010327240426
43665CB00049B/2902